CANADA THE GOOD

CANADA THE GOOD
A SHORT HISTORY OF VICE SINCE 1500

MARCEL MARTEL

WILFRID LAURIER
UNIVERSITY PRESS

Wilfrid Laurier University Press acknowledges the support of the Canada Council for the Arts for our publishing program. We acknowledge the financial support of the Government of Canada through the Canada Book Fund for our publishing activities.

Library and Archives Canada Cataloguing in Publication

Martel, Marcel, 1965–, author
    Canada the good : a short history of vice since 1500 / Marcel Martel.

Includes bibliographical references and index.
Issued in print and electronic formats.
ISBN 978-1-55458-947-0 (pbk.).—ISBN 978-1-55458-948-7 (pdf).—ISBN 978-1-55458-949-4 (epub)

    1. Canada—Moral conditions—History. 2. Canada—Social conditions—History. 3. Vice control—Canada—History. 4. Social control—Canada—History. 5. Vice—History. 6. Vices—History. I. Title.

HN110.Z9M6 2014   306.0971   C2013-906608-X
                                                              C2013-906609-8

Cover design by Sandra Friesen. Cover photo: Seizure of drugs, November 22, 1968. York University Libraries, Clara Thomas Archives & Special Collections, Toronto Telegram fonds, ASC00718. Text design by Angela Booth Malleau.

This book is printed on FSC recycled paper and is certified Ecologo. It is made from 100% post-consumer fibre, processed chlorine free, and manufactured using biogas energy.

Printed in Canada

CONTENTS

INTRODUCTION

Few people would refer to compulsive gambling, excessive drinking, and drug or sex addiction as vice. On the contrary, many believe that the inability to control drinking, drug taking, or gambling is a symptom of a disease rather than evidence of lack of self-control or of a morally weak character. However, not that long ago, these behaviours were labelled as vices, demonstrating an individual's inability to control him or herself. This inability had, according to those who denounced these behaviours, devastating consequences for individuals afflicted by these habits, and also their immediate family and surrounding community. If the term *vice* is inaccurate in today's society, although some continue to use it, Canadians are still uneasy about these behaviours. As a society, we still devote a huge amount of attention to identifying and solving these perceived social problems. And individuals are reluctant to be associated with them, even indirectly. Many financial advisers will suggest investing in vice because such an investment is a sound financial decision. Between 1965 and 2006, owning a stake in an alcohol, gambling, or tobacco company guaranteed an annual rate of return of 3.5 percent. But despite the lure of such healthy profits, individuals and mutual funds have been reluctant to invest in this type of stock, precisely because of the questionable nature of the companies' activities.[1] After all, who would take pride in supporting the tobacco industry, when it sells a deadly product? And what about gambling enterprises? Do they not bear social responsibility vis-à-vis compulsive gamblers and gambling addicts who have lost so much money that suicide sometimes becomes their preferred option?

To explain why individual and institutional investors continue to be bothered by the stigma of "vices," we need to take into consideration the more than five hundred years of debates and regulation that have conditioned Canadians' attitudes in this regard. Certain behaviours still raise controversial and divisive social issues, and questions remain about how society and governments should deal with them.

"Vice" might seem an odd word to use, since it appears to have fallen out of popular use. It is still worthwhile to define the term. According to the *Oxford English Dictionary*, vice is a "depravity or corruption of morals; evil, immoral, or wicked habits or conduct; indulgence in degrading pleasures or practices." This definition implies behaviours that are damaging, since they corrupt individuals, but also reprehensible and highly condemnable, since they are identified as immoral. Finally, the definition implies that "people who indulge in vice" are individuals who enjoy forms of pleasure that are unhealthy and disrespectful.

Based on this broad definition, what precisely constitutes a vice? Is eating chocolate a vice? The answer is obviously negative. In fact, some physicians recommend eating chocolate every day for its health benefits. Is eating an entire big box of chocolates every day a vice? One might answer that eating such a large amount of chocolate can be detrimental to an individual's health. Many would question the eater's motives. Some would interpret this behaviour as the sign of an eating disorder, especially if the habit were to become a pattern. Consumption on this scale has consequences. While it might bring pleasure to some, others would question the type of pleasure being gained. The critic would insist upon the destructive consequences for an individual who has a pattern of ingesting chocolate in excessive amounts.[2] Still others would call it gluttony, thereby invoking the Seven Deadly Sins, or Capital Vices, enumerated by Dante in his *Purgatorio*—anger, avarice, gluttony, jealousy, laziness, lust, and pride—and supported by Judeo-Christian morality.

Vice is not limited to Dante's famous list. The *Index of Christian Art*, founded by Professor Charles Rufus Morey in 1917 and now hosted on the Princeton University website, labels more than 118 behaviours and habits as vices. Besides the Seven Deadly Sins or Vices, called "deadly" by Christians because they bring death to an individual's soul, there are others that are still immoral, unhealthy, and disrespectful, such as blasphemy, drunkenness, fornication, infidelity, intemperance, pleasure, and poverty.[3]

I will not undertake to look at 118 vices—this would be a monumental task. In my brief exploration of how Canadian society has dealt with vice over the last five hundred years, I target vices that have been dealt with most extensively by state and societal institutions. I address various aspects of sexuality, such as attempts to control childbirth and to restrict sexual relations with prostitutes, same-sex partners, and unmarried persons, since at different times these were stigmatized as fornication, lust, sodomy, and infidelity. Drinking alcohol, and consequent drunkenness, was often regarded as a vice because it was a sign of intemperance. Drug use and smoking have also been identified as vices.[4] The consumption of drugs for non-medical purposes was vilified in the second half of the nineteenth century because it allowed the user to escape reality and social responsibility. Drug users, according to opponents, acquired habits that were destructive to themselves and those surrounding them. Opponents of tobacco used the term *vice* in their polemics, which started in the second half of the nineteenth century. After some serious setbacks, the anti-smoking campaign gained momentum, especially in the 1960s, when working, travelling, and exercising in a smoke-free environment came to constitute the new normal. I add gambling to the list, since it gives illicit pleasure—especially when someone makes significant financial gains without hard work, an occurrence that annoyed proponents of the Protestant work ethic—or leads to poverty, which in itself was deemed to constitute a vice. Moreover, a gambler may behave self-destructively if he or she cannot recover from significant financial losses.

Some readers may challenge the label "vice," perhaps preferring "bad habit." After all, the word *vice* has such strong Christian connotations, and Canada at the beginning of the twenty-first century is a largely secular society. The term is no longer used very much, except among those who regulate their lives according to Christian beliefs. Even among contemporary Christians from various denominations, however, some of those who call themselves liberal are reluctant to use a designation that has fallen out of fashion. Despite all this, I persist in using it, partly because Christianity has had such a profound influence on the definition of proper and unacceptable behaviours, prior to the twentieth century's secularizing processes. In sum, the label "vice" has had a powerful moral and social impact. Large numbers of people have mobilized politically to fight it. And, without ignoring the fact that many non-Christians have immigrated to Canada since the 1850s, cultural Christianity has remained a prominent feature of the social fabric. This is apparent even today in ongoing public debates on the definition of marriage and abortion.

Studying vice in a historical context enables us to analyze how individuals, religious institutions, organized social groups (such as women's organizations and, more recently, physicians and social workers), and the state have sought to regulate morality and to influence the allocation of resources to enforce this regulation. This exploration will afford an entry point into a discussion of social control and the constraints put in place by collectivities, institutions, and the state on how individuals must behave in society, and what is expected from them. People who do not comply with norms for acceptable behaviour face potential sanctions that vary according to the nature of the deviance, its frequency, and its effects on the transgressors themselves, on the people surrounding them, and on society in general.

Who has been pressing for the regulation of behaviours? In Canada, Christian theology has been hugely influential. Over the centuries, theologians developed the notion of vice as a way to discipline individuals and to regulate how they should conduct their lives; in other words, as an attempt to govern the self. The belief has persisted that vice is destructive to the self. Vice became a sign of corruption, moral weaknesses, and moral defect, and these attributes were condemnable, depraved, and degrading.[5] By internalizing the concept of Christian virtues and vices, individuals would be able to avoid transgression, because they would gain the will to choose between a righteous and a corrupt life. If internalization of these values alone did not dissuade them from bad behaviour, punishments were employed as part of a strategy to help believers stay on a righteous path. When Christians from various denominations hunted for vice, they targeted individuals and informed transgressors that they had the will to end their morally condemnable conduct. Belief in this willpower signified that Christians understood individuals to have a degree of control and responsibility for themselves and for their own conduct.

Sociologist Alan Hunt argues that members of the middle class have been instrumental in shaping the moral reform agenda, especially since the second half of the nineteenth century. Since their attempts through their own institutions and activism to regulate the lives of others have not reached their expectations and in some cases failed, these individuals and groups—called moral entrepreneurs, such as leaders of Christian churches and of the Woman's Christian Temperance Union—have come to target the state. In these circumstances, they have envisioned a greater role for the state in regulating morality. The success of their activism is also explained by the ability to broaden their appeal in order to win or to make significant gains. The concept of the "umbrella effect," which refers to individuals and groups who are generally ideologically and politically opposed on issues, but who can work together and advocate a particular regulation, is handy in analyzing this broad social mobilization.[6] The umbrella effect is evident at the end of the nineteenth century in campaigns to prohibit alcohol and gambling, to criminalize certain drugs and birth control devices, and to repress homosexuality and prostitution. For instance, the anti-drug movement at the end of the nineteenth century brought together Christian religious leaders, women's organizations, trade union leaders, and opponents of an open-door immigration policy. These individuals and groups came to work together, regardless of their ideological differences, and blamed specific immigrant groups for promoting drugs or facilitating access to them.

These mobilizations encountered strong opposition. Often regulation interfered with commercial interests (e.g., alcohol, gambling, prostitution, or smoking). Some of these opponents to regulation, such as the liquor and gambling industries, sex workers, and more recently, cigarette companies, have mobilized significant resources to prevent regulation and on certain occasions have succeeded in defeating some campaigns against vice.

The state has played a role in the regulation of vice, though, as this book demonstrates, this role has varied considerably over time. The state's changing response to the existence of vices—first to repress and more recently to control them—is indicative of its development. If, during the colonial era, the state had limited means to regulate morality and control individuals, its evolution in the wake of the Industrial Revolution in the nineteenth century in Canada led to a greater role. As the state grew in power, vice opponents who were moral entrepreneurs turned to it instead of other mechanisms for combatting vice. When other institutions failed or had limited means to regulate the conduct of others, these opponents reconciled their call for state regulation with restricting the ability of individuals to self-control. According to them, greater good would be achieved through state regulation that would be beneficial to individuals, families, and collectivities.

With the creation of police forces and the expansion of the justice system, state institutions now became the means to enforce a moral order. According to the late-nineteenth-century German philosopher and sociologist Max Weber, discipline comes with modernity. State development results in its institutions choosing strategies to discipline society. By investing resources in a school system and maintaining police forces, courts, and jails, the state reinforces its power over the people. Since the second half of the nineteenth century, scholars have used state implementation of repressive measures to substantiate the claim that the call by moral entrepreneurs for greater state involvement in the regulation of morality has triggered an era of rigid social control. In fact, the state has set firm boundaries between acceptable and unacceptable behaviours. People who questioned or transgressed these boundaries were confronted with responses from the state through its agents of control. But how effective were police forces, the justice system, and other state actors in repressing gambling, prostitution, public drunkenness, and other behaviours labelled as vices?

In her book on gambling, Suzanne Morton raises an intriguing point. She writes, "It is not always easy to determine what motivated the periodic enforcement of the law...."[7] This study of moral regulation demonstrates that the enforcement of restrictive public policies often constitutes the weakest link in the chain of efforts to suppress proscribed behaviours. Recent studies on state policy development, and in particular on implementation,[8] reveal that the state has not always allocated sufficient resources for its policies and programs targeting specific vices. Also, the state has never been a neutral agent. On the contrary, it has been the site of infighting that pits various components of the state apparatus, such as civil servants, judges, police officers, and social workers, against each other and social actors who have tried to impose their moral concerns and to influence and shape public policies. In the case of moral policies, these components are often selective in how they enforce new regulations. As Kenneth J. Meier observes, "Bureaucratic agencies, particularly those in law enforcement, have far more responsibilities than resources. Accordingly, the agencies will exercise some discretion in how enthusiastically they implement various policies."[9] But limited resources are not the only determinant. As this book illustrates, factors such as class, gender, age, ethnicity, and personal moral convictions of the supposed transgressors, clients, and patients have frequently influenced how judges, physicians, social workers, and police officers have enforced policies. At the same time, these factors and the moral convictions of judges, physicians, social workers, and police officers have shaped the enforcement of policies.

If social regulation based on moral motives has led to the expansion of state regulatory regimes and the growth of provincial and federal bureaucracies, it has, at times, been good politics for those looking to make big gains in a short time. However, such politics lead to inefficient uses of state resources for eradicating vice.[10] Prostitution is a good case in point. Since the colonial era, prostitution has been prevalent. Solutions to deal with it have ranged from moral persuasion, to re-education, to repression. Even though repression has been a widely chosen option—notably at the end of the nineteenth century, when red-light districts were closed in major Canadian cities such as Montreal and Winnipeg—prostitution has not disappeared. It has simply moved to other parts of the city, gone underground, and resurfaced when the anti-prostitution mobilization has quieted down. Police forces and other state agencies responsible for enforcing repression would turn a blind eye or extort protection fees, which would contribute to the re-emergence of sex work as a social issue calling for action.

The present study of a period of more than five hundred years starts with the encounters of two worlds: Aboriginal and European. The first chapter looks at how these encounters shaped the colonization process and how they have continued to influence the ways in which non-Aboriginals look at and construct the social realities of Aboriginal people. When the French explored North America during the sixteenth and seventeenth centuries, they encountered Aboriginal societies that had their own sets of rules and regulations for sexuality, gambling, and tobacco use, to name only a few of the behaviours that some Europeans might consider as vices. Despite missionaries' attempts to impose the Christian regulatory order, this collision of values did not prevent explorers, fur traders, and Crown representatives from entering into profitable political and economic alliances.

The second chapter looks at European settlers and the implementation of a Christian moral order that regulated sexual behaviour, gambling, and drinking. Christian churches played a decisive role in the moral regulation of their followers. Through their institutions, these churches had various means for enforcing what they defined as righteous behaviour. They strove to punish any forms of deviance. However, each Christian church—the Roman Catholic, the Anglican, the Baptist, the Methodist, and the Presbyterian—was limited in its ability to regulate its followers. The churches therefore came to rely on the state to impose a Christian moral order. Although citizens generally internalized the churches' prescriptions, as reinforced by state institutions, some individuals and communities challenged church regulations and state laws. For example, people in villages and small towns used the mechanism of the charivari to regulate sexual and reproductive behaviour. Thus social control during the colonial era was characterized by competition among communities, religious institutions, and the state.

It was in the second half of the nineteenth century that civil society began to play a greater role in regulating behaviours designated as vices. The third chapter details the massive offensive against vices that was waged by individuals, organized lobbies, and others who came to work together in a very loose coalition despite their ideological differences. These social actors pushed for laws that would constrain sexuality; restrict smoking; and prohibit drinking, drug use, and gambling. By 1918 they had made significant gains. Alcohol use was prohibited. Drugs such as opium and cocaine were made illegal and so were most gambling activities. Legitimate sexuality was reaffirmed as the act of procreation by a man and a woman within the indissoluble union of marriage. The vast social mobilization during this era succeeded because some men and women, convinced that their anti-vice campaigns were just and urgent, fought successfully for the support of the state. These social actors forced politicians to implement their social reform agenda on the belief that state interventions were legitimate despite the fact that they interfered with individual rights and ability of individuals to regulate themselves.

Militants of the social reform movement believed that vice was on the retreat at the beginning of the twentieth century. The final chapter, which looks at the regulation of vice since 1920, reveals that this triumph was illusory. During this period, vices came to be known by different names. Although churches, courts, police forces, and fellow citizens continued to condemn those who transgressed "normal" behaviours, transgressions were now often diagnosed as health issues that required treatment. The regulation of vice was increasingly in the hands of health professionals. At the same time, there were those who refused the label of illness and argued that behaviours formerly deemed as vices were well within the normal and acceptable range of human behaviour. Sex workers, drug users, those suffering from alcoholism, those seeking abortions, and homosexuals challenged narratives that negated their right to be heard. Their participation rendered the moral regulation issue more complex.

This brief historical synthesis demonstrates how moral regulation has transformed over time, how it has shaped Canadians' lives, why certain behaviours have been targeted during specific time periods, and why certain individuals and groups have felt empowered to tackle collective social issues. We can identify how the debates have changed over the years, why some—such as the controversy over the prohibition of alcohol at the end of the First World War—have almost disappeared, while others—such as abortion, gambling, marijuana use, and prostitution—have persisted and continue to divide Canadians. New disputes have emerged: for instance, the struggle at the end of the twentieth century to change the definition of marriage in order to legally acknowledge same-sex couples. Against the background of the evolution of the state, the enlargement of the body politic, and activists using courts to assert rights, the story of vice and social regulation in Canada reveals itself to be fascinating and complex.

CHAPTER 1

Different Worlds, Different Values
. Encounters from 1500 to 1700

"**A**s soon as [the Aboriginals] saw us they began to run away, making signs to us that they had come to barter with us; and held up some skins of small value, with which they clothe themselves."[1] When Jacques Cartier first met with Aboriginals in the Gaspé area on July 7, 1534, he extended a process, which had begun several decades prior to his arrival, of European interaction with First Nations on the East Coast of North America. In the course of noting in his travel diary that Aboriginals brought him small gifts, he alluded to their previous encounters with Europeans, such as the Basques, who fished along the Atlantic coast and returned home after a very profitable catch.

Other European newcomers following in the footsteps of the Basques continued this process of encounters with societies they claimed to have "discovered." Each of these two worlds had developed rules, based upon specific cultural values and understandings of society, to regulate individual behaviour. These interactions, which varied through time, introduced Aboriginals to sets of individuals who had specific interests and agendas to advance when dealing with these established communities. As agents of social control, missionaries, fur traders, and French royal authorities each attempted to operate in the "New World" according to their own values. However, when the time came for their representatives to enforce their understanding of what constituted morally acceptable behaviour, two of these institutions in particular—the Roman Catholic Church and the French crown—had limited means at their disposal.

ENCOUNTERS

In recalling his travels to Canada, Jacques Cartier commented little on the social aspects of the Aboriginal societies he encountered. He devoted much more space to descriptions of the geography, the flora, and the fauna of this new territory, and to assessing its economic potential. During his second trip to Canada, Cartier's crew spent the fall of 1535 and the winter of 1536 near Stadacona, where Quebec City now stands, and he familiarized himself with the Aboriginals living in this settlement. The few times Cartier did comment

Jacques Cartier, engraving by John Henry Walker, 1831–1899. McCord Museum, M16425.

on the social organization and living conditions of Aboriginals, he passed judgment on them.

Christianity was a central facet of Europeans' identity, and Christian cultural ideas shaped their understanding of the world. Being a French Roman Catholic, Cartier demonstrated a sense of curiosity toward Aboriginals, but at the same time he displayed his sense of cultural superiority when commenting on their religious beliefs. "This people has no belief in God that amounts to anything," he observed.[2] Cartier acknowledged that, although these Aboriginals had no knowledge of Christianity, they did have some form of spirituality. He wrote that Aboriginals believed in a spirit that communicated with them and could reveal "what the weather will be like."[3] Sometimes this spirit was angry with them and expressed his anger by throwing "dust in their eyes."[4] Cartier indicated that these Aboriginals also had a conception of what happened to their dead: they went "to the stars."[5] Despite recognizing this as a form of spirituality, Cartier viewed it as primitive and he attempted to demonstrate the superiority of his Christian faith based, among other things, on the belief that humans owed their existence and the world they inhabited to a God "Who is in Heaven, Who gives us everything we need and is the Creator of all things and that in Him alone we should believe."[6]

In his commentaries, Cartier remarked on other aspects of Aboriginal societies as well. Besides being struck by their communal way of living, he noted how relations between Aboriginal men and women were socially defined and what the boundaries of socially acceptable behaviour were. If Protestants and Roman Catholics defined marriage as an indissoluble union between a man and a woman and a fundamental social unit, this was not the case for the Aboriginals whom Cartier observed at Stadacona. "They maintain the order of marriage, except that the men take two or three wives," he wrote.[7] Although polygamy was socially acceptable, Cartier indicated that widows were not allowed to remarry. If polygamy itself was a curiosity, he condemned the practice of placing adolescent girls "in a brothel open to every one, until the girls have made a match."[8]

Cartier was definitely not an anthropologist. He had no training in cultural sensitivity and lacked empathy when meeting with individuals who belonged to a very different culture from his own. After all, Cartier was first and foremost an explorer eager to find a short passage to China and to expand the North American territory that directly belonged to the King of France. Nevertheless, he concluded that the Aboriginals he met along the St. Lawrence Valley could easily be converted to Christianity, if this were the king's desire.[9]

Several decades later, Samuel de Champlain, sent by the French king Henri IV to further explore North America, found Stadacona to be an ideal location for a permanent European settlement in 1608. "I arrived there on the 3rd of July, when I searched for a place suitable for our settlement; but I could find none more convenient or better suited than the point of Quebec."[10] Until his death in 1635, Champlain eagerly pursued the development of a system of alliances with various Aboriginal nations that he encountered along the Atlantic Coast, but in particular in the St. Lawrence Valley, the Outaouais region, and the Great Lakes. He understood that the Aboriginals who lived in these regions had created a sophisticated trade network consolidated by political alliances. He inserted the French imperial design of a permanent settlement in North America into these Aboriginal commercial and political networks.

While waging wars alongside his newfound allies, Champlain observed how these Aboriginal tribes structured their social relations and regulated the lives of their members. Still, he could not refrain from condemning practices that seemed barbarous to him, such as torturing prisoners taken in battle. After a victory with his Algonkian allies against members of the Iroquois League, twelve prisoners were tortured by tearing off their nails and burning their fingers. Champlain could not bear this spectacle and shot to death one of the tortured men. He justified his action by arguing that he had put an end to what he considered a "barbarian" practice.[11]

Prior to the arrival of Europeans, Aboriginals had developed sophisticated social structures, with their own forms of governance, trade networks, and political alliances. They belonged to different linguistic families, such as Algonkian and Iroquoian. Their distinct cultures were also partly shaped by their economic structures; some bands were nomadic hunters while others were more sedentary. The nomadic Mi'kmaq, who lived along the East Coast, depended on fishing (mostly during the summer), hunting, and gathering wild berries. Others, such as the Iroquoians, who lived in the St. Lawrence Valley and the Great Lakes area, based their economic life on hunting, and on growing beans, corn, pumpkins, and squash. In the Prairies, Ojibwa and Plains Cree were primarily hunters, and their economic and social organization was centred on the bison hunt. Finally, the various Aboriginal nations varied greatly in numbers. For instance, at the time of European contact, there were about 500 to 700 Beothuk in what is now called Newfoundland,[12] between 10,000 and 20,000 Mi'kmaq on the East Coast, up to 25,000 Hurons or Wendat in the Great Lakes area, and thousands of Plain Cree in the western Prairies.

Aboriginals had established their own sets of rules regulating members' behaviour. Their mechanisms of social control were based on the notion that the whole group was involved in dealing with transgression and deviance. Social status within each band was determined in part by the nature of the economy. For example, as hunting was a crucial activity, skilled hunters would earn the respect of other band members and enjoy a higher social status. Spirituality also played a fundamental role in social organization. Individuals called shamans, who had the ability to interact with the spiritual world or were recognized as having special attributes for communicating with the supernatural, also enjoyed an elevated status.

The social roles of women and men varied greatly among Aboriginals. In matrilineal and matrilocal societies, women played a decisive role. Among Iroquoians, women influenced the political functioning of communities by intervening in the selection of the chief and in the daily organization of the band. Among Aboriginals living along the Pacific coast, women held a less influential place. Knowledge of all these social organizations has come to us through Europeans' eyes. In their descriptions of Aboriginal people, religious representatives pursued an agenda. Besides gathering knowledge, the Jesuits, for instance, described Aboriginals "in a way that demanded their intervention as missionaries." By doing that, they tried to give a purpose and credibility for their action to Europeans by asserting their "authority over Native peoples."[13] However, scholars have deconstructed European value judgments about Aboriginal societies and have been able to understand how men and women interacted with each other, how they raised their children, and how they conversed with the spiritual world.

Nevertheless, Cartier, Champlain, and other Europeans who explored or settled in North America discovered that Aboriginals were resilient and could not be easily assimilated into European culture. Assimilation efforts began to bear fruit only when diseases struck and began to decimate Aboriginals. Brought by Europeans, smallpox killed thousands, sickened many others, undermined the shamans, and wiped out many of the elders who were leaders. It wreaked political, economic, and social havoc. These illnesses were foreign to Aboriginals. Their spiritual treatments and other traditional health practices were powerless either to contain the spread of the diseases or to cure the sick.

FREE SEXUALITY?

Explorers and missionaries who left diaries and other written testimonies of their encounters with Aboriginals would typically pay attention to such matters as eating habits, clothing, hairstyle, tattoos, means of transportation, warfare, and cosmic world view. Contemporary readers of these various written works are struck by the value judgments these observers passed—judgments that reveal a great deal about how Europeans regulated their own gender relations.

In most Aboriginal societies, marriages were monogamous, but in some, men were allowed to have several wives, especially those men who had the reputation of being good hunters. This was the case among the Cree. When Champlain commented on gender relations in Aboriginal communities, he mentioned the age of women thought to be of marrying age—"eleven, twelve, thirteen, fourteen or fifteen years of age"[14]—but insisted that they did not need the consent of their parents to develop a relationship with a man. Female Wendat, Champlain observed, could have several relationships: "It is the woman's choice and option to take and accept whoever pleases her most...."[15] Women were active in initiating sexual relations with men. Public displays of affection, including kissing, were not welcome among the Wendat. Despite these reservations, women did develop long-term relationships with men. However, this did not prevent them from having other male sexual partners, even while they were in a stable relationship with a particular man. This dynamic changed when women were pregnant. "Now the time when they do not leave their husbands is when they have children."[16]

When the Jesuit missionaries commented on the Wendat, they observed with satisfaction that these Aboriginals practised monogamy, but they did not hesitate to condemn the relative sexual freedom that these women otherwise enjoyed. Female Wendat could have premarital sex soon after puberty, choose their husband, and end their relationship with their husband with ease, simply by asking them to move out. Divorce was freely accepted.[17] Other Europeans, such as the explorer and fur trader Nicolas Perrot, noticed that in some Aboriginal societies that valued monogamy, unions between men and women would last until the death of one of the partners.[18] But the ease with which a marriage could end without the spouse's death was shocking to these European observers. Missionaries and other clergy members were especially appalled, since they were the ones entitled by their social status to enforce the Christian moral order, the set of rules that regulated gender relations and condemned any form of sexuality outside the "sacred" union between a man and a woman. Moreover, European clergy came from societies that believed that women were subordinate to men, and the notion that both women and men could choose to withdraw from a marriage challenged all European conceptions of such a union. In her analysis of the *Relations*, Carole Blackburn argues that condemnation of sexuality was indicative of the Jesuits' struggle with sexual desire and what they "were afraid of and from which they had to dissociate themselves."[19]

Nevertheless, not everyone condemned Aboriginal women's relative degree of sexual freedom and their control over their own bodies. This state of affairs suited Antoine Denis Raudot, who was the Intendant of New France from 1705 to 1710. He wrote: "The manner in which the girls live among the savages is very convenient. They are mistresses of their body until they are absolutely married."[20] Louis-Armand de Lom d'Arce, third baron de La Hontan, commented on the ability of Aboriginal women to regulate births. Having observed Aboriginal life while serving as a soldier in New France from 1683 to 1692, he mentioned in his memoirs that Aboriginals knew how to use

Cover page of *Relations des Jésuites en Canada* by John Henry Walker, 1855. McCord Museum, M930.50.7.260.

certain herbs and roots to induce an abortion.[21] Reportedly, Wendat women had no sexual relations for two or three years following the birth of a child. This allowed them to control the size of their families.[22] For their part, some French fur traders were attracted to Aboriginal women and found the idea of premarital sex very pleasing. These traders were reluctant to condemn a form of sexual freedom that was unavailable to European women.[23]

Though this aspect of societal and political behaviour escaped them initially, Europeans did eventually come to understand that sexual intercourse could be a form of diplomacy for Aboriginals. Father Pierre Biard was at the Jesuit mission of Port Royal in Acadia from 1611 to 1613. In his report, he wrote that the Mi'kmaq and the Abénaquis were not appreciative of the fact that French fur traders sought to trade more than goods when they interacted with them, since they were interested in having sexual relations with Aboriginal women. Some fur traders sought sexual relations, but left showing no concern if an Aboriginal woman became pregnant and had a child.[24] Since Aboriginals used matrimonial unions as a form of diplomacy and a means to consolidate political alliances, the behaviour of certain of these fur traders demonstrated a clear lack of understanding of Aboriginal culture. Over the years, however, Europeans began to see the benefits of developing intimate relationships with Aboriginal women. These relations facilitated their accul-turation to Aboriginal ways and reinforced political alliances concocted by Crown representatives.

Aboriginal children's relative autonomy and sexual freedom had led the Jesuits to label them as spoiled. To the great dismay of the Récollets and the Jesuits, Aboriginal parents did not inflict physical punishment. Champlain had difficulties absorbing this cultural shock as well. The lack of discipline and respect for parenthood and parental authority disturbed him. Children hit their mothers, and some of them who "have gained strength and power" hit their fathers as well. But Champlain's biographer, David Hackett Fischer, reports that the Chief Lieutenant in New France admired the Huron and reached the conclusion, after many years of relations with them, that they were "to be the equal of Europeans in their intelligence, and superior in physical strength and the proportion of their bodies."[25]

A Jesuit missionary, who was in North America between 1711 and 1717, commented on "men who dress[ed] as women" and "special friendships among men"[26] among Aboriginal groups. The prevalence of homosexual relations led religious officials to condemn these practices. However, sociol-ogist Gary Kinsman argues that cross-dressing and same-sex relations did not constitute a form of "institutionalized homosexuality." On the contrary, Aboriginal cultures did not have a clear dichotomy between homosexuality and heterosexuality. In some cultures, "cross-dressing men and women actu-ally belonged to the other gender or to a third gender that either combined male and female features or that was 'not man, not woman.'"[27]

Since sexuality captured the attention of Europeans, did those who ven-tured along the Atlantic coast, the St. Lawrence Valley, and the Great Lakes area also comment on sexually transmitted diseases? When Gabriel Théodat Sagard, who was a Récollet friar and missionary among the Wendat in 1623 and 1624, published *Le Grand Voyage du pays des Hurons* in 1632, he reported the story of a male Wendat who lived isolated from the rest of his band. This situation intrigued Sagard. Was this Aboriginal being punished? If so, what was his crime? Sagard learned that this man lived apart because of an illness affecting his testicles. By talking to him, Sagard discovered that the sick man had no hope for a cure; only death would end his suffering. Was he living apart because of the nature of his illness? If this was the case, Sagard thought this would constitute a form of moral sanction on the part of the community. But Sagard learned otherwise: that Aboriginals isolated sick individuals in order to prevent the propagation of disease.[28]

These facets of sexuality, child rearing, and relationships were in direct contrast to predominant European values and behaviours. Shaped by centuries of proscription and regulation, Europeans who interacted with Aboriginals naturally brought with them their concept of society, having internalized what church and state deemed proper and improper behaviours. Europeans valued marriage as a means to gain social acceptance, and to fulfil both societal expectations and their sexual needs, since marriage was the only context in which it was appropriate for a man and woman to have sexual relations. As stated in the Roman Catholic catechism, marriage was "a sacrament which gives grace to the married couple to love one another, and breed up their children in the fear of God."[29] European parents, church leaders, and communities expected a man and a woman to get married as a condition of intimacy, and Protestant and Catholic religious organizations played a crucial role in defining marriage as an institution and a social unit. For them, marriage involved individuals of two different sexes: a man and a woman. This was an explicit rejection of same-sex marriage and polygamy.[30]

"AN INVETERATE PASSION FOR BRANDY"[31]

One of the primary enforcers of the European moral order, the Roman Catholic Church, strongly encouraged Christians to moderate their use of alcohol. Temperance was a virtue, and Catholics had to live soberly by avoiding drunkenness. For a Catholic, abuse of alcohol meant possible damnation in the afterlife. This form of punishment was foreign to Aboriginals—especially, of course, to those who did not convert.

Prior to the arrival of Europeans in Canada, Aboriginals did not have access to alcohol and did not know how to make it. When Jacques Cartier's ships ventured into the St. Lawrence River in 1535, he noticed a large number of wild grapes growing on the island near Stadacona. The presence of these plants on Orleans Island led him to name it "Bacchus Island" in honour of the Roman god of winemaking and wine.[32] The absence of wine among Aboriginals intrigued the first missionaries who visited them. Récollet friar Gabriel Théodat Sagard could not explain why alcohol was unknown to the Wendat in spite of the fact that wild grapes grew where these Aboriginals settled.[33] But if the presence of grapevines led European settlers to believe that they could make wine using fermented fruits, the harsh climate and short growing season would soon dispel their notion and limit the development of the wine industry in New France. These realities encouraged royal authorities in the colony to favour the importation of wine and other spirits.

Alcohol came to play a prominent role in the fur trade. The supply of wild animals in the Baltic had been depleted, but Europeans' appetite for furs remained insatiable, so it became imperative to find new sources. North America possessed what the European continent could no longer offer: relatively easy access to beaver pelts that would satisfy the high demand fuelled by the emergence of new fashion trends in Europe. This demand stimulated the development of the fur trade in North America.

Access to alcohol radically changed trading relations between Europeans and Aboriginals. The French introduced alcohol as a diplomatic tool even before they began trading with Aboriginals, just as they did when interacting with other Europeans during official business and political dealings. Jacques Cartier offered alcohol and food as a gesture of goodwill when he met with Aboriginals during his first trip in 1534. Other French explorers repeated Cartier's gesture, but they were astonished by the Aboriginal response. Aboriginals were initially very cautious, as they were repulsed by the colour of red wine; they thought that the French were offering them blood to drink. When the French offered eau de vie, a colourless distilled beverage made from fruit, Aboriginals disliked this "strange" liquid that set their mouths and throats on fire after just one shot.[34] According to the first accounts about the Wendat, these Aboriginals had no interest whatsoever in drinking alcohol. For the Montagnais, alcohol was a "magical substance." Those drinking it were "possessed by powerful supernatural forces."[35] Nevertheless, Aboriginals did come to enjoy the "strange" liquid that the French generally offered before trading with them. Besides firearms, copper kettles, woollen blankets, knives, and other metallic objects, alcohol was very much prized by Aboriginals when they traded with the French and other Europeans in North America.

After their initial reactions of reluctance and distaste, Aboriginals enjoyed alcohol. Intoxication allowed them to connect with their spiritual world. According to several Europeans who lived among them, they were

> naturally very much inclined to drink and become intoxicated willingly because at this time they believe everything permitted. They are so well persuaded of this that should a drunken man break their canoes and everything that is in their cabins, they do not get angry, and, laughing, say, "he has no sense."[36]

Some Aboriginals even developed what is now referred to as alcohol addiction. Researchers have struggled to explain this growing dependence. One of the most common, but also controversial, explanations is based on the rate at which Aboriginals metabolized the substance. Others have argued that since, as mentioned above, some Aboriginals found that drinking alcohol helped them to connect with the spiritual world, becoming drunk was a very fast and therefore irresistible way to connect with the Great Spirit and other beings who inhabited the spiritual world.[37]

Although scholars no longer suggest that the introduction of alcohol was the key cause of the sharp decline and disintegration of Aboriginal societies, the chiefs of these communities condemned its use just as forcefully as did the Jesuit missionaries. Fearing for the success of their missions among the Huron and Algonquian nations, the Jesuits eagerly used the concerns expressed by Aboriginal chiefs to reinforce their own views on the issue. In the 1636 *Relations*—the Jesuits' annual report on their activities in New France—Paul Le Jeune expounded on the terrible consequences of alcohol use in North America, both among French people, but also in particular among Aboriginals. As a Christian cleric, Le Jeune viewed alcohol as a vice because it provided a source of earthly pleasure. He claimed that drunken Aboriginals would kill Frenchmen and vice versa. According to the Jesuit, what he considered alcohol abuse had horrible consequences for Aboriginal women and children. Le Jeune contended that drunken male Aboriginals deprived their families of food and "a good living" earned from the fur trade.[38]

A year later, in 1637, Le Jeune again depicted a worrisome situation: alcohol use was now widespread in the Aboriginal communities that he was familiar with. "There is scarcely a native, small or great—even among the girls and women—who does not enjoy this intoxication and who does not take these beverages when they can be had, purely and simply for the sake of getting drunk." Le Jeune was particularly preoccupied by the quantity of alcohol consumed and, without providing any figures, he noted Aboriginals drank in "great excess."[39] In reaction to the social devastation caused by alcohol use, some missionaries, with the support of Aboriginals, took it upon themselves to found villages in which alcohol was banned.

Accounts by missionaries like Le Jeune put pressure on the Roman Catholic Church to regulate access to alcohol. The church in New France reminded Catholics that they had a moral obligation to refrain from excessive drinking, and in 1658 it declared the liquor trade with Aboriginals to be a mortal sin. A mortal sin was visited with a terrible punishment, but a Catholic could redeem himself if he showed remorse and asked for forgiveness. For those who were not concerned about committing a mortal sin, the Catholic church had an even more powerful threat: excommunication. This was the harshest form of punishment and the most effective tool for regulating the lives of Roman Catholics while ensuring that they followed the precepts of the church. In a further attempt to regulate the consumption of alcohol and to remind Catholics of their obligations, in 1660 the bishop of New France declared that the liquor trade with Aboriginals was forbidden, except when a fur trader or a representative of the Crown offered one or two measures of eau de vie before the trading began.[40]

The Roman Catholic Church condemned the use of alcohol in the fur trade. Besides believing that drinking would lead individuals into sin, church officials who lived among Aboriginals often denounced their inability to exercise self-control. According to the missionaries, Aboriginals drank in excess and were not able to abstain. This reinforced their perception that Aboriginals were "savages."

While church officials were quick to denounce the effects of alcohol, not all Aboriginal leaders were merely passive observers. Some chiefs reminded church leaders that their French-speaking counterparts were responsible for this situation: "It is you ... who have taught us to drink this liquor; and now we cannot do without it. If you refuse to give it us, we will apply to the English."[41] Other times, Aboriginal leaders pleaded with French authorities to eliminate alcohol in the fur trade.

Without seeking to minimize the effects of alcohol among Aboriginals, historian Jim Miller observes that the quantity of alcohol actually reaching Aboriginal societies was probably quite limited during the seventeenth century. Liquor was a heavy and difficult commodity to transport in canoes, especially over long distances. This constrained it as a trading commodity.[42] Nevertheless, critics of alcohol as an integral tool of the fur trade during the seventeenth century demanded action. They concluded that condemnations alone were ineffective. Something else had to be done, but what precisely? The solution was prohibition. For Jesuit Paul Le Jeune, absolute prohibition would prevent death, abuse, and, ultimately, the extermination of Aboriginal societies.[43]

In one of his reports to the King of France, Jacques Duchesneau de la Doussinière et d'Ambault, the Intendant of New France from 1675 to 1682, echoed the Jesuits' concerns, when he commented on the welfare of Aboriginals and the impact of alcohol use in the Outaouais region:

> But our principal interest, and what will alone crown all our designs with success, is, according to the dictates of our duty, to establish Religion on a solid basis among those people who have any disposition thereunto. This would succeed, were those in authority in this country to chastise such as set the Indians bad example, and to forbid in accordance with the prohibition contained in the King's ordinance of the year 1679, the conveying of Brandy to the Natives, in as much as drunkenness is, among them, the greatest obstacle to religion; destroys both their health and substance, and gives rise among them to quarrels, batteries and murders, that cannot be remedied on account of the distance.[44]

For a while, religious authorities had the upper hand. As early as 1621, Champlain banned the trade of alcohol to Aboriginals. Several years later, in 1663, French royal authorities endorsed prohibition by forbidding eau de vie, the main liquor used in the fur trade. Those who were caught paid a fine for the first offence or were banished or whipped for a second offence.[45]

Nevertheless, the Roman Catholic Church, and the Jesuits especially, was stymied in its attempts to use prohibition to regulate the behaviour of Aboriginals toward liquors. Diplomatic, economic, and political factors limited the ability of the church to impose its views on how the trade with Aboriginals should be conducted. Many French traders simply ignored the views and opinions expressed by the bishop of New France. They did not want their ability to trade with Aboriginals to be compromised and particularly wished to secure friendships and seal political and economic alliances with Aboriginal groups.[46] In the traders' experience, alcohol was an indispensable tool.

Motivated by economic and diplomatic considerations, Crown representatives eventually changed their policy on alcohol use and trade with Aboriginals, despite the Roman Catholic Church's views. The system of alliances that the French developed with Aboriginals required the use of alcohol. Furthermore, the kingdoms of France and England were in competition to expand their control over North America. Since English-speaking traders used brandy in their trade, the King of France, regardless of the condemnations by missionaries and other religious officials, could not afford not to follow suit. Reason of State—or in this case Reason of the King—prevailed over moral considerations.

GAMBLING

Gambling activities were not a major concern for those who left written accounts of their interactions with Aboriginals. Most observers made brief references to gambling, taking the time to describe various activities without judging those who took part in them. For instance, there was a game involving "marked fruit stones" that were "tossed like dice in a wooden bowl."[47] Those involved played with passion, both men and women betting what they owned or even their body parts, such as hair and fingers. In the Jesuit *Relations*, there are references to Aboriginals who had their little fingers "cut off without showing any sign of pain." According to Jesuit accounts, the losing player was generally not upset and left his gambling partners singing.[48] In his analysis of the Wendat, anthropologist Bruce Trigger notes that Aboriginals who lost at gambling were not supposed to display signs of anger or displeasure. On the contrary, they were supposed to be gracious. Some, whose losses were too high, committed suicide.[49]

TOBACCO

In their accounts of Aboriginal societies, Europeans commented on various habits and customs that, in the second half of the nineteenth century, would come to be declared highly immoral and reprehensible. At the time of their early encounters, though, they mentioned these activities without condemning them. During his second voyage, Jacques Cartier commented on a "herb" that Aboriginals grew in "large quantity" for "the winter's consumption": tobacco.

> Men alone make use of it in the following manner. After drying it in the sun, they carry it around their necks in a small skin pouch in lieu of a bag.… Then at frequent intervals they crumble this plant into powder, which they place in one of the openings of the hollow instrument, and, laying a live coal on top, suck at the other end to such an extent that they fill their bodies so full of smoke that it streams out of their mouths and nostrils as from a chimney.

Cartier tried it but "one would think one had taken powdered pepper, it is so hot."[50] In the *Relations* of 1636, Paul Le Jeune made a similar observation about tobacco.[51] Several Aboriginal nations grew tobacco for their own consumption. They enjoyed smoking it "to clear the brain."[52]

Pipe (1475–1525) used by the Iroquoians in the St. Lawrence Valley. McCord Museum, M4243.

Aboriginals in different locations were more or less successful in growing tobacco, since it depended on the quality of soil and the climate. Algonkians who lived in the Ottawa Valley area traded with other Aboriginals in order to obtain tobacco. Although the Wendat grew the plant, the climate in the Georgian Bay area, where most of them lived, limited the size of their crops. The Wendat traded with Aboriginals living on the north shore of Lake Erie, where the soil was much more favourable, and thus gained access to the plant.[53]

Tobacco had sacred properties for Aboriginals. The substance was used as an offering during religious ceremonies to communicate with spirits. In other circumstances, Aboriginals offered tobacco to spirits to gain their support and sympathy. At other times, it was used as a cure for illnesses.[54] As Récollet friar Gabriel Théodat Sagard noted, some tribes offered tobacco to Europeans and other visitors as a sign of hospitality.[55] The introduction of tobacco to the French meant that, in European terms, the kingdom of France "discovered" this plant. However, the transfer of its habitual use would have "deadly long-term consequences."[56]

CONCLUSION: INTERACTING WITH ABORIGINALS

Aside from the findings of archaeological digs, knowledge of Contact-era Aboriginal societies has come to us from different groups: explorers, fur traders, and missionaries. If members of the first two groups, except for Jacques Cartier or Samuel de Champlain, did not leave many written accounts, it was a different story with missionaries. Although, at the beginning, their assessments of Aboriginal societies were sometimes harsh, historian Jim Miller argues that their judgments evolved and became much more favourable over time.

These judgments changed because European societies that established and maintained permanent contact with Aboriginal communities, in particular the French, came to develop a series of relations based on mutual dependence. This interdependence would limit the ability of those who were eager to enforce a moral order shaped by Christianity. The Jesuits concluded that they could convert souls, and incidentally impose their moral order on sexuality and alcohol use, but they could not turn Aboriginals into Frenchmen. Jim Miller observes that the "European presence in North America was dependent on Native goodwill and cooperation because the Indian was vital to the realization of all the purposes the Europeans had in coming to the continent."[57] This seriously limited the ability of the newcomers, and especially their agents of change, to Frenchify Aboriginals. Outnumbered by Aboriginals, the French, and their dreams of remodelling Aboriginal societies, were temporarily stalled, even if this situation did not prevent those who wrote about the Aboriginals from outlining what they wished they could do.

If explorers were eager to broaden territorial boundaries for their French masters, missionaries tried to convert as many Aboriginals as possible and to mitigate what they labelled as the negative impacts of trade. By introducing alcohol and firearms, explorers and traders such as Daniel Greysolon Dulhut and Médard Chouart des Groseilliers wanted to increase the trade in furs and at the same time consolidate the system of alliances that royal representatives had developed. But they also entered into conflict with the moral order that missionaries strove to implement and enforce. There was a collision between two worlds: the commercial and the spiritual. The former would prevail.

CHAPTER 2

In the Name of God, the King, and the Settlers
Regulating Behaviour during the Colonial Era (1700–1850)

The visit of Peter Kalm caught the attention of many in New France in 1749. Settlers, Roman Catholic Church officials, and the Governor General and the Intendant, who were the royal representatives in the colony, were eager to meet with the Swedish botanist and traveller. Kalm had already sojourned in the British colonies for a year, before spending the summer in New France. Upon his return to Sweden, he published a report of his travels. His recollections contained not only details about the flora and fauna in North America, but also observations of the political, social, and economic climate. French-speaking settlers intrigued him greatly, and Kalm took the time to compare them with Europeans. He commented on the institutional role that the Roman Catholic Church played in the colony and in particular in the colonists' personal lives. Insisting on the centrality of the church's role, Kalm depicted settlers as devoted churchgoers, who willingly complied with religious obligations. He wrote:

> It was both strange and amusing to see and hear how eagerly the women and soldiers said their prayers in Latin and did not themselves understand a word of what they said. When all the prayers were ended the soldiers cried *Vive le Roi*! And that is about all they understood of the prayer proceedings.... In the meantime the people are very faithful in these observances, because everyone tries by these means to put God under some obligation and intends by it to make himself deserving of some reward.[1]

For her part, British immigrant Susanna Moodie discovered that settlers had their own means for regulating the lives of others. Two years after immigrating to the Peterborough area with her husband and young daughter in 1832, she observed a charivari—a mechanism of social control used by a community against members who chose to marry contrary to social customs, despite the fact that religious and state institutions sanctioned the union. She was quite alarmed and demoralized by what she witnessed. Moody wrote that a group of people "disguise[d] themselves, blackening their faces, putting their clothes on hind part before, and wearing horrible masks, with grotesque caps on their head, adorned with cocks' feathers and bells." They walked toward the "bridegroom's house, to the sound of tin kettles, horns, and drums, cracked fiddles, and all the discordant instruments they can collect together." Members of this community organized a charivari because they disapproved of the decision by a man to marry a fourth wife, who was only sixteen years of age. The age difference between the old man and the young woman was deemed unacceptable.[2]

In North America during the period from 1700 to 1850, religion was central to an individual's identity. But, while religious organizations had a great deal of power to constrain behaviour, nascent state institutions and local communities also had ways to exert social control. Living mostly in small towns and in the countryside, inhabitants internalized notions of good behaviour through their interactions with these institutions and with each other. Individual settlers also developed their own strategies of resistance. In fact, the ways in which individuals and communities enforced their moral order sometimes collided with the agendas of the church and state.

SEXUALITY: ONLY FOR PROCREATION

Since 1627 the Roman Catholic Church had been the only church allowed in the St. Lawrence Valley, along the Mississippi River, and in Louisiana. All settlers were required to be Catholics, and, after 1685, Huguenots, or French Protestants, could no longer live in the kingdom or in any of its colonies. Though the King of France exercised nominal control, this religious institution was not totally obedient to the monarch. For example, the king, by virtue of the authority he held by divine right, contested the papal authority to appoint bishops in his kingdom. In New France, the royal authorities intervened in the establishment and territorial limits of parishes, but the bishop appointed parish priests without royal consent.[3]

No concept of popular sovereignty existed during this period, since French inhabitants had no say in the administration of the colony. This began to change with the British victories over French military forces in Quebec City and Montreal, in 1759 and 1760 respectively, and with the Constitutional Act of 1791. A group known as the Loyalists joined the few English-speaking people who had immigrated to Quebec after the British conquest. These Loyalists left the thirteen American colonies during, but mostly after, the American War of Independence, compelled by their allegiance to the British Empire. About 40,000 moved to British North America, but a few went to the Province of Quebec, formerly the colony of New France. The majority went to the colonies of Nova Scotia and New Brunswick. The few Loyalists who migrated to the Province of Quebec refused to live in the St. Lawrence Valley, where French-speaking settlers greatly outnumbered them. Instead, they settled west of the Ottawa River and agitated for a new colony where English-speaking Loyalists would form a majority of the inhabitants. Responding to these pressures, British authorities created the colonies of Upper Canada and Lower Canada (known formerly as the Province of Quebec), in 1791. Settlers began electing their own representatives in the legislative assemblies of Lower Canada and Upper Canada in 1792.

During the colonial era in New France and British North America, religion was the basis of society. This meant that, initially, Roman Catholic beliefs regulated how individuals interacted with each other, and how they understood the functioning of society and their specific places and roles. When English-speaking immigrants settled in British North America, Protestant denominations, alongside the Roman Catholic Church, exerted a similar influence.

The Roman Catholic Church had several means for enforcing its moral order. Bishops elaborated regulations, called *mandements*, designed to guide individual behaviours and social relations. The clergy enforced these *mandements*, and other proscriptions, through the school system, religious services that Catholics had to attend, and sacraments they had to receive. Since the Council of Trent, which convened in the sixteenth century, the teaching of faith had deeply preoccupied the Catholic church. The church used the catechism to explain its doctrines and dictate how Catholics should regulate their lives. Bearing witness to the confession of sins and other harmful behaviours gave priests the authority to enforce the Catholic moral order. The Lateran Council of 1215 stated that Catholics had to confess to their parish priest at least once a year.[4] The sacrament of confession allowed priests to absolve sinners and impose a penitence, which depended on the nature of the sin or transgression.

Aside from maintaining these mechanisms for developing and enforcing a moral order, the Catholic church accomplished several other tasks in New France and, after the Conquest, in British North America. It provided comfort for the soul by being a moral guardian. It recorded births, marriages, and deaths. And it was in charge of the school system, hospitals, and charitable institutions. Outlining the numerous functions of the Roman Catholic Church adds sharper definition to a crucial issue: the extent of its social control. Travellers who visited New France and British North America, and scholars who have studied these societies since then, have frequently commented upon and debated this issue.

Church officials often complained about their inability to control the inhabitants. The first bishop of New France (from 1658 to 1688), François-Xavier de Montmorency Laval, criticized settlers for playing cards, participating in horse racing, taking part in dances, and wearing clothing that he labelled as "indecent." According to Laval, the French-speaking colonists did not have a virtuous lifestyle or habits.[5] In the middle of the eighteenth century, evidence of bad behaviour was still abundant. According to reports sent to the bishop of New France, clergy members who visited Acadians living in the Maritimes saw men and women dancing together "after sunset" and settlers abusing alcohol, especially on Sundays and holy days, in the colony of Nova Scotia.[6] After the British Conquest, the clergy kept complaining about sinful behaviour. According to a visiting missionary and a parish priest residing near Rimouski, vices were so prevalent in the town that its Catholic inhabitants would have to face a punishment similar to that inflicted upon the biblical Sodom and Gomorrah. When he learned of these worrisome reports, the bishop of Quebec acted swiftly. In a letter read to the inhabitants, he threatened them with excommunication unless they abandoned their sinful conduct.[7]

Such complaints reflected how the clergy understood their spiritual work among settlers. They reminded inhabitants that the flesh was weak and could easily succumb to temptations such as uncontrolled sexual activity, excessive drinking, and gambling. By reinforcing Catholic doctrine about sins and temptations, Catholic officials appealed to the settlers' obligation to discipline themselves and highlighted the various punishments they faced by failing to do so. At the same time, the clergy emphasized the "difficulties" of their task and hoped for support on the part of their superiors.

These complaints also demonstrated the limited means at the disposal of the Roman Catholic Church to discipline Catholics effectively. There was a shortage of priests in New France, and in the St. Lawrence Valley under British rule until the Rebellions of 1837–38. In Quebec City and Montreal, priests were more numerous, and the church had a greater ability to enforce its moral order. But outside of these two cities, clergy members visited settlers and administered sacraments only once or twice a month. In 1713, the priest-to-person ratio was 1:83 in urban areas but only 1:289 in the rest of the colony. This situation did not change quickly, since four-fifths of the one hundred parishes in the colony still had no resident priests by the 1730s.[8] On the eve of the British Conquest, there were 180 priests to look after the spiritual needs of 70,000 inhabitants. Following the Conquest by the Protestant British, and with only 138 Catholic priests in place by 1766, church officials feared for their institutional survival.[9] However, British authorities granted the inhabitants the right to practise the Catholic religion. While tensions between colonists and British representatives in the thirteen American colonies reached the boiling point, Crown authorities made political concessions to inhabitants of the

Province of Quebec. The Quebec Act of 1774 recognized the Roman Catholic Church and allowed French civil law to govern social relations.

The Roman Catholic Church was not the only religious institution complaining about immorality in the colony. When Loyalists and other immigrants came to British North America after the Conquest and the implementation of British rule after 1763, Protestant officials from various denominations denounced settlers' lack of religious knowledge. They complained about their irregular attendance at religious services, their disrespect for Sunday as a day of rest, and other vices and sinful behaviours.[10]

Despite limitations to the influence of both the Roman Catholic Church and the Protestant denominations, a Christian-driven moral order prevailed after the Conquest. Settlers internalized this moral order, but this did not stop them from transgressing it, especially when it concerned sexuality.

During the French regime, marriage was both a religious sacrament and a union defined by a civil law known as the *Coutume de Paris*. For Catholics, the legitimate form of sexuality was intercourse between a married man and woman for the purpose of reproduction. "Marriage [was] the only suitable outlet for sexual desire."[11] During the fifteenth and sixteenth centuries, the Roman Catholic Church introduced a mode of regulation that condemned the pleasure of the flesh. Regardless of their social status, individuals learned that sexuality was strictly for reproduction. Referring to the Scripture, the church constrained the boundaries of acceptable sexuality. Same-sex marriage was unthinkable, since the Bible states that "a man will leave his father and mother and be united to his wife, and the two will become one flesh." Premarital sex and sexual intercourse between unmarried individuals, or between married individuals other than husbands and wives, were sinful acts. For the Catholic church, God himself traced the proper boundaries when he dictated the commandments to Moses: "Thou shalt not commit adultery" and "Thou shalt not covet thy neighbour's wife." Marriage was monogamous and indissoluble, conjugal fidelity was fundamental, and abstinence was a virtue for the unmarried. Since sexuality was confined to reproduction, sex with animals, masturbation, rape, and other nonconforming sexual acts were "crimes against nature" and sinful.[12] The age of consent for men and women was low. Pope Alexander III had intervened in the debate during the twelfth century. He specified that the minimum marrying age was twelve for women and fourteen for boys. If a girl under the age of twelve or a boy under the age of fourteen married, the marriage could be annulled.[13]

Protestants too had strict views on sexuality and marriage. Sexual intercourse was acceptable for a married couple as long as they had, or were intending to have, children. If intercourse occurred outside of marriage, or "for purposes other than reproduction," it was transgressive.[14]

The state also regulated marriage as a civil institution. In New France, the husband had total authority over the couple's well-being. He decided where the newlywed couple would live and built their house. He, not his wife, owned the property and borrowed money. Once married, a woman lost her legal capacity. This meant that she, among other things, could not own property or borrow money and needed her husband's permission to ask for a divorce. In the British colony of Nova Scotia, before the British Conquest of New France, the law explicitly stipulated that a married woman was "the sexual property of her husband."[15] Following the conquest and the creation of the British colonies in North America, in the other Maritimes colonies and in Upper Canada, a married woman "could not make a will, sell her property, sign a contract, or engage in business without her husband's consent."[16]

Despite religious condemnations of premarital sexuality, and of sexual intercourse between married individuals other than husbands and wives, individuals frequently sought extramarital sex. Prostitutes worked in *maisons closes*, or whorehouses, in Quebec City and Montreal during the French regime. Court cases, such as the case of Marguerite Leboeuf, attested to their existence. In appearance, Marguerite was a respectable woman, since she had married Gabriel Lemieux. However, other females resided in their home, and she was found guilty of using the household for prostitution in 1667. Marguerite Leboeuf pleaded that poverty and her husband's debts were the factors that led her to commit her fault. Before the Sovereign Council, a court of appeal for civil and criminal cases in the colony, she asked for clemency. She argued that a delay would give her and her husband enough time to repay their debts. However, the case was never settled, as Marguerite died in 1673.[17]

Most prostitutes worked near the Quebec City and Montreal harbours, as these were the main points of entry to the French colony. When a ship arrived at Quebec City from France or the Caribbean, its crew went looking for food, drink, and sex. As well, there were numerous soldiers stationed in these towns, since European wars and military conflicts with Aboriginals required a permanent military presence. Although settlers welcomed soldiers, they did not accept sexual relations between soldiers and prostitutes. In August 1667 two soldiers, Langevin and Champagne, learned the hard way that this type of sexual activity was not tolerated in the colony. Arrested in the company of prostitutes, these two Frenchmen were accused of desertion and rape. In order to save his life, since a conviction of rape carried the death penalty, and following the advice of his Jesuit confessor, Claude d'Ablon, Langevin changed his story. This time, he blamed the prostitutes for forcing him to desert. Furthermore, the prostitutes, whom local soldiers knew very well, had had sexual relations with three other soldiers. The rape charge was dropped.[18]

While the Catholic church impressed on settlers that they should abstain from all extramarital sexual intercourse, royal representatives contemplated the possibility of a crackdown on prostitutes. In 1687 Governor General Jacques-René de Brisay, marquis de Denonville, and Intendant Jean Bochart de Champigny promoted the idea of sending prostitutes back to France. The king rejected their proposal, because he believed he had a better plan: hard labour. A woman found guilty of prostitution would be condemned to hard labour to be performed in public. This would capture the public's imagination and dissuade and frighten women from engaging in sex work. Hard labour in public was a demonstration of the state's power and a tool of discipline designed to punish those tempted by this form of sexual transgression. Nevertheless, the king's plan did not take effect. During the seventeenth century, prostitutes and those accused of using their homes for prostitution were arrested and convicted. However, they were not accused of being prostitutes per se or of making a house available for prostitution. Rather, royal authorities accused them of other offences, as in the case of Marie Anne Vendezzeque in 1689. Her son-in-law accused Vendezzeque of allowing "questionable" individuals to stay in her home during the day and night. His claim was dismissed on the basis that he had a conflict with his mother-in-law because of her refusal to let her daughter live with him. However, Vendezzeque had additional problems with the law because of the "poor" reputation of her home. Four years later, she was convicted of selling liquor to Aboriginals and forced to pay a fine.[19]

Throughout the eighteenth century, authorities tolerated prostitution. In his study of crimes in New France, historian André Lachance writes that no prostitutes were arrested during the last decade of the French regime. Authorities intervened only when they were led to believe that prostitution was out of control. If clergy members or nobles complained about prostitution and pressured royal representatives to act, authorities would send women suspected of being prostitutes to hospitals, rather than arrest them.[20]

By 1810 there were between four hundred and six hundred prostitutes in Quebec City. In Montreal in 1825, 6 percent of women who had a "declared" profession were prostitutes.[21] The presence of prostitutes disturbed many residents in Montreal. Religious leaders, members of the elite, and people living in neighbourhoods where sex trade activities occurred openly asked for better regulation of public space. This implied that streets and parks belonged to them and not to prostitutes. A crackdown on women who "invaded" public space with their "despicable" activities was in order. According to opponents, if prostitution was to occur at all, it should take place in private spaces.

Authorities began to use vagrancy laws to crack down on street prostitution. Between 1810 and 1842, there were 2,528 recorded incidents of vagrancy in Montreal. Law enforcement scholars observe that police forces typically use their discriminatory power to target specific groups. In the case of prostitution, most of the women arrested were immigrants from lower economic classes. The Montreal case exemplifies the arbitrary enforcement of laws and bylaws by police. Class, gender, and ethnicity shaped law enforcement. Non-francophone women constituted most of the arrests. Two-thirds of these women were prostitutes. Although some prostitutes captured the public imagination, such as Mary Ann Green, who was arrested thirty-two times and sent to jail eighteen times over an eight-year period, most were first-time "offenders."[22] Sometimes, law enforcement officers launched a crackdown on prostitutes in reaction to pressure from civil society to reclaim public space. If sometimes prostitutes opposed resistance, this was not always the case. For instance, prostitutes did not resist their arrest, especially during the fall and winter seasons. If convicted, they hoped to be able to stay in a shelter for a few days or weeks. This solution, Mary Anne Poutanen writes, reflects "the degradation of their lives."[23]

Same-sex relations were another form of sexual activity that concerned authorities during the colonial era. According to Patrice Corriveau, from 1648 to 1759 only three court cases in New France involved sexual relations between men. None of these cases involved relations between adults and young persons, and all them occurred before 1700. In 1648 soldier René Huguet was accused of committing an "unnatural act" and received the death penalty. Opposed to the sentence, the Jesuits asked for a second trial. Found guilty a second time, Huguet was sent to prison. However, he spent no time in jail, because a "job opportunity" opened up. Royal authorities were seeking an executioner, and Huguet rose to the challenge.[24]

The fact that there were so few cases is puzzling. Were French settlers generally law-abiding individuals? During the seventeenth century, 21 percent of all court cases in New France involved morality. This decreased to 5 percent in the following century.[25] These data suggest that the state did not have the means to bring before justice all individuals accused of adultery, prostitution, rape, and same-sex relations. This is also an indication that victims were perhaps reluctant to press charges, since 80 percent of the inhabitants lived in small, rural communities. As it does today, living in a small community meant that most people knew each other. It is likely that victims and suspected offenders lived side by side, and the former would be reluctant to speak up. But Corriveau argues that society at the time also demonstrated a level of tolerance for these types of crimes. "The unremarkable nature of violent acts corresponded to the low rate of prosecution for them. In other words, rape, murder, and other forms of physical violence, because they were everyday occurrences, did not raise the ire of the public and the judges."[26]

Taken together, these factors could explain the paucity of cases involving individuals accused of having homosexual relations. However, these few cases are still intriguing. Does it mean that there were almost no homosexual acts and relationships in New France? The more likely reason is that court cases involved only individuals who had sex in public, and the justice system did not deal with what took place in households or other private spaces. At the same time, the small number of such cases demonstrates that there were other mechanisms of regulation for dealing with what were labelled "crimes against nature."

Again, during the British regime, few such cases were brought to the attention of the justice system. These involved individuals accused of committing "unnatural crimes." For instance, there was the case of Alexander Wood, a merchant established in York, or what is now Toronto. In 1800 Wood became a magistrate, but his career was in turmoil ten years later, when rumours of his "unorthodox" investigation techniques surfaced. In 1810 Miss Bailey accused a young man of rape. During his investigation, Wood examined the genitals of some young male suspects, since Miss Bailey claimed that she "had scratched her assailant's genitals." Denounced for what he had done, Wood left York for Scotland. He nevertheless came back later and was able to rebuild his enterprise.[27]

In 1842 the court found guilty of sodomy Samuel Moore and Patrick Kelly, a private of the 89th Regiment of Foot. They were both condemned to die but spent time in jail instead. In Gary Kinsman's view, this case demonstrates the existence of a network for men to have same-sex relations that crossed class boundaries, since some accused, in other cases, were from the elite or working class. "Working-class young men in the military may have been able to negotiate relations with elite men that not only led to erotic pleasure but also economic benefits for themselves as well."[28]

Religious institution tribunals were another instrument of regulation. Anglicans, Methodists, Baptists, and Presbyterians had the option of asking their churches to discipline their members. These tribunals heard cases dealing with various vices: horse racing, dancing, and drinking, but also adultery. With regard to sexuality, rumours that a church member was not faithful, had committed adultery, or had premarital sex were sufficient to trigger an investigation.

As Lynn Marks argues, among the Protestant denominations that dominated the religious landscape in British North America, church discipline was gendered. Despite the fact that both men and women were brought before religious tribunals, men controlled the disciplinary process. When a man or a woman was found guilty of sinful conduct, depending on the nature of the fault there were various possible punishments: public confession, temporary suspension from the congregation, or permanent expulsion. In this last instance, it was a tragedy for the guilty individual. When a Baptist or Presbyterian moved to another town, he needed a letter from his previous community in order to join a Protestant church. Anyone who had been expelled from their congregation could not join a new one, since they were unable to provide such a letter. Thus expulsion was a harsh form of punishment. Belonging to a congregation had multiple meanings for settlers: it provided comfort to the soul, facilitated the building of a social network, and gave access to social and in-kind assistance. Since the state did not offer much in the way of providing welfare, belonging to a church had material advantages.[29]

Unlike the legal system, religious disciplinary mechanisms had no double standard when they dealt with sexual misconduct and divorce. As Christians, both men and women were required to abstain from sex except in a monogamous, heterosexual marriage. In practice, however, more Protestant women than men were charged with sexual misconduct. This reflects the fact that women were overrepresented as church members in most Protestant denominations. Also, men were more likely to "disappear" from the community, rather than face church discipline. For instance, in 1835 Peterborough's Presbyterian Church heard the case of a pregnant woman. However, the congregation could do nothing with the sinful father, because "he had gone to a distant part of the country." Consequently, "no further satisfaction could now be obtained."[30] Lynn Marks observes that, notwithstanding the Protestant churches' policies of equal treatment of men and women accused of sexual offences, efforts by Baptist and Presbyterian churches to discipline their members on sexual and other matters declined in the second half of the nineteenth century.

There was a hierarchy of tribunals for Roman Catholics. Settlers could bring matters to a canon law court, but most of them chose confession. Although the clergy hoped that their flocks would confess once a month, the minimum requirement for Catholics was once a year. Anxious to prevent sinful Catholics from looking for priests who easily granted an absolution, bishops reminded priests to issue a *billet de confession*, which was a confession form that priests issued to their flocks after they heard their confession and that testified they had acknowledged their sins. Priests requested to see a *billet de confession* when an unfamiliar face asked for confession. Most of the time, priests absolved the sinner and imposed a penance that depended on the nature of the sins. Sometimes, clergy could decide on a public penance to be witnessed by parishioners. Before imposing such a public demonstration of moral control, they had to consult their bishop. For other serious sinful conduct, a bishop could ask the Vatican for advice and sanction.[31]

Sodomy and other homosexual acts were sins about which priests sought their bishop's advice. As already stated, the Roman Catholic Church defined such behaviour as a grave form of transgression. The second bishop of New France (from 1688 to 1727), Jean-Baptiste de la Croix de Chevrière de Saint-Vallier, informed his regular and secular clergy that they should not ignore this "crime against nature." On the contrary, confessors should be strict with Catholics who confessed acts of sodomy. "We wish, however, for you to make it more difficult to be absolved for the greatest sins, especially those that have a censure attached, such as setting fires, magic, sodomy, bestiality, incest."[32] The church believed that it was better equipped than the state to handle sodomy and other homosexual acts, by repressing the behaviour and reforming the sinner, who would otherwise face the courts and have his private act turned into public exposure and scandal. Unless homosexual acts were committed in public and were likely to be brought before royal justice, the church believed that the sin of sodomy committed in private should remain private. Besides the sinner, only the confessor would know about this grave sexual offence. Consequently, the clergy member who heard the confession meted out a punishment according to the nature of the sin and the degree of the sinner's sincerity not to repeat his offence.[33]

Inducing an abortion or practising birth control were mortal sins for Catholics. In *Sedes Apostolicae*, in 1591, Gregory XIV introduced the distinction between an "animated" and an "unanimated" fetus. He used the "'quickening' test, which equated the beginning of life with the time of first fetal movement." For the Pope, "quickening determined when a fetus was considered animated." The punishment for aborting a quickened fetus was excommunication.[34] For its part, the state too defined abortion as a crime. Inspired by the 1803 British legislation, New Brunswick in 1810 and Prince Edward Island in 1836 were the first colonies in British North America to legislate against the practice. Those found guilty received the death penalty if the abortion had occurred after the pregnant woman had felt any fetal movement. If she had not, the maximum sentence was a fourteen-year jail term. The colony of Upper Canada passed an anti-abortion law in 1841. Unlike New Brunswick and Prince Edward Island, Upper Canada did not include a lesser sanction in the case of an abortion occurring before a woman felt fetal movement. Abortion carried a maximum penalty of life in prison. Until 1849, none of these laws sanctioned a woman who attempted "to abort herself."[35]

Despite church views and state laws, women, in particular, and couples tried to regulate birth. A high fertility rate characterized New France. Women had an average of eight children. A significant number of these newborns did not survive the first twelve months, since about only three-quarters of newborns reached adulthood. The birth rate remained high until the mid-nineteenth century. In the second half of the nineteenth century, French-Canadian women had an average of 4.8 children. If they wanted to limit the size of their family, women used natural birth control means such as abstinence or withdrawal.

There was another means for limiting family size: infanticide. The law treated infanticide harshly. The royal declaration of 1708, which was promulgated in New France in 1722, constrained priests to regularly inform their parishioners that anyone found guilty of this crime would receive the death penalty. This penalty remained in place even after the regime change following the British Conquest. When the British Parliament amended its legislation in 1803 and substituted a jail term for the death penalty, the British North American colonies followed suit, starting with New Brunswick in 1810. During the nineteenth century, most individuals accused of infanticide were young, unmarried, working-class women. Some of them worked as domestics and tried to hide their pregnancy because they feared they would be fired if their employers found out.[36]

Some newborns died in their parents' beds. Did such deaths occur naturally? They did in some cases. In others, one of the parents crushed or choked the baby. If a newborn's death seemed suspicious, parents quickly claimed that this was an unfortunate accident. Other times, a woman would claim that her newborn was dead at birth. The justice system found it almost impossible to prosecute parents when they could invoke the "unfortunate accident" or the "dead newborn." This explains why only four women during the eighteenth century, and two the following century, were charged.[37] Roman Catholic Church officials generally refuted these excuses and suspected that the act had been deliberate. The church issued *mandements* forbidding parents from sleeping with a newborn until it reached the age of one year, hoping to prevent infanticide. By not complying with these *mandements*, parents committed a sin. They would not receive an absolution, even if they confessed to a priest. They received an absolution if they promised that they would end the practice of sleeping with their newborn.[38]

Since marriage was a prerequisite for any morally acceptable sexual act, ending a marriage was not an option for colonists. Through its canon law, the Roman Catholic Church forbade divorce. It justified its views by referring to Scripture: "What God has joined together, let man not separate." The catechism and the clergy reminded Catholics that a marriage ended only with the death of the husband or wife. However, in exceptional circumstances, a Catholic religious tribunal could grant an annulment. In order to convince the religious tribunal to hear the case, Catholics had to demonstrate that "no marriage was deemed to have ever existed."[39] In their submissions, individuals had to prove that their marriage failed due to one of the following factors: no sexual relations between the husband and the wife, "formal defect," "lack of consent," "bigamy," "failure to reach puberty," "impotence," or "kinship" (because Catholics could not marry cousins up to and including the fourth degree of consanguinity).[40] To submit a case to a tribunal was a very serious matter because the petitioners faced other punishments if they were unsuccessful: aside from the fact that they could not remarry and had to remain with their spouse, there was the possibility of a temporary or a permanent expulsion from the church. This last possibility had far-reaching negative consequences, as discussed earlier. Protestant denominations in British North America authorized divorce in exceptional circumstances. These included the disappearance of the loving relationship between a married man and woman or adultery on the part of either spouse.

There was still the possibility of getting a divorce without the consent of religious authorities. In New France, a married woman needed her husband's permission to initiate the procedure, because she had no legal capacity. Judges could grant a divorce if the wife demonstrated that she was the victim of her husband's alcoholism, if the husband was unable to provide for the family, or if he physically and verbally abused his wife. In the case of a husband's physical abuse, the plaintiff had to demonstrate that her husband was extremely violent, since he had the right "of correction over his wife."[41] Even with a favourable judgment, a divorced woman did not recover her legal capacity. On the contrary, "she continued to be subject to marital authority." She needed her former "husband's consent with respect to major decisions concerning property, and she was merely allowed to administer her property, not to dispose of it as she saw fit." If a married woman was convicted of adultery, a judge would ask her to apologize to her husband. The husband then had the option either of taking his wife back or of punishing her. If he chose the latter, he could send her either to a religious institution at his own expense, back to live with her parents, or even back to France if she was a recent immigrant.[42]

In British North America, divorces were rare because they were difficult to obtain. In the Canadas, the few that occurred were granted through a special act of the legislature. Class, wealth, and networking enabled access to this procedure. In the colony of Upper Canada, legislators granted a divorce for the first time in 1839. Between 1839 and 1867, they dealt with seven cases and granted only five divorces. Women did not initiate any of these cases.[43] New Brunswick, Nova Scotia, and Prince Edward Island had divorce courts but they heard few cases since divorce was unusual.

Secular law was punitive with respect to divorce, since it reinforced the institution of marriage and protected property. It applied a sexual double standard to women, as they were blamed and punished more severely for sexual misconduct than were men. For example, if a married man initiated the divorce proceedings on the grounds of adultery, he could win his case. If a woman asked for a divorce, adultery alone was insufficient to win her case. She had to prove that her husband was disloyal, had deserted her, or had committed other serious crimes.

Historian Andrée Lévesque notes that size matters when considering social control by communities. It was easier for small communities to enforce their moral order than for large ones.[44] The boundaries of privacy were porous, since people knew what happened in neighbouring households.[45] Hiding illegitimate births was difficult. Sexual encounters between unmarried young men and young women could not remain secret for very long, and sexual encounters outside of monogamous marriage were inexcusable. Communities themselves disciplined those who transgressed these social customs. How communities addressed transgression or dealt with bad habits varied according to the class, gender, race, and age of those accused or suspected of wrongdoing. The charivari, as mentioned earlier, was one of the community-based means of moral regulation. According to historian Natalie Zemon Davis, who has studied charivaris during the seventeenth century, this practice reflected the monitoring of the development of relationships between men and women in a community.[46] When these relationships disrupted the well-being of the larger group, members gathered and expressed their disapproval in a ritual where they made raucous noise and wore garish costumes. Held late at night, the charivari lasted until the targeted individuals emerged and met with the crowd. Those who initiated the charivari expected to receive a gift, which was often sufficient to reestablish social harmony in the community.[47]

A practice brought over by Europeans, the first recorded charivari in North America occurred after the death of François Vezier dit Laverdure, on June 7, 1683. His wife, who was twenty-five years of age, was remarried to a thirty-year-old man three weeks later. The community where these two individuals lived considered that this remarriage had occurred too soon after Laverdure's death.[48] A questionably hasty remarriage was one of the more common reasons that could prompt a charivari. Although other factors—a husband who beat his wife, adultery, a couple childless after a year of marriage, or individuals marrying for lust or wealth or marrying a foreigner—triggered charivaris, most cases in New France and British North America concerned a remarriage that a community labelled as a mismatch. This notion of mismatch was broad and included instances where individuals were seen as marrying too soon after being widowed, as in Laverdure's case, or where there was a significant age difference between the bride and the groom. A large age gap was a particularly serious cause for concern. As in France, communities in North America organized charivaris when a woman who could no longer have children married a younger man. They often did this because such unions reduced the pool of eligible bachelors available to women of child-bearing age, thereby threatening the community's ability to increase its numbers. In New France and in Lower Canada, communities that organized charivaris challenged the Roman Catholic Church's power to approve what they considered a "mismatched" union.[49]

Clearly, one of the goals of a charivari was to shame or humiliate the targeted couple. Although most charivaris did not involve physical violence, they were essentially punitive. It was a form of censorship by the community, an expression of displeasure. According to Tina Loo and Carolyn Strange, the charivari was a way of "regulating public as well as private behaviour."[50]

During the second half of the nineteenth century, the charivari also became a class-orientated social practice. Workers used charivaris to demonstrate against employers, and town and city residents used them to express their disapproval of a councillor or alderman. Newspapers, which often published reports on charivaris, tended to focus on their sensational aspects, especially when charivaris turned deadly. When the targeted victims or any bystanders who attended a charivari were killed, journalists were apt to roundly condemn this communal mechanism of social control.[51] Throughout the twentieth century, some communities would organize a charivari not to punish or expressed its displeasure over a union between a man and a woman but as a way of welcoming individuals into the community.[52]

Because marriage was a pivotal social and religious institution that it sanctioned, the Roman Catholic Church deplored charivaris in both France and New France. On July 3, 1683, Bishop Laval issued a *mandement* forbidding Catholics in New France from participating in charivaris. Afraid that many would otherwise ignore his decree, he specified that people who defied it would incur excommunication. The bishop instructed his clergy to read his *mandement* to their congregations and display it on church doors.[53]

DRINKING: VERY THIRSTY PEOPLE?

People enjoyed drinking alcohol in New France. At first, the wine, beer, cider, and eau de vie they drank was imported from Europe, but the costs of transportation, the presence of pirates, shipping delays due to stormy weather on the seas, and the possibility of losing shipments due to shipwreck were strong incentives for colonists to make their own alcohol. Nevertheless, making alcohol in the colony was not an easy endeavour. Harsh winters and a short growing season imposed severe constraints on the large-scale production of wine and discouraged all but the most optimistic among the common settlers and the elites.

In contrast to the anemic domestic wine industry, beer production was successful during the French regime. Families and religious communities made their own beer. They made cider and eau de vie as well, but domestic production remained small. This situation was due partly to competition from French producers on the European continent.[54]

Local production alone was insufficient to meet internal demand. Consequently, settlers and elites relied on imports to quench their thirst. French colonists despaired when wine barrels did not reach the port of Quebec City. Peter Kalm reported that European wars waged in North America were catastrophic for French settlers, not only on account of actual destruction and other horrors, but also because members of all classes—common settlers, nobility, and clergy—had to suffer the interruption of the alcohol trade. The Swedish traveller, who visited New France in 1749, wrote: "The people of quality here [he referred to the elites] who have been accustomed from their youth to drink nothing but wine, are greatly at a loss in time of war, when all the ships which bring wine are intercepted by the English privateers."[55]

Kalm's comments on wine drinking and "people of quality" reveal much about drinking habits in New France. Income and social status determined what inhabitants could drink. Those with higher income, such as nobles and clergy members, drank imported wine. Those with limited income, living on small farms or far away from Montreal and Quebec City, relied on domestic production. The latter drank imported wine or liquor only on special occasions.

While settlers depended on alcoholic beverages because they were intertwined with their eating habits and social customs and appreciated for their pleasurable, inebriating effects, royal representatives also relied on alcohol. The duties they collected on liquor imports paid for defence construction and financed the colonial government's operations. In her study on alcohol use in New France, historian Catherine Ferland demonstrates that duties collected by the King of France on wine, rum, and other liquor imports constituted 50 percent of colonial revenues in the 1730s and increased to above 85 percent in the following decade.[56]

Besides collecting duties, the King of France regulated several other aspects of alcohol use in the colony. In order to operate an establishment that sold alcohol, owners needed a licence. Royal authorities granted these licences quite generously, partly in order to prevent any individual from having the only licensed establishment in a certain area and a de facto monopoly on the sale of alcohol. For example, in 1744 there were 6,000 inhabitants and 40 licensed establishments in Quebec City, which was the largest urban settlement, but also the main port of entry in the colony.[57] Since the cost of importing wine and liquors was exceptionally high, the state regulated the selling price of alcohol in licensed establishments and prevented tavern owners from increasing their prices. Royal authorities did it as a way to reassure the Catholic church, which condemned excessive drinking. By controlling the price of alcohol, they had a means to control alcohol consumption in the colony.

Access to alcohol increased throughout the nineteenth century. The arrival of the Loyalists spurred the development of breweries and distilleries and increased demand for alcohol. In Upper Canada, 108 taverns served 34,600 inhabitants in 1801. Thirty-six years later, there were 1,009 taverns for a population of 400,286.[58] It might be interesting to note the corresponding ratios: 1:320 and 1:397. In the British North American colonies, domestically produced alcohol was often cheaper than tea and coffee, which remained costly until the nineteenth century. And people relied on alcoholic beverages partly because drinking water was expensive and potentially dangerous for human consumption, especially in towns and cities, because it was likely to be contaminated with dirt, garbage, and other hazards to health.[59]

Drinking was a gendered activity. Although both men and women drank during the colonial era, it was more socially acceptable for men to drink. Social conventions prevented women from drinking in public. Women could drink at home, but as historian Craig Heron writes, scholars do not say if they were drinking "before tackling the laundry, feeding the chickens, or sewing a dress."[60]

From time to time, Roman Catholic officials denounced excessive drinking and establishments such as cabarets or local bars in New France. The church was not too disturbed by drinking as such. It was excessive drinking that concerned them. Excessive drinking led individuals to commit other sins, such as having extramarital sexual relations, neglecting their wives and children, losing control of themselves, stealing, or fighting. It was morally reprehensible behaviour and society ought to address this.

The Catholic church had various means to impose its views on drinking, but in particular on drunkenness. Catholic doctrine focused on the impact of excessive drinking on the family and the community, as well as on the drunken individual's soul. Drunkenness was a mortal sin and punishable by the withholding of the sacrament until the drunkard confessed and repented. Not only did the church encourage its clergy to frequently repeat its condemnations, it also chastised merchants and tavern owners who sold alcohol on Sundays and holy days. Nevertheless, these condemnations had limited impact, as priests who worked among the Acadians reported to their bishop in 1742.[61] The church's ability to control access to alcohol was also limited by the small number of clergy in the colony. Many parishes were without resident priests.

Royal authorities in New France intervened in the hope of reducing excessive drinking. In pursuing this goal, the state attempted to use various regulatory measures. It imposed a fine or a jail sentence on those who drank to excess in public—in a licensed establishment, for example. It made owners of licensed establishments responsible for preventing drunkenness on their premises and drunken individuals from disturbing the public peace. The state imposed a fine on an owner if a patron disturbed the public space inside or outside his establishment. It also restricted specific groups' access to alcohol. Soldiers were permitted to drink only during their lunches and dinners in licensed establishments. There was an outright prohibition against serving domestics, unless their employers had given written permission to the owner of a licensed establishment. Somewhat ironically, from a modern-day perspective, construction workers were allowed to consume alcohol only when they were at work. However, the state had limited means to enforce any of these regulations.[62]

Moral and social concerns expressed by both the Catholic church and Aboriginals themselves encouraged royal authorities to regulate Aboriginal access to alcohol. During the French regime, there were several regulations. Some targeted those who made it easier for Aboriginal communities to get alcohol. There were also unsuccessful attempts to limit or prohibit alcohol exchange or sale when the French traded with Aboriginals. Officials responsible for enforcing royal edicts often ignored them or could not enforce them because they lacked resources, such as the military.

Economic and political rivalry between the French and English empires in North America did not constrain alcohol trade with Aboriginals. On the contrary, trading alcohol with Aboriginals was a small price to pay for political dominance, regardless of what church officials and other moral regulators might think. So, from the perspective of royal representatives, it was imperative not to reduce the flow of alcohol. For their part, Aboriginals informed French officials that they would trade with France's enemies in order to get access liquor. The interests of competitive trade were paramount.

In response, missionaries, and even intendants, updated their narratives in attempts to mount irrefutable arguments for putting an end to alcohol trade with Aboriginals. They pointed out that trade relations were suffering because drunken Aboriginals were poor hunters and were unable to bring "precious pelts" to the French. If the fur trade was paramount for the king, why would

French authorities turn a blind eye to how alcohol use undermined the trade's success?[63] Despite these arguments, royal authorities did not have the political motivation or will to allocate resources to enforce regulations restricting alcohol when trading with Aboriginals.

There was an exception, however. When drunken Aboriginals were found in Montreal or Quebec City, they could be fined or jailed. Moreover, the state opted to restrict the number of establishments authorized to sell alcohol to Aboriginals in Montreal. In 1710, Intendant Antoine-Denis Raudot released a list of ten establishments allowed to sell only to non-Aboriginals, and another list of nine establishments that were permitted to sell to both Aboriginals and non-Aboriginals. By restricting access, royal authorities hoped to convince religious leaders and other concerned individuals that these measures prevented public disorder, public shouting, and fights involving drunken people, especially Aboriginals. In practice, these attempts at restricting access had no real impact. In fact, royal authorities eventually reversed course and abandoned their policy of regulating Aboriginal access to alcohol.[64]

With the arrival of the Loyalists and other immigrants from Great Britain at the end of the eighteenth century, members of various Protestant denominations changed their point of view on alcohol use. The concept of self-restraint shaped their morality. From their perspective, a respectable Protestant should not drink too much because he would lose his ability to control his own actions.

Although it proved impossible to regulate drinkers, the state opted to regulate those who sold alcohol. Like state officials in New France, authorities in British North America made tavern owners responsible for their customers' good behaviour. In Upper Canada, an applicant for a licence needed declarations from other individuals indicating that he was a person of good character.[65] The state hired inspectors to visit taverns twice a year, to collect fees, and to verify if the owners complied with their obligations to maintain their establishment in good standing and prevent public disorder. Passed in 1835, the Act to Prevent the Sale of Spirituous Liquors to Indians was a new attempt to limit access. But it too proved difficult to enforce. For example, upon being charged, one tavern owner argued that he did not know that he had sold alcohol to Aboriginals, since "they were dressed like ourselves, and spoke good English."[66]

Craig Heron writes that alcohol "was central to the social life of pre-industrial colonists in New France and British North America, as a staple in their diets and as the central element in many social rituals."[67] Nevertheless, in her study of drinking in Upper Canada, Julia Roberts argues that excessive drinking was not the norm. In her calculation of drinking that excluded children, she estimates that men consumed 13.33 gallons a year, and women half that amount. This means that the average daily consumption for women was "just over a glass a day (2.3 oz.) and for men…slightly more than a gill (4.7 oz.)."[68] In Roberts's view, colonists controlled their consumption because they knew that excessive drinking affected their ability to manage their other activities. "Upper Canada may have been a drinking society by modern standards," she maintains, "but it was one in which the members had a wary respect for alcohol's potential dangers."[69]

Although there was no organized secular lobby or social movement that identified drinking as a despicable habit and tried to limit alcohol use, there were signs that alcohol use did bother some individuals. In 1785 in Philadelphia, a physician, Benjamin Rush, published the first pamphlet denouncing alcohol use. In "An Inquiry into the Effects of Ardent Spirits on the Mind and Body," Rush wrote that there was a link between heavy drinking and "jaundice," "madness," and "epilepsy." He warned that alcohol use affected an individual's health and morality, but also led to antisocial and criminal behaviours. This American physician used the term *addiction* to describe the uncontrollable desire on the part of some individuals to drink alcohol. Rush recommended that they abstain from drinking distilled spirits and consume instead "beer and wine in a temperate, or moderate, manner." His pamphlet had a limited impact, except among those concerned with excessive drinking in the United States and British North America, but it was not the last word on this issue. In Upper Canada, Peter Scholefield gave public lectures and insisted on the terrible health impacts of alcohol use. Following these observations and denunciations, in the 1820s other physicians, clergy, and members of the upper classes in British North America began to create temperance organizations, hoping to force individuals to self-regulate their use of alcohol.[70]

GAMBLING: NO "UNLAWFULL GAMES TO BE USED IN HOUSE"

Settlers gambled in New France, both during the French regime and under British rule. Despite condemnations from the Roman Catholic Church, people could take part in games of chance in a variety of places. After the British Conquest, travellers who stopped in Cataraqui, near Kingston, in 1790 could join local residents and gamble in the tavern owned by Daniel McGuinn. Those who gambled put the owner in conflict with the law, since his licence forbade drunkenness and "any other disorders or unlawfull games to be used in house."[71]

When state lotteries were introduced in the United States at the beginning of the nineteenth century, settlers in British North America were no less

attracted by the possibility of winning a jackpot than their southerly neighbours were. Newspapers published ads for these state lotteries, and colonists bought tickets until American legislators banned their sale in the United States between 1833 and 1840. Following this ban, members of the private sector in the British colonies filled the void by organizing their own lotteries. They advertised them in newspapers as a means to reach out to the greatest number of buyers.[72]

Up until about 1850, Canadians had a somewhat ambivalent attitude toward gambling. On the one hand, gambling encompassed a wide range of activities: horse racing, lotteries, raffles, dice, and card playing, for example. These activities took place in both public and private settings. Individuals who gambled were easily identified in the United States and probably in the British North America colonies. Popular imagery depicted them as well dressed, smoking cigars, and exuding a sense of confidence. In short, a gambler had class and was regarded by many as a figure to be envied.[73] On the other hand, religious groups increasingly condemned gambling activities by labelling them as sinful because they were pleasurable. Furthermore, gambling was the entry point to other serious temptations such as excessive drinking and prostitution, thereby risking damnation to a Christian soul. The loss of self-control was a grave concern for religious groups. Following the example set by the first bishop of New France (from 1658 to 1688), François de Laval, religious leaders reminded settlers that they should refrain from gambling.

The Roman Catholic Church's views on gambling were contested in the public domain. For some, gambling was a relatively minor transgression. Others believed that it was "an inevitable aspect of human nature." Since even some church organizations used gambling as a fundraising activity, it was not a particularly welcome idea to launch a campaign to outlaw it.[74]

Despite dissenting views, state authorities tackled the issue. The French king had tried to restrict gambling by forbidding certain games, such as dice and lotteries, in 1684. However, this effort was abandoned. Several years later, in 1732, authorities allowed lotteries in the colony.[75] Knowing the Roman Catholic Church's views on gambling, royal representatives during the French regime targeted owners of taverns and licensed establishments and made them responsible for prohibiting gambling activities on their premises.[76] After the British Conquest, legislators regulated gambling activities as well. In 1817 the House of Assembly in Lower Canada authorized police forces in urban centres to levy a fine on gamblers. Legislators targeted public gambling that involved members of the lower classes—"workmen, journeymen, apprentices or servants."[77] In the colony of Upper Canada, gambling activities in taverns were illegal, and in 1828 its legislature prohibited lotteries.[78] However, these measures had little or no impact, and gambling remained popular among everyone, including members of the lower classes.

TOBACCO: A "SUCCESSFUL" CULTURAL TRANSFER

Aboriginals, who introduced tobacco to the French, had used tobacco during spiritual ceremonies from time immemorial. Inspired by the British in the Thirteen Colonies, the French gave it a different cultural meaning, however, and smoking tobacco became a recreational activity. In 1749 Peter Kalm observed that everyone in New France smoked: "Boys of ten or twelve years of age, as well as the old people, run about with a pipe in their mouth." Regardless of their social status, both men and women used tobacco. According to Kalm, most inhabitants grew their own tobacco. "Every farmer plants a quantity of tobacco near his house, in proportion to the size of his family."[79] Also, they preferred Canadian tobacco to other varieties.

Tobacco use did not trigger any moral or health concerns during this period. Consequently, there were no attempts to restrict its use among children and adolescents—even the Roman Catholic Church did not condemn settlers for seeking pleasure through smoking.

CONCLUSION

The Roman Catholic Church, Protestant denominations, and the state had various means for imposing their respective moral orders on settlers' lives. Sexuality, drinking, and gambling were regulated. When, in their view, certain behaviours became excessive, intendants and religious leaders in New France developed mechanisms to prevent their propagation. As demonstrated with alcohol use and gambling, it was easy enough to proscribe these activities, but far more difficult to implement and enforce such policies. The state had limited resources, despite, for example, enlisting tavern owners and making them responsible for enforcing regulations concerning access to alcohol for Aboriginals and settlers. If we pay attention only to official discourse and regulation, we might believe that powerful institutions effectively regulated settlers' behaviour. However, as we have seen, there is abundant evidence to the contrary.

Observations by travellers and the numerous complaints by clergy demonstrate the limits to religious institutions' and the state's enforcement of a moral order. In both cases, human resources were insufficient. This did not mean that settlers were entirely free of restraints. As Foucault argues, the internalization of a moral order would cause settlers to fear the consequences of transgression, either during their life or in the afterlife. Robert Hale, a young New England doctor who visited the colony of Nova Scotia in 1731, noted in his travel log while staying with an Acadian family that "just about Bed time wee were surprize'd to see some of ye family on their Knees paying yr Devotions to ye Almighty, & others near them talking and Smoaking &c. This they do all of them (mentally not orally) every night and Morning, not altogether, but now one and then another, & sometimes 2 or 3 together, but not in Conjunction one with the other."[80] Despite the absence of clergy, settlers regulated their own lives, based not only on their Christian beliefs but also on how the community itself defined good behaviour. The charivari was one such mechanism.

Individuals, communities, churches, and the state intervened in the regulation of people's lives. The power of each of these groups and institutions was not unlimited. For example, the church was limited in its efforts to regulate alcohol use, since the state did not want it to jeopardize the careful system of alliances built with Aboriginals. For its own part, the state was limited in its ability to regulate gambling, since it had inadequate resources at its disposal. People exercised their own agency, while state regulations, religious *mandements*, and Protestant moral discipline interfered, whether overtly or through processes of unconscious internalization, with how individuals actually conducted their lives.

CHAPTER 3

Triumphs

Vices in Retreat, 1850–1920

I n her autobiography, Letitia Youmans, an emblematic figure of the temperance movement, relates the story of a family devastated by alcohol use. The father, who had the legal obligation of providing for his family, squandered much of his income on alcohol. He even brought bottles home for consumption on Sundays. His wife objected to having alcoholic beverages in the family home. Although her husband did not actually drink in the house, he did it "in the barn in winter, and in the grass in summer." One day, the children found one of their father's bottles. The mother turned the children's discovery into a valuable life lesson. The bottle that they held in their hands, she insisted, explained why they were improperly fed and clothed. The "evil" beverage was the cause of their economic misery. Consequently, the mother asked her children to kneel down and pronounce a solemn pledge: "I want you to promise— *and God will hear the vow*—that you will never taste anything that would make you a drunkard."[1] By referring to this particular story, Youmans provided hope to those who were heartbroken by the misfortune of this family or who were facing a similar situation themselves. The publication of her book helped turn the temperance cause into a popular movement that touched thousands of lives. Known for her remarkable organizational and oratory skills, Youmans explained in highly accessible terms why alcohol use was one of the evils affecting society during the Industrial Revolution.

The Industrial Revolution transformed the nature of economic activities, brought new means of transportation such as railways, and led to the growth of manufacturing and the rise of the service sector. By 1921, 50 percent of the Canadian population lived in urban centres, which were characterized by economic segregation. The wealthy tended to congregate in certain areas of a city—the Golden Square Mile in Montreal was a case in point—while individuals with limited financial means occupied districts considered slums due to deplorable living conditions.

The economic change brought by the Industrial Revolution affected everyone. Those who controlled the new means of production—business owners and investors—embraced these decades of structural transformation and became wealthy or even wealthier. Others, who had formerly controlled their own means of production, fell victim to these changes. They left their farms and moved to towns or larger urban centres in their quest for paid employment. Many travelled long distances, sometimes crossing either the Atlantic or Pacific oceans, to get a job and a better future for themselves and their families in British North America.

The Industrial Revolution changed labour practices too. Mechanization led to an increase in productivity but also to a new division of labour, since workers now had specific, segmented tasks to accomplish. People worked long hours and six days a week. Workers had few additional days off, and no job security. Many had low-paying jobs requiring no specific skills, in situations where activism and worker organization were inconceivable. Safety, wages, job security, and working hours became crucial points of contention between workers and employers.

Women and children also began to work in industrial factories. Working-class families in Halifax, Montreal, Toronto, and Hamilton justified their decision to send married women, and children as young as ten years of age, to work, because the father's income was insufficient to cover the family's living expenses. Religious leaders, factory inspectors, and journalists who condemned families that sent children and mothers to work were oblivious to these economic realities.

Gambling, alcohol use, and prostitution came to dominate social debates between 1850 and 1920. Society was in turmoil, causing widespread alarm. Among those concerned, Christian individuals and groups from various denominations promoted social reforms shaped by their religious beliefs. One such advocate and former secretary of the Dominion Alliance for the Total Suppression of the Liquor Traffic, Francis Stephens Spence, summarized in a speech in 1908, as a Manichean dichotomy, the purpose of the battles to be fought: "Wherever you find an evil of any kind, something that curses and hurts humanity, and into contact with that evil you bring men and women of Christian character, unselfish thought, and earnest purpose, there you have the elements of a moral reform."[2] In response to social and economic forces that profoundly challenged their beliefs, Christians from various denominations launched an offensive that became more sophisticated, refined, and determined over the years. In the face of their adversaries who explicitly advocated prostitution, gambling, and drug and alcohol use, Christian reformists understood the need to update their narratives and arguments justifying the repression of gambling, prostitution, abortion, homosexual acts, and drug and alcohol use. At the same time, they pursued a strategy of building coalitions with civic reformers, opponents to immigration, women's organizations, and elected officials, to broaden their support. According to Alan Hunt, a moral regulation movement succeeds if its promoters appeal to a range of social actors who can work together despite their different ideological, political, and social agendas. Hunt refers to the process of bringing together social actors from different backgrounds as the umbrella effect.[3] Christian moral reformists succeeded in creating coalitions that promoted their social agenda.

BUILDING THE KINGDOM OF GOD ON EARTH

In reaction to changes brought about by the Industrial Revolution, some Canadians became involved in moral regulation movements. Initiated within civil society—scholars have observed that members of the middle class have been the most active in these types of social movements—these mobilizations transformed a social reality into a problem that required remedial action. The movements' motives were to "influence the conduct of human agents"[4] and to affect not only how society governed people, but also how individuals governed themselves—what Alan Hunt calls the governance of "others and the self."[5] Moral regulation movements developed arguments that were part of a normative narrative. Targeted behaviours were defined as "intrinsically bad, wrong or immoral."[6] According to the promoters of regulation, society was sinking into vice. How should society prevent or reverse the disintegration of morality? Moral reformers considered various means for slowing down and hopefully reversing the degeneration process. Through their churches, they encouraged people to change their behaviour. According to Protestant morality, everyone should practise self-restraint. Many believed that religion provided much-needed moral guidance to society. However, moral reformers measured their success by their ability to govern the conduct of others. Consequently, they pressed the state to translate into law their moral-oriented reformist agenda.

Christians from various denominations could not stay inactive. Society was in turmoil, threatened by old realities—such as prostitution, gambling, and alcohol—as well as new ones—drug use and low birth rates. It was imperative to address these serious and growing moral deficiencies. A sense of urgency characterized moral reformers' actions and understanding of social issues, and the scale of problems to be addressed fuelled their campaigns. Inspired by the Gospel, moral reformers worked toward building the kingdom of God on earth. In *A Theology for the Social Gospel*, Walter Rauschenbusch argues that building the kingdom of God meant "'the establishment of a community of righteousness in mankind,' which was 'just as much a saving act of God as the salvation of an individual.'"[7] Christians from Protestant denominations came to the realization that there was no individual salvation without the collective "cleansing of society."[8] These Christians were part of, and influenced by, the Social Gospel Movement that emerged at the end of the nineteenth century. This Protestant religious movement was transnational, with roots in Great Britain and the United States, and fuelled the belief that Christians had to actively work toward the building of the kingdom of God by transforming individuals and society, establishing a better moral climate, and achieving greater social equality. Beginning in the 1880s, Methodists, Baptists, and Anglicans held meetings attended by their representatives from the English-speaking world. Attendees reflected on the significance of building the kingdom of God on earth. They debated strategies for achieving their goal and rejoiced when they had registered victories. Once an international meeting was over, they went back to their own communities and re-energized their fellow church members by reminding them that the time had come to eradicate personal, social, and cultural factors that led individuals to adopt immoral behaviours.[9] Protestant denominations, and in particular the Baptist, Methodist—which was the largest denomination in the country—and Presbyterian churches, embraced the Social Gospel Movement. New religious organizations, such as the Salvation Army, were set up to help the poor, prostitutes, and drunkards. They publicized their work as a means of social mobilization but also took the opportunity to raise funds.[10]

The Catholic church reacted somewhat differently to the social and economic challenges of the Industrial Revolution. As a highly hierarchical organization, it adopted a top-down approach. In Europe and North America, the papacy encouraged the clergy to embrace Catholic social action. In practice, this meant increasing the church's control over its flocks through the multiplication of socially oriented initiatives. After 1840, the Roman Catholic Church in British North America no longer faced a shortage of priests. Through its effective control of the school system in what became the province of Quebec in 1867, church officials could identify promising candidates for the priesthood and brotherhoods. By joining female religious orders, many women "legitimately" avoided child-bearing. Consequently, the Roman Catholic Church possessed human resources that led to a significant increase in the number of parishes in urban centres. It also encouraged workers to join Catholic trade unions, as opposed to international unions that the church considered hostile to its doctrine.

This spiritual movement energized Christians from various Protestant denominations during this period. For its supporters, the time was right to bring together the spiritual and the material and to regenerate society. The Social Gospel Movement contributed to the broader social reform movement sweeping the United States, Great Britain, and the British North American colonies.[11] These colonies—the Colonies of Canada, New Brunswick, and Nova Scotia—agreed to change their political structure and formed a new political entity, the Dominion of Canada, in 1867. Since 1867, both federal and provincial governments would be under pressure by moral entrepreneurs to regulate behaviour defined as vice.

SEXUALITY: REPRESSION AND RESISTANCE

Both church and state continued to define marriage as an indissoluble union between a man and a woman. For Christians, it was the only legitimate site for sexuality. The state did its part to maintain wedlock as a pivotal social institution by keeping access to divorce restricted. In order for the state to dissolve a marriage, Canadians had to submit a request to their member of Parliament. The process was long, but MPs were unwilling to liberalize the divorce procedure. If the number of divorces that the House of Commons actually granted is an indication, few Canadians brought their marital problems to the doorsteps of their elected officials. Between 1867 and 1900, there were seventy-one divorces in Ontario, Quebec, and Manitoba. New Brunswick, Nova Scotia, British Columbia, and Prince Edward Island had their own divorce courts prior to their entry into Confederation. These new provinces did not suspend their courts when they agreed to join Confederation, but neither did they commonly support those who sought to end their marriages. Only two hundred divorces were granted in these provinces during the same time period.[12]

During the Industrial Revolution, many Christians felt that families were under tremendous threat. Some reformists were convinced that the power of the state should be used to protect the institution of marriage. In reaction to this pressure, the state strongly opposed those who questioned the definition of marriage as a union between one man and one woman. One challenge came from a group of American immigrants, who were among the thousands attracted to Canada's prairies by propagandists promising them wealth as farmers. At the end of the 1880s, these immigrants began to settle in the future province of Alberta. This group practised polygamy and belonged to the Mormon religion. Their founder, Joseph Smith, had received "a divine revelation that some elders should take more than one wife."[13] His followers requested that they be allowed to continue this practice, but they did not receive a sympathetic hearing, either from politicians or from other Christian religious leaders.

Christian missionaries working in the Prairies and on the West Coast were concerned by the arrival of the Mormons, an influx that started in 1887. But it was the persistence of polygamy among Aboriginals that particularly bothered them. They launched a campaign against it, affirming monogamous heterosexual marriage was the cornerstone of a "stable" society. Polygamy was seen as exploitative of women and leading to promiscuity. From their point of view, if polygamy were legally condoned, it would be impossible for men to control their sexual desires.[14]

A similar debate divided American society, where Christian church leaders launched an attack on the Mormons. They claimed that the sect threatened Christianity and the family as a fundamental social unit. American politicians acted swiftly. They denounced the Mormons, and the U.S. Congress criminalized polygamy with the Edmunds Anti-Polygamy Act of 1882.

In Canada, some feared that Mormons would transform the country with their belief in plural marriage and that they would greatly increase their numbers. In order to prevent this, the 1892 Criminal Code condemned polygamy and reaffirmed marriage as the union between one man and one woman. The penalty for those who practised polygamy or celebrated plural unions was a fine of $500 and imprisonment for five years. While politicians were dealing with the Mormons, they used the opportunity to crack down on Aboriginals who practised polygamy. As Sarah Carter writes, preventing polygamy was part of the general campaign to isolate Aboriginals, confine them to live on reserves, and destroy their culture. The federal government implemented a series of repressive laws and policies in the second half of the nineteenth century. The 1876 Indian Act constituted the main piece of legislation in this arsenal. The federal government counted on the co-operation of the Protestant and Roman Catholic churches. Again, for both the state and the churches, it was necessary to reiterate support for monogamous, indissoluble marriage and to force Aboriginals to adhere to it.[15]

Other concerns about unrestrained sexual activity led several groups, and in particular religious organizations, to mobilize their forces and urge the state to take action. Their strategy was to unify societal response to vice through government intervention. No one would be able to escape the law as long as those who enforced it—police forces and courts—had the resources and the determination to do so. Since church tribunals disciplined only members belonging to their own denomination, they had difficulty bringing in the accused to the church authorities and dealing with him or her in that sphere, and dealt less and less with sexual issues during the second half of the nineteenth century. Individuals in the middle class, which was now developing, were opposed to having issues "now seen as private matters" dealt with "by those they considered their social inferiors." Furthermore, middle- and upper-class men "were particularly reluctant to submit their business practices and personal behavior to church regulation."[16] Individuals were also moving to towns and urban centres, looking for jobs and a better future, and with this migration, small communities lost their ability to enforce their understanding of appropriate sexual conduct. Consequently, moral reformers insisted that their movement's lobbying of the state to better protect men, women, children, and families and to impose self-control was timely.

One of the issues to be addressed was prostitution, which was notably present in urban centres. In 1871 there were 41 brothels in Montreal. Twenty years later 102 houses of ill repute were employing 390 prostitutes, according to the Montreal chief of police.[17] In Halifax, moral reformers estimated that there were between 600 and 1,000 prostitutes working in the 1860s. The sex trade was due to the presence of soldiers and sailors in the capital of Nova Scotia.[18]

Church leaders and moral reformers targeted prostitution because they believed that they could make a significant breakthrough in fighting interconnected social evils. The definitive resolution of the prostitution issue would undermine other social evils such as adultery and the transmission of sexual diseases. It would also curb activities that thrived on it, such as gambling and alcohol use. Prostitution was a sin and its presence challenged the proper boundaries of sexual behaviour. Prostitutes were blamed for spreading sexually transmitted diseases that threatened families and an individual's health. Furthermore, the commercialization of prostitution and in particular its visibility on the streets and in taverns, parks, and brothels irritated moral reformers. In his 1898 study of Toronto, Christopher St. George Clark argued that adultery "being public is what constitutes the sin because sin, as far as my observation has carried me, is only sin when it is found out."[19] Since Christianity confined sexual relations to marriage and the privacy of the household, the time had come to eradicate prostitution and purify neighbourhoods and cities where the sex trade took place. Tolerance was no longer an option.

In their anti-prostitution campaigns, women's groups targeted men and appealed to their ability to govern their own sexual desires. They denounced society's double sexual standard, which maintained that women should remain chaste before marriage, but readily excused men's sexual transgressions. Within the women's movement, the Woman's Christian Temperance Union (WCTU) was active on this front. Founded in the United States, the WCTU formed its first Canadian local in Picton, Ontario, in 1874. The WCTU dealt with a range of issues: women's and children's labour; poverty; sexual practices; and tobacco, drug, and alcohol use. With regard to prostitution, and sexual practices more broadly, the WCTU believed in the ability of individuals to self-govern. For instance, it launched a White Ribbon campaign, in which men "who promised to remain sexually pure" were given a small white ribbon to wear proudly as a visible sign of "their new identities."[20]

Societal response to prostitution varied. Some individuals, such as the future prime minister of Canada, William Lyon Mackenzie King, armed with their Bibles, motivated by their Christian faith, and convinced they were doing the right thing, decided to socialize with prostitutes. What did King, who was a nineteen-year-old University of Toronto undergraduate student, want to achieve by meeting with a prostitute called Edna, in February 1894? He sought to bring her back on the "right" path. He hoped that his involvement would be sufficient to convince her, and others like her, that they should abandon their sinful lifestyle. Although it is difficult to determine how many individuals repeated King's gesture, it was likely that many devout Christians tried personally to counsel prostitutes. According to his diary, King was successful in convincing some to leave the sex trade, but it is difficult to confirm this assessment.[21]

If moral persuasion failed, religious groups, which strongly encouraged prostitutes to abandon their work, sent them to shelters. This type of establishment had an explicit goal: to reform prostitutes by forcing them to adopt a "righteous" lifestyle. For instance, in 1858, with fifteen other women, Elizabeth Dunlop founded the Toronto Magdalene Asylum. Their goal was to "eliminate prostitution by rehabilitating prostitutes." The admission process required the rescued to sever ties with their prostitute friends. The Toronto Magdalene Asylum taught that domesticity and Christianity were the prostitutes' path to redemption.[22] Also other new institutions destined to reform prostitutes mushroomed throughout the country. For instance, reform schools were run by lay organizations, or sometimes, as in Montreal, by religious orders.[23]

Moral reformers pushing the anti-prostitution agenda sought to document their case, in an attempt to "measure" scientifically the prevalence of immoral behaviours. Between 1911 and 1915, they requested that vice surveys be conducted in urban centres. Moral reformers expected that those collecting empirical data for the surveys would have irreproachable credentials and be acquainted with the Social Gospel movement. Suspecting that some data collectors, hired by cities, lacked impeccable moral character, churches undertook to conduct surveys themselves. In 1913, the Board of Temperance and Moral Reform of the Methodist Church and the Board of Social Service and Evangelism of the Presbyterian Church conducted surveys in several Canadian cities: Hamilton, London, Regina, Sydney, Vancouver, and Winnipeg. At other times, moral and social reformers pressed cities to appoint a commission on social vice in order to undertake a "moral" survey, as did the city of Toronto in 1913. These civic initiatives were part of an urban phenomenon that had started south of the border, in Chicago, in 1911.[24]

Based on these surveys, moral reformers identified social, economic, and personal factors that could lead a woman to become a prostitute. Sometimes they blamed prostitutes themselves, claiming that they coveted an expensive lifestyle. In 1886 John Grierson, who was a missionary for the Halifax City Mission, claimed that women chose this immoral way of life because of their "extravagant tastes and lack of industrious habits."[25] Others proclaimed that women did not wish to become prostitutes; on the contrary, they were the victims of unscrupulous individuals and criminal elements. Newspapers, religious leaders, and moral reformers disseminated stories raising fears that a number of innocent young white girls, having left their families and towns for employment, had disappeared once they reached the city. The accusation was that non-white individuals—Chinese, Italians, and Blacks—had kidnapped these girls and forced them into prostitution. The "white slave traffic" panic echoed sentiment in the United States.

Many reformers failed to realize that some women were driven to work in the sex trade by the lack of other opportunities for employment. Knowledge about prostitutes—social background, origins, age, and marital status—is scarce because few of them, including brothel owners, left records. Scholars have started using census data to document the sex trade as in the case of Victoria in British Columbia. According to the 1891 and 1901 census records, most female prostitutes were in their mid-twenties, came mostly from the United States, and were married.[26] As for the motives to be in the sex trade, there were few "legitimate" options for women besides domestic services in a city like Halifax. In larger urban centres, such as Toronto and Montreal, women could find employment in factories making cigars, shoes, or clothing, but they faced long working hours and low wages. Prostitution paid much more money compared to these jobs.[27]

Working conditions in the sex trade varied considerably. Brothels had regular customers, and prostitutes could have four or five customers every night. Prostitutes working on the street could have more, but the number was unpredictable. Regardless of where they worked, there were dangers. Besides physical violence, prostitutes faced the possibility of sexually transmitted diseases, pregnancy, and abortion.[28]

Prostitutes developed their own strategies of resistance. Brothel owners, who were often prostitutes or former prostitutes themselves, bribed police officers in order to keep them at bay.[29] Other owners hired their own security guards in order to keep unruly customers from their premises. Pimps, who offered protection to prostitutes, but often victimized and abused them, also joined the business.

Proposed solutions to prostitution varied. Some moral reformers asked for a crackdown while others preferred to target prostitutes and to reform them. Depending on the intensity of lobbying by moral reformers, cities reacted differently. Some cities opened institutions to reform prostitutes, while others launched crackdowns on street prostitutes. These campaigns, however, often lasted only a short period of time. In other cities, officials opted for what they thought was a permanent solution, since their attempts to control prostitution had failed. At the beginning of the twentieth century, inspired by similar initiatives in American cities, several Canadian municipal councils closed their red-light districts, where prostitution was tolerated, and police forces arrested and charged prostitutes and brothel owners.

The prostitution issue came and went, depending on the strength of the anti-prostitution forces in a given area. Often a campaign would emerge in a town or a city such as Halifax, Montreal, Regina, Toronto, Vancouver, or Winnipeg, when worrisome news, complaints by moral reformers to city officials, and a perception of inactivity on the part of elected officials and police forces fuelled a moral crisis. Sometimes, moral reformers won, and city officials put in place repressive measures and forced police forces to act.

Opponents to prostitution could count on the support of physicians, some of whom wondered if repression was the best approach. Other physicians agreed that sexually transmitted diseases (STDs) were a concern and suggested that prostitutes should be routinely tested to contain the spread of these infections. In their view, instead of launching sporadic crackdowns on prostitutes, society should let them work in peace and threaten them only when they were ill in order to prevent them from infecting others.

Others challenged the narrative developed by moral reformers. In his survey of Toronto, journalist C.S. Clark took issue with moral reformers by arguing that repression did not work as a public policy when it came to prostitution. "Houses of ill-fame," he wrote, "are absolutely necessary in, not Toronto alone, but every city in America." Knowing that moral reformers would reject what they qualified as ill-conceived advice, he argued that his views mattered because he "reflect[ed] public opinion more than any so called public moralist." Clark envisioned a policy allowing brothels in North American cities to be licensed by health boards. Physicians would visit the licensed brothels and test prostitutes for STDs. In the case of a positive result, a prostitute would receive medical treatment. Clark claimed that his policy would eliminate the violence surrounding the sex trade, since prostitutes would work in safe establishments, and the possibility of being infected would disappear.[30]

In some cities, moral reformers failed to persuade voters that prostitution was a problem that required such radical solutions as massive arrests, closures of brothels, and allocating financial resources to rescue prostitutes. As the cases of Winnipeg and Montreal demonstrate, residents were not always bothered by the sex trade and sometimes adopted an attitude of tolerance. However, attitudes changed when prostitutes moved into their neighbourhoods; this migration occurred partly because of crackdowns in other parts of these cities. Residents who shared public space with the newly arrived prostitutes now began to pay attention to the moral reformers' arguments. This explains why city officials in Winnipeg and Montreal occasionally appointed commissions of inquiry to report on prostitution. In response, police officers would become "suddenly" zealous in enforcing municipal bylaws and laws, especially when brothels did not have a licence to sell liquor.[31]

There was an ongoing struggle between moral reformers and law enforcement agencies. Municipalities and police forces had legal instruments for arresting prostitutes, people running a bawdy house, or those who frequented such establishments. The state could charge prostitutes for vagrancy, disorderly behaviour, drunkenness, or causing public fights. In 1869, the federal Parliament passed the "Act respecting Vagrants." It defined prostitution as a crime punishable by up to two months in jail. Among those who found themselves targeted by the law were

> All common prostitutes, or night walkers wandering in the fields, public streets or highways, lanes or places of public meeting or gathering of people, not giving a satisfactory account of themselves;
>
> All keepers of bawdy houses and houses of ill-fame, or houses for the resort of prostitutes, and persons in the habit of frequenting such houses, not giving a satisfactory account of themselves; and
>
> All persons who have no peaceable profession or calling to maintain themselves by, but who do for the most part support themselves by the avails of prostitution.[32]

In many cities and towns, nevertheless, an unofficial policy of tolerance made laws and bylaws ineffectual. Those in charge of enforcement often questioned the repressive approach. Many police officers believed that prostitution was a fact of life and that repression achieved nothing. Others realized that they could benefit from this vice by charging "protection fees" to brothel owners and those involved in the sex trade. For their part, some judges believed that prostitution was "a necessary social evil" and that repression was a poor choice of public policy.[33] Such attitudes on the part of law enforcement officers and the judiciary profoundly shocked and disappointed those fighting prostitution.

Although the law identified prostitutes and customers, police officers enforced it only sporadically and they rarely arrested customers. They did it because they came under pressure from individuals and groups opposed to prostitution. In 1894 the Ontario WCTU threatened to release the names of men who had sex with prostitutes if police did not target them. But this threat did not affect how police officers enforced the law. "In the latter half of the nineteenth century, women prostitutes represented 97.5 per cent of those charged, while the number of male customers registered only a paltry 2.5 per cent."[34] Since 1869 the vagrancy offence had also applied to male prostitutes, but few were ever charged.

When police did enforce vagrancy and federal laws against prostitution, gender, race, religion, and class influenced who was targeted in certain communities. Certain groups of women were overrepresented among those arrested and convicted. In British Columbia, where anti-Asian sentiment was strong, Chinese and Japanese women were disproportionately arrested. In Halifax and Regina, Afro-Canadians were a particular target. And in other parts of the country, Catholic Irish women were most often charged. Furthermore, politicians contributed to the ethnic and class war on prostitution. In the 1880s, the federal Parliament passed laws dealing specifically with Aboriginals and prostitution. Brothel owners who employed Aboriginal prostitutes faced severe penalties. In the case of Aboriginal men, they could "be convicted for merely 'frequenting' or being 'found' on the premises, while other customers had to be proved to be 'habitual frequenters.'"[35]

Other aspects of sex triggered strong reactions from moral reformers. Christian churches were opposed to abortion and birth control. Among them, the Roman Catholic Church was very militant. In the 1869 bull *Apostolicae Sedis moderationi*, Pope Pius IX reminded Catholics that abortion—at any stage of pregnancy—was a serious offence and a mortal sin and that the penalty was excommunication.

In their campaigns to regulate sex, Roman Catholic and Protestant Church officials counted on physicians to be their allies. In the second half of the nineteenth century, physicians expanded their control over the treatment of the body and became engaged social actors. Colleges of physicians and surgeons were established and granted licences to individuals who could practise medicine. The institutionalization of medicine coincided with a campaign to eliminate individuals who practised medicine with no scientific training. With the professionalization of medicine, physicians claimed that their scientific approach adequately equipped them to deal with illnesses and other health issues. Physicians, but also new health professionals such as hygienists, psychologists, and sex experts, shared the view that the Industrial Revolution was radically transforming how individuals lived and how they interacted among themselves and with their environment. They feared for the future of the "race," especially when certain ethnic groups, labelled as "inferior," were mixing with Anglo-Saxons. The impoverishment of urban centres, data demonstrating that working poor families lived in abject and shameful social and health conditions, the spread of illnesses, and continuing alcohol abuse made health experts worried for the people's well-being. By linking science to their professions, health experts improved their social capital and built their image of respectability.[36]

Health professionals relabelled some behaviours, dispensing with the term *vice*. Various sexual behaviours were deemed to be signs of mental illness or of mental states that required medical treatment. Practitioners defined their work as instrumental in addressing both social and health issues. They supported groups that advocated for a crackdown on abortion by denouncing midwives, herbalists, homeopaths, and traditional healers as charlatans. At the same time, they justified their right to control the birth process by arguing that their scientific approach constituted a step forward, as opposed to the unscientific methods used by those they called imposters.[37]

In this context, physicians pushed for harsher penalties for those who assisted a woman in ending her pregnancy. Some of them became activists and pressed their colleagues not to perform the procedure. Dr. Alfred A. Andrews published an article on this topic in the medical journal *Canada Lancet*, in 1875. He wrote:

> When we consider the terrible penalties inflicted by society on the female sex for incontinence, we need not wonder at the desperate efforts young girls make to escape them. When you are solicited to interfere for the relief of these poor wretches, pity them, pity them with your whole hearts; ... meet their entreaties with prompt, decided refusal.[38]

The abortion debate was connected to the controversy over the declining birth rate. The fact that Canadians were having fewer children fuelled social anxiety. While the infant mortality rate was relatively low in Ontario, it was high in Quebec, especially among French-Canadian newborns in Montreal, with an overall decline in the fertility rate. The reduction of family size was "noticeable in the urban centers and among the middle classes."[39] The general birth rate was 189 per thousand in 1871, but 144 per thousand twenty years later (the fertility rate refers to the average number of children born to each woman; the birth rate is the number of births in an area per 1,000 of the population in a year). Women had an average of 4.1 children in 1871, and 2.0 forty years later. Catholic and Protestant church officials, women's groups, and physicians feared for the survival of the white race. They believed that, to reverse what they considered a dangerous trend, individuals should be prevented from attempting to control pregnancies or to induce abortions. For its part, the eugenics movement, which believed that the human race could be improved by eliminating deficiencies, joined the campaign to limit access to birth control for certain groups. Its members believed that the "unfit"— individuals who had a mental deficiency or belonged to the lower economic classes—should not be allowed to procreate, while the upper classes should be discouraged from using birth control. They pushed for programs to sterilize the "feebleminded." In response, the governments of British Columbia and Alberta introduced sterilization programs, but the governments of Ontario, Quebec, and Manitoba, provinces where lobbying from the Catholic church was relatively strong, especially in Quebec, rejected them.[40]

During this period, several physicians opposed birth control. They argued that the means to regulate births were unnatural and prevented women from fulfilling societal expectations: embracing motherhood by having children. Although physicians conceded that sexuality should be controlled but not repressed, they did not approve of women and couples who voluntarily limited the size of their families. Some physicians accepted that women used abstinence or interrupted sexual intercourse as birth control methods, but most agreed that birth control devices and information should not be made available.[41]

Meanwhile, the state kept abortion as a crime and criminalized birth control in 1892. Section 179 (c) of the Criminal Code (1892, 55–56 Victoria Chap. 29) made the sale, advertisement, and publication of information on both birth control and abortion a crime. The penalty was imprisonment for two years. In the case of abortion, Section 272 stipulated that anyone who assisted a woman would face up to imprisonment for life. If a woman terminated her own pregnancy, Section 273 imposed a sentence of up to seven years' imprisonment. Since several physicians denounced abortions and, in particular, individuals who assisted women in terminating their pregnancies, the federal government took their views into consideration.

Women's organizations had a different perspective on this public policy choice. At the time, the feminist movement was concerned with limiting the degree of control that men had over women's bodies. If access to abortion and birth control were facilitated, feminists feared that men would "take greater sexual advantage of women."[42] Despite repressive state policies and views from women's groups, women continued to find ways of terminating unwanted pregnancies. They relied on informal advice and word of mouth in order to find drugs, herbs, and other products, or individuals who could help to induce an abortion. Despite the threat of a criminal charge, some physicians continued to help women end their unwanted pregnancies.

Law enforcement of abortion offences was selective. Carolyn Strange observes that in Toronto between 1880 and 1930, women who sought abortions were rarely prosecuted. Police forces preferred to arrest the abortionists, whether male or female. On the other hand, as Andrée Lévesque has noticed, in Montreal between 1919 and 1939, police were reluctant to arrest either abortionists or their patients, since the police officers themselves might want to send a female friend or colleague to someone who offered the procedure. Accordingly, the court system rarely dealt with abortion cases. For instance in British Columbia between 1886 and 1939, judges generally only heard about abortions that went wrong—those with serious medical complications that obliged a woman to request additional health resources, or those where a pregnant woman died following an abortion. When accused individuals faced the wrath of the justice system, about 50 percent of them were found guilty.[43]

In spite of the legal obstacles put in place by moral reformers, the dissemination of information about birth control did not disappear. Families and women continued to seek information by talking to friends, writing to experts such as the American birth control activist Margaret Sanger, going to pharmacies, or buying products—such as the "Ladies Safe Remedy: Apioline," of Lyman and Sons of Montreal—that were advertised in newspapers, claiming to enable women to regulate their cycle. In its 1901 catalogue, Eaton's department store advertised the "Every Woman Marvel Whirling Spray," which was a vaginal spray (some believed that vaginal sprays could induce an abortion).[44]

The repression of extramarital sex included same-sex relations. Christian religious institutions condemned homosexuality as a sin, but educators, magistrates, and physicians, who had become the new moral entrepreneurs, constructed homosexuality as "deviance." At the end of the nineteenth century, they created new terms for tracing the boundaries of acceptable sexuality. The word *homosexual*, first used by Swiss doctor Karoly Maria Benkert in 1869, characterized a form of improper sexuality. According to D'Emilio and Freedman, physical intimacy among women was tolerated. However, the new emphasis on motherhood and reproduction meant that intimate friendships among women triggered some warnings. Men who displayed similar feelings were considered deviant. The fears surrounding homosexuality led some physicians and moral reformers to warn young boys to stay away from older men who could prey on them sexually.[45]

Inspired by the British example, Canada criminalized homosexual acts. Section 178 of the Criminal Code (1892, 55–56 Victoria, Chap. 29) associated homosexuality with gross indecency:

Every male person is guilty of an indictable offence and liable to five years' imprisonment and to be whipped who in public or private, commits, or is a party to the commission of, or procures or attempts to procure the commission by any male person of, any act of gross indecency with another male person.

The legislator did not define the term *gross*, assuming that the meaning was self-evident. Indeed, the word captured the public imagination. The broad definition allowed considerable flexibility to police officers and judges in their interpretation of "gross indecency." Consequently, enforcement varied immensely throughout the country. In Montreal, judges' own moral values determined whether clemency or severe punishment would result from the charge, but all "gross indecency" cases heard by the courts involved sexual relations with minors in public.[46]

Although moral reformers pursued an agenda of limiting acceptable sexual acts to the privacy of the household, these did not include homosexuality. This sinful behaviour—a crime against nature for the Roman Catholic Church—continued to be considered deviant. The privacy of the household could not excuse this abnormal form of sexuality, since heterosexuality was the norm.

DRINKING: CHASING THE LIQUOR DEMON

Opponents of alcohol use no longer denounced only excessive drinking; rather, they deplored drinking itself. The battle for temperance, and subsequently for prohibition, came to mobilize various social actors over the years, and arguments changed as more individuals and groups joined in. At first, temperance societies, several of which emerged at the end of the 1820s, led the movement. They aimed to reform individuals by strongly encouraging them to make a pledge to abstain from alcohol use. They focused on individual efforts, and their strategy relied on moral persuasion. The promotion of Christian values—restraint and moderation—was at the core of an interventionist strategy destined to alter radically how Canadians related to drinking. These societies appealed to both men and women, regardless of their class, ethnicity, or religion.[47]

Initially, the novelty of the movement captured the interest of various regular and occasional drinkers. By the 1840s, several thousand of them had answered the call and taken the pledge. In French Canada, Father Charles Chiniquy became the figurehead of the temperance movement. Between 1848 and 1850, almost 45 percent or 400,000 French Canadians took the pledge. Tavern owners and liquor producers noticed a significant reduction

Group of men smoking and drinking in Calgary, Alberta, ca. 1893–94. Robert Randolph Bruce, McCord Museum, MP-0000.583.38.

in consumption, and the Molson's distillery registered a large financial loss during this period. However, Chiniquy's success came to an abrupt halt. Bishop Ignace Bourget of Montreal asked the temperance advocate to stop working in his diocese, following allegations of sexual misconduct with women. Chiniquy left Canada for the United States, and the liquor industry rejoiced as alcohol consumption rebounded. Thomas Molson could go ahead with his expansion plan for his distillery in Montreal.[48] But, despite the Chiniquy episode and the resurgence in demand, the popular response to their campaigns convinced temperance advocates that a dry society was no longer an altogether distant possibility.

However, enthusiasm for the temperance cause and moral persuasion faded by the 1840s. Words and promises were not sufficient. The concept of self-improvement, the pressure to take the pledge, and enthusiasm for the cause lost their appeal and effectiveness. The temperance movement with its strategies and tactics was no match for well-entrenched cultural habits and society's use of alcohol.

Once again, though, a new initiative from the United States injected hope among opponents of alcohol use. The arrival of temperance lodges, such as the Independent Order of Good Templars, and the Sons of Temperance, founded in New York City in 1842 by reformed drunkards, allied sobriety and sociability. Their first lodge in British North America was founded in St. Stephen, New Brunswick, in 1847. Temperance advocates realized that drinking was more than just a way for individuals to quench their thirst. Those studying drinking habits observed that men went to taverns for more than just drinks. These locations were meeting places. Customers went to socialize with co-workers, neighbours, or other regulars. Reverend Foster Almon of St. George's Anglican church in Halifax acknowledged that "young men did not frequent dram shops for the love of liquor only." They went there for "the love of sociability that gathered around it."[49]

In keeping with this social function, temperance lodges became hugely popular among members of the working class, as a substitute for the taverns. Lodges organized social events and offered mutual benefits such as covering the cost of a funeral or giving assistance in case of sickness or accident to

Crest of Society of Temperance, Canada East, John Henry Walker (1831–1899), ca. 1852. McCord Museum, M930.51.1.378.

their members as long as they abstained from alcohol. However, the lodges ultimately had their limitations. Many members of the working class, who had enthusiastically joined the lodges, abandoned them in the 1860s when they ceased to provide mutual benefits.[50]

Women had been part of the broad campaign since its beginnings, and they too joined temperance societies and lodges in large numbers. In the second half of the nineteenth century, the WCTU in particular came to symbolize female participation. Because of her organizational and oratorical skills, Letitia Youmans led the movement in Canada. Her experience, indirectly through observation, of the liquor demon shaped her involvement. The physical, emotional, and financial hardship and desolation that drinking caused families horrified her. She felt compelled to aid those whom she called the innocent victims of the drunkards. For her, to do nothing was criminal. Thousands of women, inspired by Youmans's determination and conviction, decided to do something. They joined the WCTU, attended lectures on alcohol use, and became involved in direct action. They signed petitions demanding prohibition of the liquor trade. Armed with their bibles, they visited taverns and saloons, where they sang hymns and tried to enroll customers in their anti-alcohol cause.[51]

The involvement of evangelical Protestant churches invigorated the temperance movement. Many Presbyterian, Methodist, and Baptist ministers forcefully condemned alcohol use from the pulpit. Malcolm Bethune, a Presbyterian minister and father of physician and communist activist Norman Bethune, denounced drinking in the strongest terms. Motivated by religious factors and family circumstances—he blamed alcohol for his own father's misfortune—Malcolm Bethune proclaimed that drinking was the source of all evils. This colourful clergyman went on a speaking tour in Ontario, hoping to rally thousands in the fight against the liquor demon.[52] Although the Anglican Church was not officially involved, some of its members also joined the cause.

While alcohol consumption was declining in some parts of British North America, it was still widespread. Previous efforts to achieve a dry society had not lived up to the activists' expectations. A new approach was in the works: prohibition. The politicization of the issue was inevitable following the 1851 Maine law prohibiting the manufacture and sale of alcohol in that state. The success of this public policy convinced temperance advocates in British North American colonies that it was time to use the law to enforce the prohibition of all manufacturing and sale of alcohol. For these advocates, prohibition was the only means for achieving the overall goal pursued since the 1820s. Although prohibition interfered with individuals and their ability to govern themselves in a society based on the principle of freedom, its supporters believed that using state power to restrict individual liberty was legitimate since the goal was the well-being of the community.

The politicization of the liquor traffic issue led temperance advocates, Protestant churches, and women's groups to agree, in 1877, to unite their forces and form the Dominion Alliance for the Total Suppression of the Liquor Traffic. Although women's organizations were not the driving force, they co-operated with the Alliance, which had the goal of co-ordinating all the anti-alcohol forces. The Alliance drew its support mainly from members of the middle class living in urban centres. At one point, its leaders contemplated founding a single-issue political party, but soon abandoned the idea.[53]

Notwithstanding the growing enthusiasm of prohibition advocates, the Dominion Alliance encountered some challenges in pursuing its mission. The presence of Protestant churches in the organization created tensions and conflicts within the temperance movement. Co-operation with the Roman Catholic Church became almost impossible at the institutional level. In the eyes of Catholic officials, the temperance movement had become a vehicle for Protestant proselytism. For them, temperance was a much better option than prohibition.

The founding of the Dominion Alliance allowed the social actors involved in the prohibition campaign to refine their narrative. Proponents of a "dry" Canada challenged the notion that drunkenness and alcohol use were acceptable behaviours. In deconstructing the dominant narrative, these anti-alcohol proponents defined those who favoured liquor use as promoters of family violence, economic hardship, and poverty. Consequently, drinking became a destructive habit and, even worse, a vice. Drunken individuals disturbed public order. Saloons and taverns were places that encouraged people to drink and get drunk. Individuals who drank had poor work ethics—drunken people should not be working under the influence of alcohol—and they lowered national morals—drunken people could harm children, women, and families. Alcohol use led to social, moral, and economic destitution for families. Individuals under the influence of alcohol could become violent and harm their wives and children. Furthermore, drinking loosened morality. Under the influence of alcohol, individuals committed sinful acts—having sex with a prostitute—which they would not do if sober. Anticipating criticism from those who insisted that the liquor industry created jobs, the Dominion Alliance counter-argued that the industry actually drained financial resources that could have created a greater number of jobs if invested in other industries.[54]

Moral reformers used various means to disseminate their views. From the pulpit they warned about the dangers of alcohol use and educated church-goers politically. They organized rallies and speaking tours. They produced

This advertisement captures some of the arguments used by temperance forces. John Henry Walker, 1859, gift of Mr. David Ross McCord, McCord Museum, M930.50.3.147.

and distributed a variety of publications. They drew up petitions and sent them to elected officials. They visited politicians and pressed them to let the people decide on the prohibition issue by holding referenda. They tried, but often failed, to close down licensed establishments. After all, the state granted the licences, but enforcement of municipal bylaws and provincial legislation varied tremendously, depending on the commitment and resources at the disposal of law enforcement officers.

Because drinking played a role in class identity formation, alcohol use divided society. For the working class, "the right to drink with other men became a major component in their class identity."[55] But it was also how members of the working class managed their leisure time. Spending hours in a saloon was part of a worker's class identity, since it provided an opportunity to socialize and to create a lasting bond with co-workers. For some members of the middle and upper classes, alcohol use was a disturbing behaviour. In their view, hours spent at a saloon were a terrible waste. They maintained that these fathers should be at home with their wives and children instead of spending the family budget on liquors. Their judgment on how members of the working class should regulate their lives and spend their leisure time did not go unnoticed. Some observed that those who promoted a "dry" Canada were quick to target workers and their detrimental drinking habits but were almost silent on members of the bourgeoisie who spent their leisure time drinking with their fellow "good bodies" in private clubs.

Drinking played a role in gender identities, as well. For proponents, young men drank to prove their "manhood" and to take part in the "vital ritual of one man's taking a drink with another man."[56] For women, temperance advocates argued that drinking was evidence of a failure of femininity. According to opponents, drinking revealed the true nature of a person's character. Under the influence of alcohol, men could become violent and harm friends, loved ones, and the community. A drinking woman did not live up to her obligation to be fully in control of her emotions and capable of complying with societal expectations. As abstinence from alcohol became the new norm, public drinking by women disappeared, and women who wanted to drink had to hide their habit.[57]

Women with a regular drinking habit concerned some physicians, who considered them to be bad mothers and fallen individuals. Some doctors warned women that drinking while pregnant could have dire consequences for the fetus. According to British physician Elizabeth Chesser,

> a drunken motherhood mean[t] children handicapped physically, mentally and morally. The problem of infant mortality includes also the problem of drink. The woman who takes alcohol [...] when she is pregnant, is imperiling her unborn child. If a woman ruins her constitution with alcohol, how can she bear healthy children? How can she nurse them? And what chances have they of surviving the first few months of infant life?[58]

Comments such as these contributed to the emergence of the societal expectation that women should not drink. This repressive discourse on women and alcohol had consequences for those who drank. Regardless of the nature of the relation that women had with alcohol—casual, heavy drinker, or addicted—they were reluctant to seek help. After all, seeking assistance was an admission of moral weakness and a sign of lack of control on the part of a woman with a liquor problem. As long as a woman could conceal her alcohol consumption, she could convince herself that there was nothing wrong.[59]

Physicians' warnings about the harmful effects of alcohol alarmed society, but they were also concerned with the manner in which the medical community dealt with the liquor issue. Some of them prescribed alcohol for medicinal purposes: to relieve pain or to cure some illnesses. According to physicians hostile to alcohol use, these members of the medical community encouraged men's and women's drinking habits while social groups were arguing for abstinence. Consequently, those physicians preoccupied by alcohol use put pressure on the medical community to act on this issue.[60]

In other parts of the country, promoting a "dry" Canada meant targeting visible minority groups to reinforce anti-immigrant views and racism. In British Columbia, temperance forces counted on the support of individuals and organizations opposed to the presence of Chinese, Japanese, and other Asians.

Already blamed for undermining the national fabric and defined as not fitting well in a Christian Anglo-Saxon society, Chinese and Japanese were portrayed as behaving immorally while under the influence of alcohol. Others claimed that these recent immigrants deprived the state of revenue by selling alcohol on their premises without a licence. Attempting to increase societal support for their movement, temperance voices tapped into anti-Asian sentiment in the westernmost province.[61]

Many perceived the new narrative on alcohol use as a threat, and the politicization of drinking was a highly contested issue. Besides the Catholic Church, which as we've seen favoured temperance over prohibition, there were numerous other opponents of prohibition, such as farmers; owners and workers in the transportation, beer, and liquor industries; and tavern and saloon owners and their employees. They believed that this public policy was a radical solution threatening the livelihood of many and that the state should not be in the business of regulating lives and interfering with the rights of individuals in managing their time and activities.

Although alcohol use was framed as a social problem requiring a political solution, elected officials were generally reluctant to tackle the issue. Some politicians promoted the prohibition cause among other elected officials, but everyone knew that this was a divisive issue. The movement for prohibition, which was seen as a necessity by some and as a dangerous, radical public policy by others, made the search for a compromise extremely difficult. Furthermore, alcohol production and sale constituted valuable sources of revenue for governments. Any attempt to curb alcohol use would have a negative impact not only on the ability of governments to balance their books, but also on the economy in general. In its 1895 report, the Royal Commission on the Liquor Traffic, appointed by the federal government in 1892, pointed to the consequences of shutting down the liquor industry. This was "a multi-million dollar complex of industries that could not be shut down abruptly without significant economic disruption in many parts of the country."[62] Politicians knew that, aside from jeopardizing the Canadian economy, prohibiting alcohol use would be self-defeating. Free drinks rallied supporters and convinced undecided electors to support the "right" candidates on election day. Since alcohol was a conspicuous lubricant of political machines and an essential component of how election campaigns were fought and won, politicians were reluctant to restrict liquor access. Prohibition would cause a further headache to politicians, since liquor permits and the granting of positions as liquor inspectors were valuable instruments of political patronage.

Despite politicians' reservations, the state made some attempts to address the situation in order to restore social peace. In its dealings with Aboriginals, the state renewed its past approach. In the 1876 Indian Act, it targeted Aboriginals' access to liquor, by prohibiting the sale of alcohol. As had happened during the French regime and when the British authorities administered the colonies, tavern owners had the responsibility of not selling to Aboriginals. If they were caught, they faced penalties of a fine or a jail term of up to six months. However, law enforcement varied throughout the country. Church missionaries working among Aboriginals and federal representatives justified the ban by exploiting the image of the "drunken Aboriginal." Although alcohol use was widespread in all of Canadian society, Aboriginal drinking habits were distorted in the popular imagination. In the eyes of those promoting a "dry" society, "drunken Aboriginals" were unable to provide for their families, undermined the notion that a man was the family breadwinner, and spent their income unwisely.[63]

In 1878, federal politicians found a way to withdraw from the battle over prohibition. By passing the Canada Temperance Act (CTA), known as the Scott Act and inspired by the 1864 Dunkin Act, which applied only to Quebec and Ontario, the federal government empowered citizens to request local elected officials to hold referenda on the prohibition of liquor sales. This new legal ammunition sent the "dry" and "wet" camps into the trenches, as some municipalities and counties began to implement prohibition within their boundaries. However, the CTA did not prohibit alcohol production, trade, and possession. Furthermore, individuals could buy alcohol for medicinal purposes, by showing a prescription issued by a physician, or wine for religious reasons, with a clergyman's certificate. The liquor industry was not too affected, despite the fact that "per capita sales of alcohol declined from roughly six liters in 1871 to less than four for most of the 1890s and remained between three and four until after World War II."[64]

Many parts of Canada went dry, especially in the Maritimes, but this did not put an end to the debate. Moncton offers a compelling case. Even when, in 1879, the residents chose to prohibit the sale of alcohol, the "dry" camp remained vigilant. They looked for tavern owners who broke the law and put pressure on police forces to arrest them. Those who were arrested and convicted challenged the constitutionality of the CTA, but in 1882, the Judicial Committee of the Privy Council ruled that the legislation was constitutional. Although Moncton was officially dry beginning in 1881, the sale of alcohol remained a fact of life, partly because municipal politicians were reluctant to enforce prohibition, arguing financial considerations. In reaction, a group of citizens formed the United Temperance Committee. Since the CTA allowed a private party to initiate legal action, these prohibition proponents assumed the cost and sued violators in municipal court after the police arrested them.

As part of an agreement with the city, the committee collected fines imposed on those who were convicted.[65]

The citizens' initiative to sue violators of the 1878 law was a success. There were 32, 57, and 45 cases before the municipal police court in 1886, 1887, and 1888, respectively. Sixty-four percent of the cases resulted in convictions, compared to a success rate of only 38 percent in the 1881–85 period.[66]

Despite its success, the United Temperance Committee in Moncton ended its activities in 1888. Its members explained that they could no longer assume an obligation that truly belonged to the city. What they did not add was that it took considerable time and financial resources to get a conviction. They discovered what the city probably knew before the committee came into existence: that finding witnesses willing to testify in court was almost impossible. If they were found, witnesses often had a change of heart and refused to testify or their recollection of the events became "suddenly" vague when they were questioned by lawyers from both parties. Also the committee discovered that owners of licensed establishments would sometimes mount a vigorous defence that led to their acquittal or the payment of a small fine. In the event of a guilty verdict, some moved out of the city for the short or long term and thus escaped the reach of the law.[67]

Moncton's officially dry status did not ease tensions within the community. The zeal of the "dry" side, led by the United Temperance Committee, re-ignited tensions over how to manage alcohol use in the public sphere. Verbal confrontations and physical altercations broke out between dry and wet groups. In their pursuit of a dry society, prohibition proponents disturbed the public peace, which raised concerns among elected officials and police officers. Several of them questioned the wisdom of attempting to govern the conduct of others when many individuals were clearly willing to break the law in order to have a drink. Although consumption declined in Moncton, it did not disappear.[68]

Prohibition opponents discovered that the CTA had some unintended consequences. Following the dismantling of the United Temperance Committee, the city of Moncton once again brought law violators to justice. In the years that followed, municipal politicians and liquor sellers reached a tacit agreement: the city enforced the law and imposed fines on law violators, but liquor sellers were allowed to remain in operation. In other words, the fines became a sort of protection tax, imposed by the court and sanctioned by the city. These fines constituted between 2 and 5 percent of the town's revenues from 1889 to 1893. While the city remained officially dry, Moncton tolerated the sale of liquor and the city's coffers reaped the benefits. This type of arrangement was not uncommon in other parts of Canada as well.[69]

If the CTA was designed to bring prohibition to the country, it was a qualified failure by the 1890s. Only certain counties and towns had voted to become alcohol-free, and even in these places, alcohol use did not disappear. The sale of alcohol and its consumption might no longer be visible, since stores were not allowed to advertise, but hotels and taverns had rooms that regulars could access through a back door. Enforcement was still a serious problem. However, these setbacks did not deter prohibition proponents. On the contrary, the failure proved to them that the elimination of the alcohol trade required a viable national solution.

When the federal Liberal Party, led by Wilfrid Laurier, took office in 1896, it promised a national referendum on prohibition. Held two years later, the referendum revealed deep social divisions. The "dry" side insisted on the terrible social consequences of alcohol use on individuals, families, and communities. For its part, the "wet" side affirmed that government would need new sources of revenue, probably an income tax, if prohibition was implemented. Although 51.3 percent of those who voted (only male property owners were eligible) favoured prohibition, Prime Minister Laurier refused to legislate. Only 44 percent of the electorate had bothered to cast their ballots. Furthermore, this referendum revealed deep regional and national differences. Quebec voters had massively rejected it. Bishops in Quebec had refused to make any official statement on the issue.[70] French-speaking communities in other parts of Canada, notably in New Brunswick, and Catholics also strongly opposed a "Protestant-fuelled public policy." Although those who voted in the Maritimes overwhelmingly favoured prohibition (the results in Prince Edward Island supported the "dry" side by 89.2 percent), the support was not as strong in British Columbia and Ontario, where, respectively, 54.6 percent and 57.3 percent of eligible voters agreed with the option of a "dry" Canada.[71]

The defeat did not deter prohibition's forces. On the contrary, they turned their attention to provincial governments. In Quebec, Dominion Alliance representatives met with Montreal bishop Paul Bruchési. Convinced that alcohol use was an urgent matter, the Montreal bishop agreed to launch a public temperance campaign in his diocese, an initiative that other Quebec bishops decided to emulate. The campaign in the province was a success. More than one million individuals joined the movement. They committed themselves to curbing alcohol consumption, and their efforts appeared to achieve some success. Between 1905 and 1914, there was a significant decline in the number of establishments selling alcohol in the province. However, 50 percent of all licensed establishments were located in Montreal, and for the moment, the largest city in Canada resisted the trend.[72]

The First World War provided a window of opportunity for social reformers and prohibition forces in particular. According to moral reformer and women's political rights activist Nellie McClung, the war offered society an opportunity for regeneration: "Without the shedding of blood, there is no remission of sin."[73] Since the government asked Canadians to make sacrifices in supporting the war effort, prohibition forces perceived the war as a catalyst for winning public opinion once and for all, and forcing the hands of elected officials. In its new range of activities, the state would also be a moral enforcer on the alcohol front.

Before launching the final battle, prohibition forces updated their narrative. The war provided them with new ammunition. Since war propaganda insisted upon sacrifices and efficiency, prohibition forces questioned the legitimacy of diverting grain crops to produce alcohol. Was it not more appropriate to use all available grain to feed Canadian soldiers and Canadian allies, instead of using it to make alcohol? Soldiers also had to be fit for duty, and alcohol use undermined the army's ability to wage a successful war. Furthermore, drunken soldiers could easily succumb to the temptations of the flesh. Having sex with a prostitute increased the risk of getting a sexually transmitted disease, and sick soldiers would then be unfit for combat. Reformers urged the federal government to "cut out" soldiers from "the damned beer."[74] Finally, war required workers in domestic industries to be productive. Working under the influence of alcohol undermined the war effort and the ability of the Canadian army and its allies to win the war.

Prohibition forces won new allies. The Anglican Church, Orange Lodges, the Imperial Order of the Daughters of the Empire, and various ethnic organizations agreed that the war created exceptional circumstances. Consequently, prohibition of alcohol became a necessity and a sound public policy.

Besides updating their narrative and gaining new allies, prohibition forces now won a series of provincial referenda. Alberta, Manitoba, and Saskatchewan implemented prohibition in 1915. Although provincial prohibition limited access to alcohol, it did not affect interprovincial trade, since this was under the jurisdiction of the federal government. Many residents took advantage of this and purchased liquor from outside their dry province. Nevertheless, the dry option gained momentum even in Quebec. In 1916, it became harder for those living outside of Quebec City, Montreal, Saint-Hyacinthe, and Valleyfield to have access to alcohol, since these cities were the only remaining wet centres.[75] Two years later, the Quebec provincial government imposed prohibition throughout the province with some exceptions—citizens could buy liquor for medical reasons, and the industry could still produce it.[76]

An argument for prohibition. The cartoonist reminds voters that prohibition would benefit the family as opposed to the liquor industry. *Vote for Us*, temperance cartoon, Victoria, no date. Image D-07520 courtesy of Royal BC Museum, BC Archives.

The newly elected Union Government enacted prohibition for twelve months, beginning April 1, 1918. As stated earlier, the war provided an opening for anti-alcohol forces, and prohibition became a viable public policy. Politicians came to support it. During the war, being drunk was neither respectable nor patriotic. Already victorious in Canada, liquor opponents targeted the world community. With the help of Americans, they organized the World League Against Alcoholism in 1919 in the hopes of enlisting the international community in their cause and to undermine the liquor industry in the world.[77]

GAMBLING: A DISRESPECTFUL ACTIVITY

Gambling was also in the sights of moral reformers. Certain aspects of gambling culture annoyed Christians from various denominations who were actively pursuing their agenda of building the kingdom of God on earth. Most gamblers were men; though a few women did gamble occasionally in taverns, gambling dens, or sporting venues, most of them preferred the privacy of their homes in company of other women, "shielded from the scrutiny" of moral

Group of men gambling, 1900. Image C-05231 courtesy of Royal BC Museum, BC Archives.

reformers. In her study of three rural small towns in Southern Ontario between 1870 and 1914, Rebecca Beausaert observed that women played cards and gambled. Local newspapers published news articles about American female gambling at home, denouncing the practice and hoping that this would suffice to discourage Canadian women from doing the same.[78] Furthermore, some non-European ethnic groups—the Chinese in particular—were in the gambling business. This made gambling a concern for those actively lobbying for a more restrictive immigration policy that would bar specific ethnic groups, such as Asians, from entering the country.[79]

The proponents of the moral reform movement developed a narrative that defined gambling as a bad habit that was unrespectable and morally condemnable. According to them, gambling undermined individuals' and families' righteous character. Married men who gambled could not only lose money but also seriously compromise their wives' and children's future. The imagined ideal family relied upon a well-defined role for each member: the husband was the breadwinner and the wife looked after children. Gambling, by undermining the breadwinner's ability to provide for his family, constituted an additional threat to families, which were already under siege during the Industrial Revolution. Furthermore, Christian reformers disseminated the belief that gambling ran contrary to the work ethic. Gaining enormous riches without having to work for them was sinful. Working hard was the only morally acceptable means to make a living. Spending family income on gambling instead of legitimate economic activities was highly reprehensible. Finally, there was a risk of addiction and of adopting criminal behaviours if gamblers had to resort to stealing and other crimes to offset their financial losses.[80] In developing their narrative, Protestant churches and the WCTU took considerable pains to link gambling to other vices. Gambling took place in establishments that sold alcohol, and where prostitutes worked. Since the liquor demon and prostitution were already under attack, moral reformers believed that targeting gambling would help achieve the overall goal of getting rid of immoral behaviour.[81]

Under pressure from various groups, the government decided to adopt a repressive policy toward gambling. Domestic and foreign lotteries and raffles had been allowed until 1856. Thereafter, it became illegal to sell tickets, except in Canada East or in Quebec. Those found guilty of breaking the lottery ban paid a fine. However, elected officials observed that it was difficult to enforce laws prohibiting gambling activities, without considering cultural and linguistic factors. The Catholic church rejected repression as the best course of action. Although Catholic officials viewed gambling as a bad habit, they accepted that human beings had difficulties controlling themselves. On the issue of vices and public policy, the Roman Catholic Church had contradictory views. Recognizing that the flesh was weak when it came to sex, the church strongly supported the state in its attempts to repress sexual activities outside of marriage and any forms of birth control. When it came to gambling, however, church officials used the argument that individuals lacked self-control as a reason for rejecting repression as a public policy. The willingness of the Roman Catholic Church to make allowances for individuals' weakness with respect to gambling cannot be dissociated from the fact that the church used gambling as a fundraising means for some of its institutions. Roman Catholic officials believed that the government should make an exception for charitable gambling activities. Lotteries organized by Catholic charities should be legal, since the proceeds went to a "good" cause.[82] If politicians were still not convinced by these arguments, the Roman Catholic Church added, as it did on the drinking issue, that the anti-gambling campaign was part of the moral reformers' agenda, itself a plot to enforce Evangelical Protestant morality.

In 1860, the colony of Canada, which included at the time Canada East, or Quebec, and Canada West, or Ontario, amended its 1856 legislation on gambling. Henceforth, the state would allow lotteries organized by charitable groups. The Roman Catholic Church took advantage of this notable victory by launching a series of lotteries for charitable purposes: building or repairing churches, schools, and colleges.[83] In 1869, after Confederation, the Quebec Legislative Assembly passed legislation to forbid foreign lotteries. This did not affect lotteries organized by the Roman Catholic Church. On the contrary, this provincial legislation abolished restrictions on the value of prizes.[84] Nevertheless, provincial politicians lost the power to regulate gambling activities. On June 1, 1892, in a court decision on the constitutionality of the federal government initiative making lotteries and gaming houses illegal, Judge Dugas stated that the federal government had the power to legislate on this issue, since the British North America Act allowed this level of government to "to make laws for the Peace, Order, and good Government of Canada."[85]

For its part, as a result of strong lobby from gambling opponents, the federal government chose repression in its attempt to handle the gambling issue. In 1875, it suppressed gaming houses and, three years later, gambling activities were forbidden on trains, steamboats, and other means of transportation. In 1892, the federal Criminal Code prohibited lotteries and gaming houses, but assigned to the provincial governments the responsibility to enforce prohibition. The federal Criminal Code marked a decisive victory for moral reformers but gambling did not cease to exist. On the contrary, the federal government legitimized raffles "not exceeding $50.00" as fundraising activities at "religious and charitable bazaars" in 1900. The anti-gambling lobby mounted a campaign that led to the introduction of a private member's bill in the House of Commons to suppress betting on horse-racing tracks in 1909. Although the bill was defeated by a single vote, proponents of gambling on sporting events claimed that this was a respectable activity.[86] Despite protests, the federal government revisited its gambling policy and relented, allowing certain activities. In 1925, agricultural fairs and exhibitions were entitled to organize gambling activities. In her study of gambling, Susan Morton argues that federal public policy officially condemned gambling while tolerating it for certain classes. Although state repression affected workers' gambling activities, this was not the case for members of the bourgeoisie, who successfully put pressure on politicians and prevented the criminalization of gambling at racetracks. This situation was similar to the alcohol use debate during the same period. Members of the upper and middle classes were quick to judge workers' drinking habit and how they managed their leisure time; a similar attitude prevailed when the state criminalized certain gambling activities on the ground that members of the less privileged class could not govern themselves.[87]

The prohibition approach did not eradicate gambling—quite the contrary, since individuals clearly had a tenacious appetite for it. Like alcohol consumption during prohibition, gambling was no longer seen in public. In large urban centres such as Montreal, criminal elements took control and imposed their own rules. From time to time, newspapers broke the silence surrounding gambling, by publishing stories about police officers who protected gaming houses and corrupt municipal politicians who were unwilling to step in. In reaction to these stories, moral reformers pressed for better enforcement and a cleansing of municipal politics in certain cities.[88]

DRUGS: GETTING RID OF THEM

During the second half of the nineteenth century, narcotics and hallucinogenic drugs such as cocaine, heroin, morphine, and opium were readily available. Physicians prescribed them relatively easily. Some people used them for pleasure and to escape reality for a few hours and others bought them to treat various health problems: asthma, coughs, toothache, or pain. This new phenomenon meant that some individuals developed an addiction—Clayton Mosher reports that between 200,000 and 2 million Americans were addicted. However, we do not know about corresponding Canadian numbers.[89]

Moral reformers targeted drugs and denounced those who used them for their euphoric effects. They accused drug users of trying to escape reality. Reformers feared the dangers of addiction, which had been noticed and documented by physicians. Accounts of such cases were disseminated in medical journals and raised grave concerns among the reformers. Moral reformers were especially concerned with women's addiction: female addiction was a threat to society, since an addicted woman would be unable to fulfil her primary obligation: being a caring mother for her children. The anti-drug lobby proclaimed that drug-taking could become habit forming, and that those unable to stop had a weak will, as was the case with those who formed a drinking habit. The overall goal of criminalizing drugs was part of the campaign to build a society free of vice.[90]

The campaign to get rid of drugs attracted women's groups, Protestant churches, and other moral reformers. Nationalist groups and trade unions also supported drug criminalization. Moral reformers linked the use of certain types of drugs, such as opium, to ethnic groups like the Chinese. This provided ammunition to nationalist groups, which sought to promote Canada as a white society, and trade unions, which saw certain ethnic groups as competition driving down wages. Both elements joined the anti-drug campaign as a means to suppress non-white groups. It was in British Columbia that the campaign to restrict Asian immigration was the most heated. Most Asians who immigrated to Canada settled in British Columbia during and after the gold rush at the end of the nineteenth century. The various groups and individuals opposed to drug use pursued different agendas, but were united on this issue. The racist

"Just a whiff of opium": cannery worker in British Columbia smoking opium on the job, 1913.
Courtesy of Royal BC Museum, BC Archives, E-05065.

element in the criminalization of drugs played a pivotal role in motivating certain social actors. However, the anti-drug campaigns were part of a larger movement to pressure the state to restrict immigration and close the doors on "unwanted" immigrants.

Opium was the first drug to be targeted. Anti-drug campaigners insisted it had a severe social and economic toll on individuals and families. They also raised the spectre of its association with the white slave trade, by arguing that vulnerable young women, attracted by opportunities for employment in cities such as Vancouver and Victoria, would succumb to opium's charm and would have to prostitute themselves to satisfy their insatiable addiction to the drugs they consumed in dens operated by Chinese. Drug opponents disseminated these stories and used the "vulnerable-young-women-addicted-to-opium" and the "dangerous-Chinese-who-do-not-belong here" narratives to create an atmosphere of fear and put pressure on legislators to criminalize the poppy-based narcotic.

In pressing the state to criminalize opium, the anti-drug coalition counted on the support of individuals in positions of authority. This was the case with William Lyon Mackenzie King. As deputy minister of labour, King was appointed to assess Japanese and Chinese residents' losses during the 1907 anti-Asian riots in Vancouver. During the investigation, two claims submitted by Chinese opium manufacturers intrigued him. Two opium manufacturers had submitted a claim of $600 each for "loss of business for six days" because their businesses were closed for six days during the riot. King went on a fact-finding mission. He visited opium dens, witnessed people buying opium, and decided to buy the substance himself. In his alarming report submitted to the federal government, which echoed the anti-drug narrative, King's conclusion was crystal clear: the state should suppress the importation, manufacture, and sale of opium, except for medicinal purposes. According to King, opium was an evil substance consumed by both Caucasians and non-Caucasians. The deputy minister was careful to note in his report that some members of the Chinese community also asked for the suppression of the opium traffic in Canada.[91]

The anti-drug coalition registered its first legal success in 1908. Canada was among the first countries to make the importation, manufacture, and sale of opium criminal offences, except for medical purposes. The penalties were a fine not exceeding $1,000 and/or a jail term not exceeding three years. Three years later, the federal government criminalized cocaine and morphine. The 1911 Opium and Narcotic Drug Act authorized the federal government to add more drugs to the list of prohibited substances when their use became widespread. The federal legislation made possession of these drugs, unlike alcohol use, a criminal offence, as it pursued its repressive anti-drug agenda.

Various social actors favoured the criminalization of cocaine. Newspapers published, for a brief time, sensational reports on the popularity of the stimu-lant. These reports set the tone of the public debate by creating an atmosphere of moral panic. An episode of moral panic occurs when individuals identify a particular behaviour they label as reprehensible—in this case drug consump-tion—exaggerate its frequency and popularity, and distort the facts in such a way that the issue is raised to the rank of a social and moral crisis that would force anyone in a position of authority to concur that something has to be done. In other words, repression and suppression of this immoral behaviour were required responses. Nor could other authorities who had a role in enforc-ing the moral order, or in supporting those who enforced it, ignore the sit-uation. For instance, the Children's Aid Society of Montreal urged citizens to write to their elected officials and press them to take decisive action. The Catholic archbishop of Montreal, the Anglican bishop of Montreal, and other religious leaders from other parts of the country wrote to Mackenzie King, who was in charge of the anti-drug legislation. They warned him that cocaine was in high demand from people of all ages and walks of life: young, old, respectable citizens, and foreigners. In the context of the moral panic, which characterized the public debate, the legislator chose what seemed the best course of action: repression.[92]

From the point of view of the anti-drug coalition, however, these domestic victories were insufficient. They believed that immigrants were responsible for importing drugs and that the drug problem was international in scope. Consequently, the anti-drug lobby pursued its campaign outside of Canada's borders, as Canadian dry voices in the debate over prohibition did. However, opponents of drugs were more successful. Along with similar American groups, they enlisted the international community in their battle for the prohibition of drugs. Since it was difficult to convince the international community to put in place mechanisms designed to control the international movement of people, they advocated the containment of the flow of drugs instead. Affected countries, such as Canada and the United States, argued that they were suffering from the reluctance of producing countries, and European nations that supported them, to agree to restrict and repress the production of opium and other substances used for their psychoactive properties.

Prime Minister Wilfrid Laurier sent King, who was a newly elected member of Parliament, to the international opium conference in Shanghai in 1909. The prime minister considered King to be the best qualified to represent the country, following his investigation of Vancouver opium dens. King had already alerted the federal government to the mounting international campaign against opium in his report submitted one year earlier. In Shanghai, he was one of five British delegates. Other delegates, notably Canadian-born bishop Charles Henry Brent, who was appointed an Episcopal bishop in the United States, played a key role in enlisting the international community to adopt repression and criminalization as the pillars of government anti-drugs policies. The Shanghai conference was the first step in the development and implementation of international agreements, such as the 1912 International Opium Convention, destined to control the production, distribution, and use of drugs.

Unlike drinking, the drug issue did not cause an extensive public debate. Proponents were disorganized, disenfranchised, and in survival mode. The Chinese community faced an attack on several fronts. The federal government restricted their immigration by charging a head tax, starting in 1885. Over the years, it increased the head tax and revised its policy by closing Canada's doors to Chinese immigrants in 1923. The campaign to discourage Chinese from settling included disenfranchisement—they lost the right to vote in provincial elections in 1872 and in federal elections, thirteen years later—and restriction from working for government agencies. Occasional anti-Asian riots at the beginning of the twentieth century were an indication of the prevalence of racist attitudes toward Asians, particularly on the West Coast.

For their part, as they had done around the birth control issue, physicians were keen to establish their power by allying themselves with moral reformers. Although some physicians became reticent, most of them continued to prescribe drugs such as cocaine and morphine to their patients. At the same time, they were well aware that some of the prescribed drugs, such as morphine, were addictive. They used their status, based on their scientific knowledge, to claim they ought to be the ones to control these substances and prescribe them for legitimate uses. Yet even some physicians themselves abused drugs and developed addictions, and they might have been in denial over their own drug dependency.

The federal government's criminalization of opium and other drugs did not eliminate their consumption. Rather, like the prohibition of gambling and alcohol, criminalization led mainly to a crackdown on dens and other venues where people consumed drugs. Nevertheless, Canadians looking for drugs continued to find them. The doors were opened to criminal elements who came to control the drug trade. As well, unlike legally traded pharmaceuticals, substances sold illegally were often contaminated.[93]

TOBACCO: A FASHIONABLE HABIT

In the second half of the nineteenth century, smoking was fashionable and an indicator of class identity. The bourgeois could afford to smoke cigars, while members of lower classes chewed tobacco or smoked it in pipes. Tobacco smokers had an image of respectability. Smoking was a habit that males acquired as part of the process of growing up and becoming a man. It was natural that a respectable man would acquire the habit of smoking.

The arrival of cigarettes revolutionized smoking culture in the second half of the nineteenth century, by reducing the cost of smoking and increasing accessibility among men. In 1888, the Davis family of Montreal, known for its brand of cigars, acquired a licence to manufacture cigarettes. However, the habit of smoking cigarettes was slow to develop. Most men in Canada, as opposed to the United States, still preferred smoking tobacco in pipes at the beginning of the twentieth century. It was after the First World War that large numbers of men embraced smoking cigarettes, as did women.[94]

According to social norms, women were supposed to abstain from smoking. Any respectable woman was expected to refuse to smoke either in public or in private. However, women came to develop the habit of smoking cigarettes. Was this due to a successful marketing campaign on the part of tobacco companies? Some scholars think so, but others have argued that women picked up the habit of smoking as part of the phenomenon of the "new woman," who challenged gender inequality before and during the First World War as women began to work in factories and the service sector. Smoking in public became acceptable.[95] For her part, Cook argues that both causes played a role since cigarette manufacturers were eager to expand their market and some women decided to smoke cigarettes, which illustrates "the complex connections between smoking and women's lived motivations and experiences."[96]

Male smokers' image of respectability irked moral reformers, who were anxious to restrict, and in some cases ban, smoking. Their action on the smoking front was linked to their campaigns against gambling, alcohol, and drug abuse. In an atmosphere of fear and the belief that the white race was facing tremendous challenges to its ability to perpetuate itself, smoking was defined as part of a degenerative process affecting society. Opponents of smoking believed that tobacco users would try other drugs. They claimed that tobacco stimulated smokers to drink, since nicotine and alcohol had "a similar impact on the nervous system."[97] Anti-smoking advocates were particularly disturbed by the pleasure individuals derived from smoking. There was a strong belief that God demanded humans to refrain not only from drinking but also from drugs, gambling, and smoking because "the body is 'a living temple' owned by God, not by the individual 'tenant' who happens to live in it, and so it ought to be kept clean."[98]

The Salvation Army and in particular the Woman's Christian Temperance Union were at the forefront of this movement. Anti-smoking books such as *The Sin of Tobacco Smoking and Chewing Together with an Effective Cure for These Habits* by Reverend Albert Sims in 1878 began to make an appearance. When campaigning for individuals to pledge their opposition to alcohol, drugs, and gambling, the WCTU also included tobacco products as something that must be avoided. Individuals would declare: "I solemnly promise, God being my helper, not to use intoxicating liquors of any kind, not to use tobacco in any form, and never to use bad language."[99]

Tobacco use divided the medical community. Historian Jarrett Rudy found reports on the health dangers of tobacco use. According to German pathologist Dr. Jankau in an article published in *L'Union médicale du Canada* in 1896, "excessive consumption could burn the stomach." However, tobacco had some health benefits since it "disinfected the mouth, depressed the 'genital functions,' and acted as a sedative on the central nervous system." In 1909, an article in a Montreal medical journal stated that individuals who abused tobacco would face serious health ailments, including "tobacco heart," "smoker's cancer (lip cancer)," and "memory loss." In the case of a female smoker, abuse could induce an abortion.[100] On the other hand, some medical journal articles listed health benefits. Tobacco use appeared to help those suffering from constipation and those who suffered from digestive problems. Some journals even encouraged victims of tuberculosis to begin smoking if they had not already developed the habit.

Despite the lack of consensus on the dangers of smoking, the medical community agreed that there was a correlation between the frequency of smoking and its risks and benefits. If adults smoked in moderation, which meant smoking between ten and twelve cigarettes a day, they were told not to worry. At the time, the medical community believed that men smokers were better than women at controlling their consumption of tobacco products. As in the case of liquors, women's lack of willpower limited their ability to use a substance such as tobacco in moderation.[101] Despite these gender differences, someone abusing tobacco products would have serious health problems. Although the medical community agreed that abusing tobacco was a serious issue, its members could not agree on what level of consumption constituted a risk.

There was one aspect of the medical debate on the health consequences of smoking that physicians could agree upon. For boys, smoking was a serious health concern. Most physicians believed that boys should not smoke. In fact, boys should wait until they had attained adulthood before picking up the smoking habit.[102] Smoking opponents paid close attention to these arguments in their efforts to ban the practice.

Canadians read conflicting reports on the benefits and dangers of smoking on an individual's health. Some news reports insisted on dire consequences such as a man who had his tongue removed because of cancer resulting from "excessive cigar smoking" in 1904. Another case, reported a year later, concerned a woman who killed herself because she was unable to quit smoking. During the Spanish influenza epidemic, a news article in the *Toronto Star* reported that many, especially among smokers, believed that smoking prevented the deadly flu.[103] Another report claimed that the "Millburn's Heart and nerve pills," which was already credited for benefiting anyone with a heart condition, could help people to quit smoking.[104]

In contrast to other anti-vice campaigns, women and other social reformers opposed to smoking had difficulty reaching out to potential allies among Protestant churches. Although they could count on the support of the Presbyterian and Methodist churches, the Anglican Church remained opposed to a smoking ban. At the end of the nineteenth century, their officials in Montreal wondered if the state should be involved in the business of governing the conduct of others on moral grounds when it came to smoking. For its part, the Roman Catholic Church was sensitive to the argument that boys should not smoke, because of the risks to their health. When it came to debate the merits of legislating tobacco use, the Roman Catholic Church in Montreal questioned the label of "vice" in characterizing smoking. The church officials did not believe that smoking was a vice. Since tobacco opponents pushed for legislation, the Roman Catholic Church rejected prohibition as too extreme a public policy, which was consistent with their positions on alcohol and gambling. They opposed as well the call for age restrictions on access to tobacco products. They justified their opposition by portraying state regulation of smoking and access to tobacco products as an attempt to deprive the Roman Catholic Church of its right and ability to regulate the conduct of Catholics. Some Protestant groups sought to increase the role of the state in the regulation of individuals' lives. In contrast, Roman Catholic Church officials pleaded for the preservation of their own sphere of influence and activity.[105]

Alongside opposition from some Christian churches, newspapers voiced their concerns. When tobacco opponents agitated for the state to impose age restrictions, Montreal newspapers, such as *The Gazette* and *La Patrie*, argued against them. For these dailies, attempts to regulate access to tobacco products constituted a direct attack on parents and their right to educate their children. After all, parents should be free to raise their children the way they wanted, and it was up to them to decide if their male children should smoke cigarettes or use other tobacco products. These dailies warned politicians that they should refrain from legislating on an issue that properly concerned only individuals and parents.[106]

In spite of their efforts, tobacco opponents failed to mount a massive campaign between 1892 and 1914. While they opposed smoking in general, tobacco opponents did not press too hard for a complete ban, knowing that their call for state intervention would fail. Instead, they acted more strategically and targeted one tobacco product in particular: cigarettes. After all, this new product on the market was not yet very popular among tobacco consumers. Making headway on cigarettes could pave the way for other successes. For a time, tobacco opponents promoted the prohibition of the manufacture, importation, and sale of cigarettes. The movement pressed provincial elected officials and, between 1903 and 1908, MPs to act. MPs debated the principle but concluded that prohibition was a bad choice. Although most MPs agreed that young people should not smoke, they supported Prime Minister Laurier's views that preventing everyone from smoking would be a terrible public policy. Since Canadians were not convinced that smoking was bad, it would be impossible to enforce prohibition under these circumstances. According to Laurier in 1904, "It was always an evil in a community to pass a law that would not be accepted by the respectable part of the community."[107] The WCTU became impatient with MPs who talked about the issue but did not act. The organization met with Prime Minister Laurier in 1907 and suggested that if the federal government was unwilling to legislate, perhaps it should authorize the provinces to do so.[108]

Since physicians pointed to smoking by boys as a health risk, the anti-smoking movement refined its arguments further, and argued for an age restriction on access to tobacco products. Between 1890 and 1901, most provinces introduced legislation forbidding the sale of tobacco products to minors, except in Manitoba and Quebec. The lack of legislation in Quebec reflected the weakness of the anti-smoking lobby in that province. For its part, the federal government also imposed age restrictions. Beginning in 1908, the Tobacco Restraint Act stipulated that individuals under the age of sixteen could no longer buy tobacco products and were banned from smoking. "Maximum fines were set at $10 for a first offence, $25 for a second, and $100 for a third."[109] During the First World War, an increasing number of men and women developed the smoking habit. Despite that, moral reformers concentrated their attacks on drinking rather than smoking. Thus, state activism, limited as it was, did not greatly affect the tobacco social culture.[110]

CONCLUSION

Between 1850 and 1920, moral reformers launched strong attacks on several fronts: prostitution, abortion, birth control, homosexuality, alcohol, gambling, drug use, and tobacco. They succeeded in imposing their views and narratives on Canadians who debated these issues. The values of sobriety, self-discipline, cleanliness, family life, and hard work dominated the reformers' discourses.

When moral reformers looked back at more than seventy years of activism, there was a sense of "mission accomplished." Most of the targeted vices were in retreat, because the state had criminalized and prohibited them. One moral reformer and former secretary of the Dominion Alliance for the Total Suppression of the Liquor Traffic, Francis Spence, claimed in his 1908 address:

> The temperance cause is winning; the temperance cause will win. Lack of confidence in this certainty is the result of a failure to understand the end of the movement. That movement is not a mere human invention or fake, created by some novelty-seeking cranks. It is the inevitable result of great universal conditions and forces.[111]

Although the intensity and outcomes of the battles to control vices varied, moral reformers proclaimed victories at the end. They achieved the prohibition of alcohol and the criminalization of drugs. Most gambling activities were forbidden. Abortion was already a crime, but now the dissemination of information on and the sale of birth control devices also became crimes. Marriage as a Christian institution was protected, and those who challenged its definition (Mormons) or resisted it (Aboriginals) faced legal consequences. On the drug front, the national battle was transferred to the international stage. Canada and the United States enrolled the world in their anti-drug strategy by discussing and implementing international agreements that would restrict certain drugs for medical purposes. The status of tobacco remained virtually unchanged, but not because moral reformers did not target it. On the contrary, reformers tried, but they were unsuccessful in building a broad coalition such as they had forged on the alcohol, prostitution, and drug issues.

There was still much unfinished business. If the laws of the country made these various vices a crime, enforcement remained critical. As moral reformers observed, those in charge of enforcement often ignored violations and did not zealously seek out people committing vicious crimes. Vigilance on the part of moral reformers was a weapon and remained so as long as adequate state resources were not allocated and law enforcement remained uncommitted. Only social mobilization could maintain the pressure, since critics of using state power to enforce a morally based order saw such legislation as inappropriate state intervention.

CHAPTER 4

No Longer Vices—Call Them Health Issues
1920 to the Present

At the beginning of the twenty-first century, a female sex worker from the Maritimes explained her job to university researchers: "If you're bringing in $1,000 a night, you're off welfare and you're off their back. Your kids got a babysitter; your kids got food; your kids got clothes, and your kids got love."[1] As a sex worker, she made much more money than she would if she worked at a "respectable" nine-to-five job where she would earn the minimum wage or barely above it. At the same time, her work—though consistently condemned by large segments of society—allowed her to be a responsible parent, which society has always valued. Consequently, she requested to be left "alone" and argued that society, and in particular the state, should not regulate her trade. In demanding that the governance of the self be left to individuals, instead of to the state and non-state institutions, she echoed a growing resentment of social control and of those who believed they had a right to govern the conduct of others.

Sex workers joined their voices to those of other social agents to challenge moral reformers who favoured the regulation of behaviours defined as vices. However, from 1920 to the present, vices gradually ceased to be called "vices," and health professionals and experts from social sciences played a significant role in their renaming and redefinition. By regarding behaviours such as alcohol and drug use, gambling, or homosexuality as indicative of mental illness or other pathological conditions, these experts increased their control over the interpretation of these behaviours and over how society, and governments in particular, had to deal with them. Medicalization led health and social work "professionals" to press for new approaches and regulations. Meanwhile, moral reformers were not entirely silenced; their activism on the abortion issue persisted till the latter part of the twentieth century. Nevertheless, they were not as influential as they used to be.

In December 1967, Justice Minister Pierre E. Trudeau proclaimed, "There's no place for the state in the bedrooms of the nation." He used these words in summarizing the goal of his omnibus bill, which enacted changes to laws on birth control, abortion, gambling, and same-sex activity. Thus, he explicitly acknowledged and legitimized state activism in the development of morally based public policies. Even though Trudeau asserted that the state had no business breaching the privacy of the household, it has nevertheless continued to intervene in the field of moral regulation during the twentieth and into the twenty-first century. Since the 1920s, drinking, drugs, gambling, sex, and tobacco have been revisited, leading to stronger or weaker regulation, in dynamic interaction with coalitions and lobby groups and their ability to mobilize and broaden their support.

DIFFERENT VALUES AND SEXUAL OPENNESS

The Criminal Code continued to regulate various aspects of sexuality. Abortion, birth control, and same-sex activity were crimes, and marriage continued to be defined as a union between a man and a woman. Nevertheless, over the course of the twentieth century, society engaged in debates over aspects of sexuality and redefined the boundaries of acceptable sexual behaviour.

Although abortion was a crime, women, as they had since time immemorial, still sought ways to prevent unwanted or unplanned pregnancies. They relied on friends, relatives, and neighbours, but also on birth control activists and some members of the medical profession.[2] Although the medical establishment played a crucial role in requiring harsher penalties for those who helped women to terminate their pregnancy, many physicians did not comply with the wishes of their professional associations and were willing to terminate pregnancies when requested.

Law enforcement varied considerably on the abortion issue. Police officers tended not to intervene, becoming active only when they were under pressure from abortion opponents. In these cases, they might arrest physicians and midwives, though not necessarily the women who sought the abortion or terminated their pregnancy.

Assessing how many women terminated their pregnancy before the federal government amended its abortion policy in 1969 is a difficult task. Relying on court cases is an inadequate indicator. As indicated in Table 1, there were few cases were brought before judges, since law enforcement was sporadic. Other factors further explain the lack of court activism. In her study of abortion in Quebec, historian Andrée Lévesque observes: "The difficulty of establishing proof and producing witnesses partly explains the infrequency of trials for abortion."[3] If police forces were reluctant to intervene, justice officials were reluctant to prosecute. Angus McLaren observes that those who might have been aware of or have heard rumours of someone helping a woman obtain an abortion, often did not bother to press charges or denounce abortionists. "If few abortions were reported, it was because many members of the law and medical professions felt there was little to be gained in prosecuting desperate women who sought by dangerous means to end their pregnancies."[4]

Nevertheless, the law stated that any woman who was found to have terminated a pregnancy, and those who had helped her, could be arrested, charged, and prosecuted. Of the few cases that caught the attention of the justice system, most involved abortions that had gone terribly wrong and resulted in hospitalization or even the mother's death. As Table 1 reveals, the percentage of individuals who were charged and convicted increased between 1900 and 1970, but there was still a significant percentage who were acquitted, at least until 1930. Juries had a tendency to acquit because of the pregnant woman's trying social, personal, and economic circumstances that led them to abort their fetus. Since abortionists and other practitioners were more likely than their patients to be arrested and charged, they were also more likely to receive what McLaren calls "savage punishments" as a deterrent and a demonstration of the state's ability to govern individuals and control women's sexuality and bodies.[5]

Although abortion was an option for women, it remained an unsafe practice. A woman's health was on the line when she sought help. Deaths from abortion "averaged 12.3 [percent] each year between 1958 and 1969."[6] Accessibility constituted another serious obstacle. Not only did women have to pay for the procedure or for products that could induce an abortion, they also often had to travel long distances to find a provider. This could even entail going to the United States. For those with limited financial means, abortion could be out of reach.

Table 1   Criminal Charges and Convictions for Induced Abortion, Canada, 1900–70

Year	Charges	Convictions	Percent Convictions/Charges
1900–10	97	33	34.0
1911–20	172	87	50.6
1921–30	210	115	54.8
1931–40	427	271	63.5
1941–50	358	243	67.9
1951–60	254	194	76.4
1961–70	267	204	76.4

Source: Report of the Committee on the Operation of the Abortion Law (Ottawa: Minister of Supply and Services Canada, 1977), p. 68.

The abortion issue highlighted the challenge that both women and men faced in regulating birth and getting access to birth control information and devices. Since 1892, section 207c of the Criminal Code had made the dissemination of information about birth control and the sale of contraceptives a crime. In spite of this, many Canadians disregarded the law and sought information in newspapers, books, and magazines and from druggists. They also found ways to buy birth control devices.

One of the sources of information was the birth control movement. Born in the United States, the movement was intensely active in Canada during the Great Depression. As individuals and families struggled with dire economic conditions, limiting the size of a family was a significant concern. Canadians could obtain birth control information and contraceptives from the Parents' Information Bureau, which was founded in 1933 and operated birth control clinics in Toronto and Windsor. The staff travelled outside of these urban centres and offered much-needed information to those wanting to limit the size of their families. This organization gained notoriety when one of its nurses, Dorothea Palmer, was arrested and charged with the crime of distributing birth control information and devices to a Franco-Ontarian family from Eastview, near Ottawa. However, Palmer was acquitted, on March 17, 1937. The Criminal Code did allow the dissemination of birth control information for the "public good." Her lawyer argued and the judge agreed that "the public good was served by 'the acts alleged to have been done'—namely, providing conception prevention to women who were poor, received relief, had large families, were of lesser intelligence, and, in this particular case, were francophone and Catholic.[7] In McLaren's view this trial constituted a "breakthrough" for the birth control movement. Media coverage made more Canadians aware that there were concerned citizens who could assist women in not having children. By affirming that Palmer had indeed contributed to "the public good," the acquittal also legitimized the work that people like her were doing.

The birth control movement counted on a range of supporters. Some help came from Protestant clergy members, such as A. H. Tyrer, who disagreed with the official stand of their churches and promoted birth control. More broadly, women supported this initiative. Women who believed in birth control did so because they thought they had a responsibility to help women and families to limit births and to prevent miscarriages and maternal deaths. There was a kind of class bias in the decision to help women with unwanted pregnancies. Women who were involved in helping families to limit births believed it made no sense for parents with limited financial resources to have a large family. As well, members of the eugenics movement supported and promoted birth control as a means to prevent individuals termed "unfit," because of mental illness or inadequate financial resources, from having children. Palmer's boss at the Parents' Information Bureau was Alvin Ratz Kaufman. A supporter of eugenics theories, Kaufman was preoccupied with the low birth rate among the middle class and the tendency among the poor and the working class to have large families. He believed this demographic imbalance had to be corrected by disseminating birth control information among the lower classes, the "unintelligent and penniless."[8]

The position of Christian churches remained unchanged. Having officially condemned contraception, the Worldwide Anglican Church repeated this injunction in 1920.[9] The Catholic church was similarly, and characteristically, uncompromising. In 1930, Pope Pius XI reiterated the church's condemnation of and punishments for transgressors. The encyclical *Casti Connubii* stated that "any use whatsoever of matrimony exercised in such a way that the act is deliberately frustrated in its natural power to generate life is an offence against the law of God and of nature, and those who indulge in such are branded with the guilt of a grave sin."[10]

Many Christians ignored their churches' condemnations and chose to use birth control anyway. Aware of this rejection of church policy, the Anglican Church revisited the issue and, at the 1930 Lambeth Conference, softened its position by allowing married couples to use birth control if factors such as age or illness made having children undesirable. The United Church of Canada actually approved birth control, in 1936.[11] The Catholic church did the same, but much later, by introducing a distinction between natural and artificial means of birth control. In September 1958, Pius XII condemned oral hormone birth control, but acknowledged the reality that Catholics worldwide were regulating births. If married couples had legitimate reasons for regulating conception, he encouraged them to use "natural" means, such as the Knaus-Ogino, or rhythm, method.[12]

Physicians were generally reluctant to encourage married couples to use birth control. Nevertheless, in 1937, the Canadian Medical Association heard some of its members make a case for birth control. They identified a series of benefits, such as reducing the number of "maternal deaths, better maternal health, fewer infant deaths," and a decreased number of abortions. Because the medical profession was divided, the American Medical Association tried to reassure physicians that it was worth debating the issue since birth control was a "reputable subject of scientific medical research."[13] These purported "benefits" failed to rally the majority of physicians, who strongly believed that motherhood was the highest ideal for women and, accordingly, that women should refrain from using methods and devices that prevented them from having children.

In the 1960s, a series of events suggested that the industrialized world was going through a sexual revolution, and the debate on birth control and abortion re-emerged. On May 11, 1960, the American Food and Drug Administration authorized the sale of the anovulant pill, which became known as "the pill" in the United States. Women, especially married ones, took the pill because it gave them greater sexual autonomy. The availability of the pill coincided with the coming of age of the baby boomer generation and the emergence of the counterculture. This social, cultural, and political movement that emerged in the sixties shook the Western hemisphere, challenged mainstream social values categorized as conservative, and championed new values based on equality, openness, and freedom. However, Canadian women still had to fight to obtain the pill, as the sale of contraceptives still constituted a criminal offence. If some pharmacists and physicians were willing to break the law in the case of a married woman, they were reluctant to be as accommodating for single women.[14] This prompted women and liberal baby boomers of both sexes to criticize the existing social order. They saw it as particularly conservative, because of its restrictive conceptions of sexuality, relations between men and women, and a role for women that confined them to domesticity and motherhood. By redrawing the boundaries of sexuality, challenging those who would restrict acceptable sexual relations to procreation, and advocating greater sexual openness and curiosity, women and baby boomers triggered a debate on the ability of individuals to govern themselves.

Within the wider counterculture movement, Canadian feminists took part in the debate by denouncing societal expectations and state regulation of sexual practices. Feminists argued that it was time for religious institutions, the medical establishment—who had become prominent moral entrepreneurs—and the state to back off. Feminists vehemently claimed that only women should govern their own bodies. The governance of the self was central to the debate over the accessibility of birth control information, contraceptives, and abortion.

These contests pitted women and their supporters against religious institutions, physicians and other health experts, and politicians. Women were very active in organizing themselves and reflecting on the social, economic, and ideological factors that led to their subordination. Feminist intellectuals—like Simone de Beauvoir, Shulamith Firestone, Betty Friedan, and Gloria Steinem—sustained women in their quest to recognize and challenge the laws, policies, and regulations that oppressed them, denied them control over their bodies, and perceived them as unable to govern themselves. By disseminating the *Birth Control Handbook* in Canadian colleges and universities in 1968,

"You Have Heard of the Pill, Haven't You?", John Collins, ca. 1968. McCord Museum, M965.199.6725.

the women who produced it were committing a criminal offence, an absurd one, in their view. Institutions of higher education became a hotbed of activism regarding birth control. Students tried to obtain birth control services by forming information committees, referring individuals to physicians who provided contraceptives, and holding birth control teach-ins.[15] On the national stage, the National Council of Women of Canada pushed for the legalization of birth control and abortion.

Women were involved in the development of a new narrative centred on notions of sexual liberation, self-determination, and gender equality. Translated into public policy, this narrative advocated for the decriminalization of birth control and abortion. Proponents argued that the latter had to be free, safe, and accessible. Women should no longer have to put their lives on the line when they sought to terminate their pregnancies, and nobody should question a woman's motives, since abortion was a right. The state's role should be limited strictly to guaranteeing that women could freely exercise this right.

Other events also fuelled the debate. In 1961, the Planned Parenthood Association of Toronto was founded following the case of a Toronto pharmacist, Harold Samuel Fine, who had been charged, convicted, and fined for selling contraceptives. According to the judge, Fine failed to demonstrate that he served "the public good" by advertising and selling birth control. In reaction to Fine's case, the Planned Parenthood Association pursued the goal of amending the Criminal Code.[16]

In the context of the sexual revolution and the counterculture movement, the birth control issue divided Christian churches. Some Protestant churches softened their position and conceded that married couples could use birth control methods and contraceptives. The United Church of Canada agreed that contraceptives were "a moral necessity."[17] Similarly, the Anglican Church acknowledged that married men and women should have access to birth control information and contraceptives. Protestant churches encouraged the state to decriminalize birth control, but only in part. Although married couples were deemed responsible enough to use birth control, the openness of the churches ended with this group. They continued to assert that unmarried individuals should not have access to birth control information and devices. In the case of the Roman Catholic Church, liberal Catholics had high hopes when, in March 1963, Pope John XXIII appointed the Pontifical Commission on Population, Family and Birth-rate, known as the birth control commission and made up of lay people, experts, and clerics, to examine sex and the regulation of births. Many interpreted this decision as a clear indication that church authorities would lift the ban on contraception and approve the use of contraceptives for married Catholics. This change in policy would have meant that the Roman Catholic Church had recognized its inability to govern the sexual behaviour of its flock and was therefore adapting its doctrine to the new reality triggered by the sexual revolution and the greater availability and social acceptance of contraceptives. In an interview with the *Globe and Mail* on April 9, 1966, Gregory Baum, from St. Michael's College in Toronto, who had attended the Vatican II Council, disseminated this belief in liberalism by stating that Catholics could now use contraceptives. A year later, Baum claimed that renewed criticism, on the part of the church, of artificial contraception was irrelevant.[18] However, when Pope Paul VI released *Humanae Vitae* on July 25, 1968, he crushed the hopes of those who believed that the church was changing course. The pope refused to amend the church doctrine and reiterated that Catholics using contraceptives were committing a mortal sin. The purpose of marriage was still procreation and the education of children. Many members of the committee felt betrayed, and the pope's document constituted a considerable blow to progressive Catholics.[19]

While Protestant churches had softened their position on birth control, most of them, including Baptists and Pentecostals, remained firmly opposed to the legalization of abortion. Some United Church of Canada congregations were strongly divided. In 1971, the meeting of the church's General Council resolved "that an abortion should be a private matter between a woman and her doctor, without prejudice to the need for consulting her male partner, where possible." It called on the federal government "to remove from the present Criminal Code all sections relating to abortion."[20] Not everyone rallied to this position. A year later, the United Church issued a new statement:

> We do not support "abortion on demand." We believe that prior to twelve weeks of gestation … abortion should be a personal matter between a woman and her doctor. After that period of time, abortion should only be performed following consultation with a second doctor. We further believe that her male partner and/or other supportive people have a responsibility to both the woman and the fetus and should be involved in the decision wherever possible.[21]

The Anglican Church of Canada also advocated more liberal laws. It rejected "abortion on demand," but also stood against "the absolute prohibition of all abortion."[22] In other words, it believed that a woman should be able to obtain an abortion if her pregnancy threatened her health.

For its part, on February 7, 1968, the Canadian Conference of Catholic Bishops issued a pastoral statement noting that the church "condemn[ed] the direct taking of foetal life, but not treatments needed to save a mother's life even if they sometimes result in the unwanted and unsought death of the foetus."[23] However, Canadian bishops insisted that the protection of life was paramount regardless of the circumstances, including when a pregnancy threatened a mother's mental or physical health. For them, the role of the state was to protect and respect life, not to terminate it. A few months later, as we've seen, Pope Paul VI categorically repeated the church's opposition to abortion, even for therapeutic reasons, in *Humanae Vitae*, in July 1968. The punishment for deviance was still excommunication.[24] Despite this strong condemnation, Canadian bishops decided not to impose their views on politicians.[25]

The medical community softened its stand on birth control and abortion during the 1960s. The Canadian Medical Association agreed that contraception was legitimate, and most of its members ceased to define the issue as a moral and ethical one. In the context of the sexual revolution, but also in response to a growing fear of global overpopulation, the medical establishment saw some benefits in prescribing the pill. With regard to abortion, the Canadian Medical Association pressed the government to liberalize the law in order to protect physicians from criminal charges, since those carrying out the procedure were the most likely to be charged.[26]

On the abortion question, the Canadian Bar Association supported an amendment to the Criminal Code. In justifying its position, the national organization questioned the motives of a public policy based on moral considerations. It discouraged the state from attempting to regulate the lives of others on religious grounds. The association argued that "it would be wrong to impose moral laws derived from religious beliefs on those who did not share those beliefs."[27] According to one study, a majority of Canadian lawyers believed that "it was wrong for the Criminal law to enforce moral behaviour," a stand shared by other law organizations, such as the Congress of Penal Law at its Ninth International Congress in 1964. For the Canadian Bar Association, law should be used if abortion caused "notable harm to the public good."[28]

Since the 1950s, the Gallup Poll had probed the views of Canadians on various aspects of the birth control and abortion issues. According to three successive polls, an increasing number of Canadians supported birth control. In 1952, 1961, and 1965, 48, 55, and 66 percent, respectively, of Canadians believed that birth control was not morally wrong. In June 1967, 61 percent of interviewees agreed that birth control pills should be freely available to women with limited financial resources and still of childbearing age, while only 26 percent were opposed. A year later, in December 1968, 69 percent of interviewees who were Catholics and 85 percent of those who were Protestants supported the dissemination of birth control information.[29]

In the case of abortion, Canadians interviewed by the Gallup Poll were mostly favourable. A 1965 poll revealed that 71 percent of those who were interviewed supported abortion to save a mother's life or to preserve her physical and mental health. Four years later, the percentage was 73. The percentage opposed was 17 in 1965, and only slightly higher, at 18, four years later. However, the wording of the questions did not echo the women's movement's argument that abortion was a right and should be free and accessible on demand.[30]

According to historian John English, Pierre Trudeau was instrumental in reforming the Criminal Code and in changing how the government dealt with issues that were still defined on moral grounds by some social actors.[31] In 1967, Trudeau, then minister of justice, introduced an omnibus bill—the Criminal Law Amendment Act—setting forth a series of changes to the Code. After being elected leader of the Liberal Party and winning the 1968 federal election, Trudeau became prime minister. So it was the new justice minister, John Turner, who continued to pilot the omnibus bill.

However, Turner was not a strong supporter of the bill. He felt that it dealt with too many highly sensitive and divisive issues at the same time: abortion, birth control, divorce, gambling, and homosexuality. Politically, he preferred a "piecemeal" approach. Turner contemplated the possibility of dividing the omnibus legislation into smaller bills and permitting free votes that would allow members of Parliament to vote according to their conscience or their constituents' views. Being a Catholic, he was especially uncomfortable with the abortion issue.[32] He struggled with the appeal to "public authorities" that Pope Paul VI included in *Humanae Vitae*. The pope had insisted that "public authorities" should

> never allow the morals of your peoples to be undermined. The family is the primary unit in the state; do not tolerate any legislation which would introduce into the family those practices which are opposed to the natural law of God.[33]

Trudeau rejected Turner's approach. Although he too was a Catholic, Trudeau felt "sin [was] to be settled with God; crimes [were] the concern of Caesar."[34] For his conscience, Turner received conflicting advice. An expert in church law at the University of Toronto, Reverend Robert W. Crooker, insisted that no faithful Catholic could vote for the proposed changes. Since Turner was a cabinet minister, however, Crooker argued that the change to the Criminal Code was not sufficient for Turner to "break ranks" with the government. A Dominican theologian at Laval University reassured the anxious Turner: "The duty of a Catholic legislator in a pluralistic society was to serve the common good by finding a peaceable reconciliation of diverse views."[35]

Turner met with the Canadian Conference of Catholic Bishops in 1968. The justice minister was careful to reassure his audience that the proposed legislation was not too transformative, since the government was not setting out to legalize abortion. The proposed changes, Turner argued, just amended the Criminal Code in order to reflect current practices. After Turner's presentation, the president of the conference, Bishop Alexander Carter, concluded: "Gentlemen, I think John has convinced us. Let's have a drink."[36]

Section 251 of the amended Criminal Code (1970, Chap. C-34) stipulated that a woman needed the approval of a therapeutic abortion committee consisting of three doctors, who would allow an abortion if the pregnancy threatened the woman's life or health. Abortion had to be carried out by a "qualified medical practitioner, other than a member of a therapeutic abortion committee" in a hospital. Failure to follow this procedure meant that an individual charged with inducing an abortion would face a sentence of life in prison. In the case of a woman charged with interrupting her pregnancy, the sentence would be a two-year jail term.

The change to abortion legislation did not bring about social harmony. On the contrary, abortion remained a contentious issue in the public arena. Meanwhile, the new legal framework helped make the procedure safe, and "the rate rose from 3 per 100 live births in 1969, clearly a reflection of underreporting of an illegal activity, to 14.9 in 1975 and 18.6 in 1978."[37] Women still did not have any real control. Even under the circumstances allowed by the amended Code, hospitals continued to refuse to perform abortions in many provinces. According to the *Report of the Committee on the Operation of the Abortion Law*, there were no therapeutic abortion committees in Alberta, the Northwest Territories, Prince Edward Island, Saskatchewan, and Yukon, in 1974.[38] This meant that women, particularly those living in these provinces and territories, had to go elsewhere in the country or even to the United States to get an abortion. For the women's movement, this situation demonstrated that the amendments to the Criminal Code had solved nothing. Women reiterated their demands: abortion should be legal, free, and accessible anywhere in Canada, because it was a right. As part of their campaign, in the spring of 1970 some members of the Vancouver Women's Caucus organized the Abortion Caravan, which left Vancouver for Ottawa. The caravan's goal was to pressure politicians to revisit the abortion issue and get them to guarantee free abortion on demand.[39] On May 11, once in the national capital, some of the participants sat in the House of Commons area reserved for the public, chained themselves to seats, and succeeded in shutting down the session.

The abortion debate came to be dominated by the judicial saga of Dr. Henry Morgentaler. Morgentaler challenged the legal requirement that abortions be performed only in hospitals by opening a private clinic in Montreal in 1969. He was arrested and charged but was acquitted by a jury in 1973. The Crown appealed the decision, and subsequently the Court of Appeal and the Supreme Court of Canada found him guilty. Therefore, Morgentaler spent time in jail for 18 months starting in 1975.

Following Morgentaler's conviction, women in the Comité de lutte pour l'avortement libre et gratuit, founded in 1974, mobilized their resources. The

Demonstration near Queen's Park, Toronto, denouncing recent amendments to the Criminal Code and demanding free abortion. Photo published in the *Toronto Telegram*, May 10, 1971, York University Libraries, Clara Thomas Archives & Special Collections, Toronto Telegram fonds, ASC00738.

election of the Parti Québécois in 1976 allowed the Comité with other Quebec women's groups to pressure the newly elected government, led by René Lévesque, to drop charges against Morgentaler. Since provincial attorneys general had to press charges, the Comité questioned the logic of doing so, especially in the case of a political party committed to the independence of Quebec or, at least, to radically transform Canadian federalism. Why should a government, led by the Parti Québécois, participate in the enforcement of a section of the federal Criminal Code? The Comité counted on pro-abortion voices within the Parti Québécois to echo its demand. Under pressure, the Lévesque government dropped charges against Morgentaler.[40]

With two other physicians, Morgentaler opened a private clinic in Toronto. In 1983, the Toronto Police arrested all three. A year later, a jury found them not guilty, but the Crown appealed the verdict. For his part, Morgentaler asked the Supreme Court of Canada to rule on the constitutionality of the changes to the law on abortion in the amended Criminal Code of 1969. In January 1988, the Supreme Court of Canada declared that section 251 was unconstitutional. Chief Justice Dickson wrote:

Forcing a woman, by threat of criminal sanction, to carry a foetus to term unless she meets certain criteria unrelated to her own priorities and aspirations, is a profound interference with a woman's body and thus an infringement of security of the person.[41]

De facto, this Supreme Court judgment made abortion a legal procedure. Federal politicians have not reopened the issue since, despite strong pressure from the pro-life movement and various religious groups. Nevertheless, access to abortion has remained a controversial issue. At the initiative of individuals, the courts have intervened in order to guarantee free access to abortion. When Morgentaler opened a private clinic in Halifax in 1990, the Nova Scotia government tried unsuccessfully to shut down his practice. Three years later the Supreme Court of Canada upheld decisions by lower courts. The province's 1989 Medical Services Act and the Medical Services Designation Regulation were ruled unconstitutional because the provincial government had intervened in a federal area of responsibility. The Nova Scotia legislation had restricted abortion procedures to hospitals and denied health insurance coverage to women who ended their pregnancies at private clinics.[42]

Despite this victory, the situation did not improve for women living in the Maritimes. Accessibility continued to be a problem for those living in the North, too, and for those living far from large urban centres. *Globe and Mail* journalist Ingrid Peritz wrote: "For some, the right to choose is diminished by roadblocks: doctor's referrals, out-of-province travel, cash payments." As late as 2010 there were no abortion providers on Prince Edward Island. Anyone in that province seeking an abortion had to travel elsewhere. In the case of Aboriginal women living in the North in 2010, the federal government "pays to fly them south for the procedure." In New Brunswick in 2010, a woman needed the written consent of two physicians for an abortion, and it had to be performed exclusively in a hospital. This policy prompted Morgentaler, who had a private clinic in Fredericton, to sue the province, since women could not be reimbursed for abortions at his facility.[43]

Just as with abortion, prostitution re-emerged as a moral and social issue after the 1920s. It was partly due to the political mobilization and social activism of individuals, groups, and institutions opposed to the commercialization of sex and its public presence and, more recently, to the interventions of sex workers themselves. Even though there were existing laws that gave municipalities and police forces the power to crack down on prostitutes and on those who lived off the avails of prostitution, sex trade opponents increased pressure on municipal politicians and police forces to be more proactive and to rid their streets and neighbourhoods of sex workers.

During the Second World War, military officials worried about the spread of sexually transmitted diseases and their impact on men in uniform. They launched a campaign against prostitutes. For them, "fallen women" were responsible for the spread of venereal diseases that made soldiers unfit for duty. In their campaign, military officials counted on the active support of municipal authorities, such as Vancouver mayor Lyle Telford, who strongly believed in the repression of prostitution as the best public policy. This support led municipalities to renew their efforts to clear their towns and cities of prostitutes. In Montreal in January 1944, military officials threatened municipal authorities that they would forbid soldiers from going to bars and other entertainment facilities located in their territory if nothing was done about prostitutes.[44]

Despite social condemnation and repression, prostitution remained a sensitive issue after the Second World War. Moral reformers, such as Pacifique Plante and the Ligue du Sacré-Coeur, pressed city authorities to clean up Montreal streets. They documented the state of prostitution to substantiate their claim that Montreal had a significant prostitution problem. They insisted—or, according to their critics, exaggerated the contention—that most prostitutes were underage. Consequently, they cast city authorities and police forces in the role of supporting the sexual exploitation of teenagers if they did not act. Police reports and city court cases offer a more nuanced portrait. Based on these documents, Danielle Lacasse's study of female prostitution in Montreal between 1945 and 1970 reveals that most prostitutes were between the ages of 16 and 30, and few of them above 30.[45] City court records for the same time also reveal that the majority of persons arrested and charged with prostitution were single. About a quarter of them were married and another quarter were divorced or widowed.[46]

While moral reformers claimed weak moral character as one of the key causes that led individuals to become prostitutes, they also identified poverty as a cause. Montreal court records for 1945 to 1970 reveal the economic conditions for sex workers. They show that 64 percent of female prostitutes were working full-time in the sex trade. Allowing for the inherent limitations of using city court records to document the sex trade, since, presumably, many prostitutes were not arrested and charged, it would appear, based on the documents, that more than a third of the sex workers had some sort of additional part-time or full-time paid employment. For these, prostitution offered a way to complement their modest income.[47] One researcher's analysis of prostitution in Windsor in the 1950s demonstrates that several prostitutes listed working as a domestic, a waitress or in a factory as employment.[48]

Contemporary sex workers confirm what historians have found in these decades-old court cases. A study of sex workers in the Maritimes in the early twenty-first century demonstrated that prostitution offered a way to make "good" money and escape demeaning and devalued jobs, for which women and men were underpaid. In other instances, prostitution offered a "quick and easy" way to supplement low social assistance payments or to obtain income to support a drug addiction.[49]

Aside from the street, cabarets, and brothels, new venues for prostitution developed in the post-1945 era. Massage parlours and escort agencies proliferated. As for prostitutes working from home, they could be charged for using their house or apartment as a bawdy house if disapproving neighbours or moral reformers discovered them. Regardless of the type or location of their activities, risks have remained a significant concern for sex workers. Those who work on the street, especially, have faced violence, both physical and psychological, from customers, pimps, and moral opponents.

Learning about these new venues for the trade, through news reports or individuals' investigations, opponents became increasingly agitated and pressed authorities into action. Towns and cities launched sporadic crackdowns, clearly indicating that their officials were taking the prostitution problem seriously, but still, prostitution did not disappear. If the Montreal scene was an indication of what was happening elsewhere in the country, any episode of moral panic that led to a crackdown simply altered how prostitution operated. According to Lacasse, episodes of repression in Montreal led to an even greater level of control over prostitutes by pimps, the Mafia, or other criminal elements.[50]

The rising sex trade on the street re-ignited the issue of public space and how to share it with sex workers. Some of these workers, particularly those interviewed for the 2003 study, acknowledged that the nature of their activities constituted a nuisance for residents, and even that sex activities with johns should not occur in neighbourhoods where children lived. Conflicts erupted in several Canadians cities. For instance, residents organized groups in Darmouth, Toronto, St. John, and Vancouver after their petitions and representations to municipal officials and complaints to police failed to generate action. These groups worked at night when sex workers were out on sidewalks; they wrote down the licence plate numbers of customers' cars and threatened to reveal the identity of clients, harassed sex workers, and pressed them to move out of their neighbourhoods. Some carried flashlights and pointed them at customers and sex workers. Their social and political activism has not necessarily been motivated by moral concerns. These groups have argued that the presence of prostitutes has had a negative impact on the value of their property. Also, they feared for their personal safety and have complained about the disturbance caused by car traffic. When HIV/AIDS became a matter of social concern in the 1980s, these groups of neighbours and concerned citizens updated their rationale for chasing prostitutes out of their neighbourhood. They began to argue that used condoms and needles on sidewalks or front yards constituted a threat of infection to children, adults, and pets.[51]

In response, city authorities pressed police forces to increase their presence at night. At times, police officers have increased patrols and forced prostitutes to move, temporarily or permanently, elsewhere. Sometimes neighbourhoods have claimed victory, when sex workers have vanished. These changes have resulted partly from the gentrification process that has affected some neighbourhoods in several cities. Some city politicians have considered the possibility of creating official "red-light" districts. For example, Toronto city councillor Giorgio Mammoliti suggested in 2011 that a red-light district should be established on Toronto Island, which can be reached by ferry services, water taxi, or private boats. For Mammoliti, this plan would not only provide the sex industry with a remote and sparsely populated environment where it could thrive and be tolerated, but also become a source of revenue for a cash-strapped city like Toronto. A Toronto Island resident interviewed by CBC rejected the proposal unequivocally, because she did not want a red-light district in her own "backyard."[52]

Through examination of state law enforcement, it becomes clear that most police officers did not believe in repression in principle, but rather tried to manage prostitution by containing it spatially or repressing its public nuisance aspect. In twenty-first century Halifax, police officers have interacted with prostitutes in order to gather intelligence on pimps and other criminal elements. At other times, Halifax police officers have taken sex workers in for a "talk" at the station. Since the 1990s, some police forces have invested resources in "john schools." This initiative, developed in San Francisco in 1995, gives arrested customers a choice: to pay a fine and go to a "school" program, during which police officers, nurses, and residents explain what is wrong with the sex trade, or to go to trial. Despite their successes, such programs are controversial. The people who attend john schools are most often members of lower social classes, rather than elites who have the financial means to hire high-class sex workers who do not operate on the streets. Such high-class johns have not been bothered by law enforcement to the same extent.[53]

With regard to the justice system, Lacasse's study of Montreal prostitution reveals that most prostitutes who were arrested and charged were women, but that few received a jail term. Judges preferred to impose a fine or a suspended sentence pending a stay in an institution that would reform them, as had been the case before the 1970s. Customers were rarely arrested. If they were charged and convicted, they received a fine. On the other hand, using the law both as a deterrent and as a way to shape public perception, the courts continued to hand out prison terms to pimps and others charged with living off the avails of prostitution.[54]

With the development of social work as a profession before the Second World War, the justice system began to send some prostitutes to another arm of the state. Social workers aimed to socially rehabilitate prostitutes. Depending on the prostitute's age, rehabilitation meant helping them to find other forms of paid employment, to get married, to re-establish lines of communications with parents, and, if they were underage, to go back to live with their parents.[55]

With regard to public policy options, both legalization and decriminalization have been debated. The National Canadian Organization for the Rights of Prostitutes (CORP), some individual sex workers, and other advocates for prostitutes' rights opposed the legalization of prostitution. Instead, they advocated the decriminalization of the sex trade. For them, decriminalization would increase sex workers' safety and limit the state's attempts to govern their conduct.

Sex workers' own voices became more audible over the years. A movement defending the rights of sex workers emerged in the United States. In California, in 1973, COYOTE or Cut Off Your Old Tired Ethics offered an opportunity to sex workers to intervene and take a stand. This movement led to the foundation of the International Committee for Prostitutes' Rights, in 1984. Inspired by this international movement, sex workers in Canada developed their own narrative in order to fight those who had patronized them, denied their right to speak up, or questioned their motives, morality, and self-esteem. Their strategy of "discursive resistance" included a challenge to those who labelled them with derogatory and degrading terms. Notwithstanding the violence and health dangers associated with the sex trade, they have insisted on naming what they do as "work." They have demanded to be recognized as legitimate workers, and not to be viewed as exploited individuals or as people who have chosen debauchery as a way of life.[56]

In participating in the debate on prostitution and public policy, the feminist movement has displayed its divisions. Some women's groups and some individual feminists have refused to accept the definition of prostitution as a career.[57] Several women's groups insisted on the exploitive aspects of prostitution and the risks associated with it. For example, at a workshop on prostitution and the state, held at the University of Toronto in 2011, a female participant asked: Who would take pride in announcing that their daughter had chosen sex work as a career?

Until the 1960s, the Vagrancy Act was the principal weapon used by Canadian authorities to manage the prostitution issue. In response to social activism on the part of prostitution's opponents, the federal government amended the Criminal Code by criminalizing public solicitation for the purposes of prostitution in 1972. Six years later, this controversial legislative change led the Supreme Court of Canada to define solicitation as an offence when an individual was pressing or persistent.[58] Fearing that this restrictive definition of solicitation would facilitate rather than restrict the sex trade, municipalities and provinces passed anti-prostitution bylaws and other legislation. In reaction, the federal government appointed the Fraser Committee, which, in 1985, recommended the partial decriminalization of prostitution, notably for the indoor sex trade. The government ignored the recommendation and amended Section 213 of the Criminal Code to stipulate the following:

1) Every person who in a public place or in any place open to public view
   a) stops or attempts to stop any motor vehicle,
   b) impedes the free flow of pedestrian or vehicular traffic or ingress to or egress from premises adjacent to that place, or
   c) stops or attempts to stop any person or in any manner communicates or attempts to communicate with any person for the purpose of engaging in prostitution or of obtaining the sexual services of a prostitute is guilty of an offence punishable on summary conviction.

As it did with abortion, civilian activism through the justice system has forced the state to revisit the issue. In September 2010, the Ontario Superior Court struck down the sections of the Criminal Code concerning running a bawdy house, living off the avails of prostitution, and communicating for the purposes of prostitution. According to the litigants, Terri-Jean Bedford, Valerie Scott, and Amy Lebovitch, these sections of the Code put sex workers at greater risk. Judge Susan Himel sided with them, agreeing that it was safer to ply the sex trade in an indoor setting where sex workers could screen their clients and hire security guards for their personal safety. "I find that the danger faced by prostitutes," Judge Himel wrote in her 131-page ruling, "greatly outweighs any harm which may be faced by the public."[59] The federal and Ontario governments have appealed and the results are still pending.

Like abortion and prostitution, homosexuality drew much public attention over the course of the twentieth century. Initially, opponents justified its repression by calling it an act of gross indecency. When the federal government amended the Criminal Code in 1892, the charge of gross indecency was applied to any public or private sexual acts between men. In 1953–54, the reference to men was abandoned, and whipping was no longer part of the sentence.[60] Homosexuals could also be prosecuted for other offences, such as buggery, which carried a sentence of fourteen years in jail.

Repression varied throughout the country. In the post-1945 period, the RCMP launched a secret campaign against homosexuals. Influenced by a parallel campaign in the United States, its main goal was to identify homosexuals working for the federal government, because they were deemed a security risk. According to the RCMP, homosexuals were morally weak, since they tried to conceal their sexuality identity. Because they hid their sexual orientation, homosexuals were susceptible to blackmail and likely to reveal secrets that would undermine national security and the authority of the state. This campaign led the RCMP to open files on more than 8,000 individuals, less than 3,000 of whom worked for the federal bureaucracy.[61] At the end of the 1950s, the federal police were using a method, the Pupillary Response Test but called the "fruit machine" by the RCMP, to detect homosexuals working in the federal bureaucracy. "Test subjects peered through an opening in a box and were shown pictures while a camera photographed pupil dilation and eye movement at half-second intervals."[62] By the beginning of the 1960s, "113 civil servants had already been dismissed or forced into resignation."[63]

For other law enforcement officers, homosexuality was seen as a sexual threat, since people could become homosexuals. In its report submitted in 1959, the Royal Commission on the Criminal Law Relating to Criminal Sexual Psychopaths cited the testimony of Toronto Police Force chief John Chisholm. He justified repression on the grounds that homosexuals "corrupt others and are constantly recruiting youths into their fraternity."[64] At the same time, media stories of indecent acts in public places fuelled fears that homosexuals undermined social values, were sexual predators, targeted vulnerable young people, and constituted a serious deviance from the heterosexual norm.

Members of the medical community and in particular psychiatrists offered a solution to those fearing that anyone could become a homosexual, especially if he was young, impressionable, and surrounded by older homosexuals. They defined homosexuality as a disease and, consequently, suggested treatments. These included psychotherapy, electroshock therapy, and even lobotomy, which was performed on homosexuals at Hôpital Saint-Jean de Dieu, a psychiatric establishment in Montreal. Some psychiatrists believed that lobotomy would eliminate homosexual impulses. They justified their decision by pointing to the fact that one of the most important medical professional organizations, the American Psychiatric Association, had labelled homosexuality as a psychological disorder in 1952. This narrative was part of the medicalization of sexual deviance, which posed alternatives to the imprisonment of individuals, mostly men, who formerly would have been charged and imprisoned for homosexual behaviour. The justice system paid attention to medical experts' understanding and treatment of homosexuality. As a part of sentencing, homosexuals were now sometimes sent to mental institutions or forced to undergo other kinds of medical treatment, in order to make them heterosexuals.[65] It was only in 1973 that the American Psychiatric Association removed homosexuality from its list of mental disorders.

In the context of the sexual revolution, homosexuality triggered another debate on the law and the role of the state in governing conduct. Already Alfred Charles Kinsey's studies on sexuality, conducted in the late 1940s and the early 1950s in the United States, had demonstrated that about 37 percent of the male population had engaged in homosexual relations at some point in their lives. In Kinsey's view, homosexual acts should therefore not be considered "crimes against nature" since same-sex relations were fairly common.[66]

In 1957, the British *Report of the Departmental Committee on Homosexual Offences and Prostitution*, better known as the Wolfenden Report, recommended the decriminalization of homosexuality. Its authors argued that the role of the state was not to interfere with private lives, but that governments could still use the law to protect public order and space. This report received media coverage in Canada, and some gay organizations, such as the Vancouver-based Association for Social Knowledge, used it as a weapon to attack the anti-homosexual narrative. It questioned the premises used to justify the repression and medical treatment of homosexuality. In 1964, NDP MP Arnold Peters introduced a private member's bill to decriminalize homosexual relations between consenting adults in the privacy of their household. It did not pass.[67]

Following a decision by the Supreme Court of Canada in November 1967, it became even more urgent to question state regulation of sexuality. The judges of the highest court examined the case of Everett George Klippert, a gay man who was accused of having sex with other men, was found guilty, and then sentenced to a three-year jail term. During his imprisonment, two psychiatrists concluded that Klippert would never cause "injury, pain or other evil to any person." They nevertheless labelled him a "dangerous sexual offender," because he was likely to have sex with other men again. Although the Supreme Court judges were split, a majority ruled that Klippert should be incarcerated indefinitely, because he was a "dangerous sexual offender."[68] In their continuing struggle against conservative, normative heterosexuality, homosexuals used this case to demonstrate the profound discrepancy between the crime and the sentence. As for Klippert, he finally was released from prison in 1971.

In tabling the omnibus bill in December 1967, Minister of Justice Trudeau indicated how the state would regulate sexuality and where it would draw the boundaries in the private/public dichotomy. Same-sex activity was no longer to be considered a crime when sexual acts were performed between consenting adults above 21 years of age in the privacy of their home. Trudeau believed that this legislative change was highly desirable. He personally knew several gay individuals who had lost their jobs or had been denied a promotion in their workplace because of their sexual orientation. During a press conference, he argued that the omnibus bill and its homosexuality provision was an attempt to bring "the laws of the land up to contemporary society."[69] For Trudeau, morality should not guide state action in "the bedrooms of the nation." Sexual orientation was a civil right. Nevertheless, the government still had to intervene "when [sexuality] becomes public" or "relates to minors."[70]

Although the legal change was not spectacular and it fuelled further activism on the part of homosexuals, Trudeau had defied broader public opinion in proposing it. Historian Ian McKay writes that in his hometown of Sarnia, many residents were adamantly opposed to the homosexuality provision: "Christians in Sarnia circulated pamphlets depicting the faces of the degenerate damned, howling in horror as they were licked by the eternal flames of hell. One of my high-school teachers, well known for dalliances with his female students, interrupted his physics lesson for a red-faced denunciation of the bill, which was for him the beginning of the decline and fall of Western civilization."[71] A poll conducted for the government on the omnibus bill revealed that Canadians overwhelmingly supported the divorce (83 percent) and abortion reforms (73 percent) but rejected at 76 percent the proposed legal change to the status of homosexuality.[72]

In their attempts to explain the motives behind the decriminalization of same-sex activity, opponents launched personal attacks on Trudeau. The minister of justice's own sexual orientation came under suspicion and fed the rumour mill. Opponents alleged that Trudeau, already in his late forties but still a bachelor, introduced the provision on homosexuality because he was gay. Biographer John English refutes this claim, but it was repeated frequently at the time. During the June 1968 election, "right-wing newsletters openly claimed that he [Trudeau] was gay. The Ottawa gossip even suggested that his close relationship with his bachelor assistant and friend Michael Pitfield was homosexual in character." Rumours about Trudeau's sexual orientation resurfaced during the 1970 October Crisis. The FLQ referred to him as "*la tapette*" ("the pansy") in their manifesto. Even American president Richard Nixon thought that Trudeau was gay.[73]

Homosexuals continued to mobilize. They founded organizations such as the Community Homophile Association of Toronto, the Gay Alliance Toward Equality (GATE) in Vancouver, and the Front de libération homosexuelle in Montreal. Inspired by the Stonewall riots in New York City, Canadian homosexuals held demonstrations, notably in August 1971 on Parliament Hill. The "We Demand" brief listed a series of demands, such as the removal from the

Criminal Code of the terms *gross indecency* and *buggery*, lowering the age of consent from 21 to the age of majority, equal access to all public service employment including the military, removal of homosexual acts as legal grounds for divorce, and an end to the RCMP campaign against homosexuals working for the government.[74]

These demands rallied the gay movement, but the state responded slowly. Gay activism brought cases to the courts. When judges ruled in their favour, it added pressure on governments to act. In 1977, Quebec became the first province to include sexual orientation in its human rights code. A year later, the federal government amended its immigration policy and removed homosexuals as a category of individuals who were denied admission. In the 1980s, members of Parliament Pat Carney and Svend Robinson failed to convince a majority of MPs to include sexual orientation in the Canadian Human Rights Act. Robinson's efforts to broaden the definition of spouse to include same-sex partners in the Income Tax Act and Canada Pension Plan Act suffered a similar fate. Homosexuals had to wait until 1992 to serve openly in the armed forces and four more years before the federal government included sexual orientation in the Canadian Human Rights Act. In 2000, Bill C-23 gave same-sex couples social and tax benefits similar to those of heterosexuals in common-law relationships.

The issue of social and tax benefits for same-sex couples brought the existing legal definition of marriage into question. The traditional definition of marriage—a union between a man and a woman—was discriminatory, since same-sex couples were excluded. This inherent discrimination and the refusal on the part of politicians to address this issue by amending the definition of marriage further fuelled gay and lesbian activism.

This continuing activism took various forms. Besides writing letters, drawing up petitions, and mounting demonstrations, some same-sex couples attempted to register their marriages in spite of the law, as Richard North and Chris Vogel did in Manitoba in 1974 and Todd Layland and Pierre Beaulne did in Ontario in 1992. However, a year later the Ontario Divisional Court upheld the definition of marriage as a union between a man and a woman.[75] Counting on the complicity of a gay-positive church, homosexuals issued another challenge in 2000. Reverend Brent Hawkes of the Metropolitan Community church of Toronto informed his congregation that he would perform same-sex wedding ceremonies for Elaine and Anne Vautour and Joe Varnell and Kevin Bourassa. Since marriage was not only a civil but also a religious institution, Hawkes chose the religious route, hoping to force the state to recognize that "what therefore God hath joined together, let not man [and woman] put asunder." As Richard North and Chris Vogel did in 1974 in a Winnipeg Unitarian

Church, he used the old custom of readings the "banns of marriage," whereby a clergyman would announce to his congregation the impending marriage between two individuals. Three Sundays in a row, he would read out the names of those who planned to tie the knot in a religious ceremony. Unless someone objected, the wedding would be celebrated. The religious ceremony for both weddings took place on January 14, 2001. Beforehand, the Ontario minister of consumer and commercial relations, Robert Runciman, warned that the upcoming wedding celebrations did not comply with the law. Informed by the media that the government of Ontario would not recognize the forms sent to the Registrar General for Ontario, the newlyweds and the Metropolitan Community Church launched a court challenge on January 24, 2001.[76] Court challenges on similar grounds proceeded in other provinces as well.

In July 2002, the Ontario Divisional Court rejected the existing definition of marriage as being a union strictly between a man and a woman. In the Court's view, the legal definition of marriage violated Section 15 on equality rights of the Canadian Charter of Rights and Freedoms. The Court gave the federal government 24 months to amend its legislation. Two months later, the Superior Court of Quebec also ruled that the legal definition of marriage was restrictive, and questioned the notion that marriage was a heterosexual union for the sole purpose of procreation.[77] In 2003, the Ontario Court of Appeal upheld the decision rendered a year before by the Ontario Divisional Court. In June 2003, the Ontario government announced that it would register same-sex marriages. The British Columbia government made a similar announcement the following month.

Although federal politicians had reaffirmed in 1999 that marriage was between a man and a woman, the federal government now invited the Supreme Court of Canada to weigh in. In 2003, the Court reviewed a proposed bill, The Act Respecting Certain Aspects of Legal Capacity for Marriage for Civil Purposes. The federal government asked the Court if the government had the authority to define marriage as a union between two individuals, without specifying their gender. Also it invited the judges to indicate if religious institutions would have the obligation to perform same-sex ceremonies despite the fact that they were contrary to institutions' beliefs.

In December 2004, the Supreme Court of Canada stated that the federal government had the authority to legalize same-sex marriage. The Court defused the growing fear, exploited and disseminated by religious groups and institutions, that they would be forced to perform same-sex ceremonies. Religious groups could refuse to perform them.[78]

In February 2005, the minority Liberal government of Prime Minister Paul Martin introduced bill C-38, An Act Respecting Certain Aspects of Legal

Capacity for Marriage for Civil Purposes, which recognized same-sex unions. Knowing that the bill was unpopular among religious groups, Martin took considerable pains to reassure them that "no church, no temple, no synagogue, no mosque, no religious official will be asked or forced to perform a marriage that is contrary to their beliefs."[79] The Liberals, who faced some opposition to the bill from within their caucus, counted on the support of most of the Bloc Québécois and the NDP members to ensure its passage. The vast majority of members of the official opposition, the Conservative Party of Canada, opposed the bill. The Conservatives ran ads targeting socially conservative ethnic communities and portraying their leader, Stephen Harper, as a true defender of the "traditional" definition of marriage.[80] Despite strong opposition both inside and outside Parliament, Bill C-38 was adopted.

The redefinition of marriage divided Canadians. Polls conducted in the 1990s revealed that only 37 percent of interviewees supported same-sex marriage. It was at the end of the twentieth century that a majority of Canadians began to favour same-sex unions. In 1996, 49 percent of Canadians favoured same-sex marriage. Three years later, it was 53 percent.[81] When the House of Commons debated the Liberal bill, an EKOS poll showed that 42 percent of Canadians approved same-sex marriage and 40 percent opposed it. There was a significant group of respondents—17 per cent—who neither supported nor opposed such marriages.[82]

Churches were divided. The Roman Catholic Church was resolutely opposed. It insisted that the federal government should protect the "traditional" definition of marriage, by using the notwithstanding clause in the Canadian Charter of Rights and Freedoms. This clause allowed the government to uphold legislation that was otherwise unconstitutional as law for a period of five years, and this could be renewed for additional five-year terms by subsequent Parliaments. In 2005, Justice Minister Irwin Cotler rebutted the Catholics by reminding Toronto archbishop Aloysius Ambrozic that "rights are rights are rights."[83] Before Ambrozic's involvement, other Catholic church authorities had expressed their opposition. In 2003, the bishop of Calgary, Fred Henry, warned Prime Minister Jean Chrétien, a Catholic himself, that he would put "at risk his eternal salvation" if his government legalized same-sex marriage.[84] For the Catholic church, a marriage was still a divine institution as defined by biblical interpretation. Nevertheless, within the church there was some dissension and resistance that occasionally reached the media. In 2003, the archbishop of St. John's, Brendan O'Brien, disciplined one of his priests, Paul Lundrigan, for criticizing the church's opposition to same-sex marriage. In front of his parishioners, the archbishop denied Lundrigan's right to talk publicly about the issue unless he was supporting the church's official position.[85]

Since the 1980s, members of the United Church of Canada had debated homosexuality, the role of homosexuals in their church, their ordination, and their right to marry. These debates generated tensions, and some members left when, in 1988, the United Church approved the ordination of homosexuals and, in 2003, same-sex marriage.[86] The Anglican Church of Canada carried on a similarly divisive debate. On the issue of the ordination of homosexuals, several members denounced their church and joined more conservative religious congregations. In 2005, although unable to reach a decision on the same-sex marriage issue, the Anglican Church nevertheless decided to pursue the discussion.[87] Two years later, the House of Bishops released a statement to the members of the Anglican General Synod. In their document, the authors stated that the Anglican Church would "develop the most generous pastoral response possible within the current teaching of the church," which excluded "nuptial blessing" of same-sex relations.[88]

Another challenge to the definition of marriage emerged in 2009. Winston Blackmore and James Oler, leaders of the Fundamentalist Church of Jesus Christ of Latter-Day Saints community in Bountiful, British Columbia, were charged with one count each of polygamy. They appealed their case before the British Columbia Supreme Court, while opponents warned of the grave consequences of legalizing polygamy. According to the British Columbia and federal governments, polygamy was harmful to women and children, and since Canada was not an isolated island, any attempt to legalize polygamy would set a dangerous precedent. Canada would become the first country in the Western hemisphere to do so, and both governments feared that polygamists throughout the world would be drawn en masse to Canada. Consequently, opponents argued that the federal government should not be compelled to amend section 293 of the Criminal Code. Proponents, including the British Columbia Civil Liberties Association, argued that individuals, and not the state, should choose their marriage arrangement, provided that their lifestyle choice did not harm others. In its decision, the B.C. Supreme Court concurred with intervenors who argued that polygamy physically and psychologically harmed women. The Court found that Section 293 of the Criminal Code "seeks to advance the institution of monogamous marriage, a fundamental value in Western society from the earliest of times. It seeks to protect against the many harms which are reasonably apprehended to arise out of the practice of polygamy."[89]

Although same-sex marriage was apparently settled as a matter of law, debate reappeared in the media at the beginning of 2012. It involved non-residents coming to Canada for religious or civil same-sex ceremonies. In a divorce case between two foreign women, Justice Department officials argued that same-sex marriages were only legal for non-residents if their home countries recognized this type of union. In the face of growing concern, the Harper government introduced legislation to recognize these marriages for all non-residents regardless of the laws of their home countries. The "gap in the law," as it was referred to by government officials, had now been closed.[90]

ALCOHOL: STATE MONOPOLY AND RESPONSIBLE DRINKING

Anti-alcohol forces saw their goal of living in a dry Canada begin to recede following the repeal of prohibition. At the end of the First World War, the federal government gave the provinces jurisdiction over this emotionally charged and highly divisive issue and progressively abandoned prohibition as a public policy. Provincial governments preferred, instead, to monopolize the distribution and the sale of liquors. Quebec and British Columbia were the first to take control of alcohol, and the other provinces followed suit. The last to repeal prohibition within its territorial boundaries was Prince Edward Island, in 1948.

The failure of prohibition due to problems with enforcement justified this new public policy. Since prohibition did not criminalize the possession of alcohol, many Canadians chose to make their own alcoholic beverages and became adept brewers, wine makers, or distillers. At the same time, as historian Craig Heron observes, prohibition provoked a mass movement of political disobedience. Canadians wanted to have access to booze, and they used a variety of means to obtain alcohol. The federal legislation permitted alcohol use for medical purposes. Physicians now noticed a significant increase in the number of patients seeking prescriptions for various illnesses whose treatment required a shot of gin or other liquor. Even if physicians generally did not object to this sudden surge in demand, the civil disobedience movement demonstrated that the moral reformers' attempts to control individuals' choices by using state power were unsuccessful.[91]

The enforcement of prohibition had occurred at a time when the Western hemisphere was battling a pandemic that became known as the Spanish flu. This disease proliferated during repatriation following the end of the First World War, when soldiers, whose immune systems were already weakened, endured crowded conditions on returning ships. They became carriers of the disease, and the home country had to battle a foreign health invasion. Hospitals were overwhelmed. Physicians commonly prescribed liquor to prevent or combat the fatal illness. Nevertheless, more than 50,000 Canadians died of the flu in 1918 and 1919. In the context of alcohol being a useful way to fight the deadly flu, prohibition was a bad public policy according to proponents of alcohol.

While provinces took control of distribution and sale, they left manufacturing to the private sector. Aside from supplying the domestic market, Canadian alcohol producers benefited from the prohibition law enforced in the United States from 1920 to 1933. Prohibition south of the border made the fortunes of a number of Canadian distillers, brewers, and other alcohol manufacturers, such as Seagram. The prevention of spirits and other alcoholic beverages reaching the United States became a controversial issue for both countries. The Canadian government dragged its feet, arguing that it was almost impossible to curb the liquor traffic, since the liquor industry controlled the production of alcohol and was at liberty to sell where its interests dictated. The American government deployed numerous agents on the Canadian-American border to stop shipments. Nevertheless, alcohol smuggling became an extremely profitable business, especially in border towns such as Windsor, Detroit, and Sault Ste. Marie in both Ontario and Michigan.[92]

State monopoly of distribution and sale meant that the government did not relinquish its ability to regulate the conduct of individuals. Through a series of measures guided by a strategy of harm reduction, provincial governments put in place a system of liquor control. Knowing that if access was unrestricted some individuals would develop a dependency, governments had to find ways to limit that availability. A delicate balance had to be found between increasing revenue through alcohol sales and simultaneously controlling access. In order to appease moral reformers, who recognized that the state had an inherent interest in facilitating the sale of alcohol, government officials implemented policies that demonstrated a commitment to reducing the harm caused by excessive drinking. At the same time, these policies favoured accessibility since prohibition demonstrated that individuals were willing to defy the law in order to secure a way to access their favourite beverage. Harm reduction policies were dictated by what Line Beauchesne calls the state's responsibility "to use its public policies to act as a guardian of public order and a protector of non-autonomous persons, *but also the responsibility to maintain a common morality within society.*"[93]

In their attempts to control the consumption of liquor, provincial governments developed a range of programs addressing accessibility. In every province, bureaucrats determined the number and location of outlets and their hours of operation. For instance, provinces forbade the sale of alcohol in their stores on Sundays and public holidays. Employees selling alcohol in state-controlled stores could regulate access to their products by passing judgment, sometimes determined by class, gender, and ethnic bias, on customers and their perceived ability to govern themselves since consumers needed, except in Quebec and New Brunswick, to get a personal permit to buy alcohol until

1970.[94] They could refuse to sell alcohol to specific groups: Aboriginals, immigrants, and people who, according to store employees, led a questionable lifestyle. For the victims of these decisions, there was no process of appeal. Direct complaints to the employee himself were usually unsuccessful. Other options included attempts to change their lifestyle, if that was the main reason for the denial of service, buying from a more lenient employee, or trying to make a purchase in another liquor store. However, going to another liquor store was not an option for those living in an area where there was only one to begin with.

Since provincial governments issued licences to establishments, the venues where Canadians drank—beer parlours, bars, and taverns—became a battleground for "wet" and "dry" voices. The wet camp, which included workers, unions, businesses, and the Moderation League, asked for fewer regulations, while the "dry" voices, such as the WCTU and some religious officials, pleaded for restrictions based on gender and age. To borrow Mariana Valverde's phrase, "governing spaces of consumption"[95] became a local, regional, and provincial issue. For instance, starting in 1927 in Ontario, people could buy liquor from state-owned stores, but public drinking—in taverns, for example—was still prohibited. Once that aspect of the prohibition regime was abandoned in 1934, a new battle emerged over who would and should be allowed in beer parlours and other public drinking spaces. Taverns, hotels, and other establishments where people could drink questioned how the state could, on the one hand, license accessibility but, at the same time, "maintain a common morality." Wet voices promoted the idea of "beer by the glass" as a respectable way of letting individuals drink in the company of others, instead of forcing them to go to underground drinking establishments. Once the notion that drinking in public was respectable, the wet voices wondered if young individuals should be prohibited from licensed establishments. And what about women? Canadians debated the division of space by gender. Women could not drink in taverns in Quebec. In Alberta, it was in urban beer parlours. In British Columbia, women could drink in a separate section of a beer parlour. These regulations demonstrated the influence of the dry and wet voices. Dry voices and some clergymen argued that respectable women should not indulge in drinking the company of men in these public spaces of consumption. Others, among them, not surprisingly, women who wanted to drink, thought otherwise and instigated the creation of separate women's drinking rooms.[96]

A number of times since the 1960s, provincial governments have reviewed policies to control access to alcohol. Liquor opponents have argued that any increase in accessibility would unduly encourage drinking; proponents have been skeptical of the relationship between greater accessibility and increased consumption. At the same time as consumption rates were rising after 1945,

Beer parlour at the Nobel Hotel in Calgary, Alberta, ca. 1940. Glenbow Archives, NA-2479-13.

moderate drinking was gaining social acceptance, which led to the development of what became known as cocktail lounges where customers could get drinks and food and enjoy entertainment.

Meanwhile, governments took other initiatives in response to the 1960s counterculture and to an ongoing contestation of state authority to regulate access. For example, they set the legal drinking age at 21. Then, between 1970 and 1972, in response to the counterculture movement, provincial governments lowered the drinking age from 21 to 18 or 19. Liquor store employees and workers in licensed establishments would henceforth have to ask individuals who appeared underage to present official government-issued documentation attesting that they were legally entitled to buy or drink alcohol. If some did not mind showing their ID, others perceived the drinking age policy as a form of state intrusion in their lives. Governments opened self-serve liquor stores, which minimized the power of government employees to deny, on discriminatory grounds, the sale of alcohol to some customers. In 1978, customers in Quebec enjoyed longer opening hours in provincial liquor stores. In 1993, the Alberta government abandoned its monopoly on the sale of liquor and privatized its 208 stores. Since then, the number of stores has increased significantly; there were 1,158 liquor stores in the province by 2009.[97] In 2013, the Atlantic Convenience Stores Association pressed governments in the four Maritimes provinces to allow corner stores to sell alcohol.[98] A year before, the Ontario Convenience Stores Association (OCSA) asked the provincial government to allow OCSA members to sell beer and wine. Its president justified this demand by arguing that Ontarians were "responsible adults who want the simple convenience of leaving the car at home and walking to their neighbourhood store to get wine for dinner or drinks for the barbecue."[99] A petition, started by the owner of a general store south of Brantford, garnered more than 112,500 signatures. In fact, 214 convenience stores already had the right to sell alcohol as agencies, because the Liquor Control Board of Ontario (LCBO) chose not to operate stores in small communities. The association asked that all its members be accorded the same privilege. This was not a new issue. In the 1980s, the David Peterson Liberal government had contemplated allowing corner stores to sell alcohol. In the 1990s, the Progressive Conservatives under Mike Harris included the privatization of the LCBO in their electoral platform known as the Common Sense Revolution. Nevertheless, once elected in 1995, they abandoned the idea. Three years later, Premier Harris acknowledged that the LCBO had performed relatively well and constituted a great government asset. According to him, the LCBO has "been a tremendous success story." At the time, it was the "third largest contributor of revenue to the government, after taxes and vehicle-driver registration fee."[100] Later on, the Liberal government of Dalton McGuinty would wonder if greater accessibility to alcohol would truly serve "the public interest." His successor, Kathleen Wynne, rejected the proposal to allow the sale of alcohol in corner stores in 2013.[101]

Governments have also used taxation as a means to control alcohol consumption. Those who have argued that the state has a moral responsibility to limit consumption have consistently applauded tax increases, on the supposition that they will negatively affect sales. On the other hand, some have criticized politicians for introducing such disincentives and warned them that tax increases could encourage cross-border shopping. Consumers will go wherever they can pay less for their alcohol. Be that as it may, no provincial government could readily afford to abandon the revenues generated by its taxes on liquor, wine, and beer. In 2010, for example, the Alberta government collected $2 billion in alcohol and gambling revenues, more than it collected that year on oil and gas royalties. In Ontario, the provincial government collected a dividend of $1.63 billion from the Liquor Control Board of Ontario (LCBO) in 2010–11.[102]

After the Second World War, a new narrative had emerged to redefine the condition of those who could not control their alcohol use. No longer labelled a vice, a sign of weak willpower, or of moral failing, the uncontrollable thirst for alcohol was characterized as an "inborn, physiological addiction" that led to a "physical addiction."[103] Drunkenness and excessive drinking became symptoms of an illness called alcoholism. American physiologist Elvin Morton "Bunky" Jellinek, who worked briefly in Ontario and Alberta between 1958 and 1962, was instrumental in transforming the medical and social construction of alcoholism. For alcoholics who were unhappy with their state of dependence, this new perspective was extremely encouraging. Clinics began to offer treatments. An interesting sidelight on this phase of treatment and experimentation occurred during the 1950s in Saskatchewan, when Abraham Hoffer and Humphry Osmond used lysergic acid diethylamide, a drug that came to be better known as LSD, in the treatment of alcoholism. They believed that LSD "would chemically alter the patient's metabolic makeup and cure a neurological process that, they believed, caused alcohol addiction."[104] They pursued their research on alcoholism and LSD until the federal government classified LSD as a restricted drug in the 1960s.

The rise of Alcoholics Anonymous also played a role in the development of the narrative of alcoholism as an illness. Formed in the United States in 1935 by Bill Wilson, the movement was based on the notion that, with the help of others facing similar drinking problems, alcoholics could reform themselves and end their dependence.[105] The liquor industry supported the new narrative because "the problem of alcoholism was not in the bottle but in the minority of drinkers with physiological defects."[106]

This new narrative prompted the state to wonder if repression was still the best approach to dealing with habitually drunken individuals. Judges had previously convicted and sent them to jail for the crime of drunkenness, but beginning in the 1960s, the courts became more lenient. Those found guilty of excessive drinking paid a fine, and judges suggested treatments to those who exhibited signs of alcoholism. However, many destitute people continued serve jail time because they could not afford to pay a fine.

Another change occurred when the liquor industry developed marketing strategies based on the concept of responsible drinking. Mothers Against Drunk Driving (MADD), an American lobby group founded in 1980, shaped these strategies. MADD founder Candace Lynne "Candy" Lightner was an American woman who had faced a personal tragedy: a drunk driver had killed her daughter. She launched a campaign of raising awareness and pressuring governments to deal with this issue. MADD spread like wildfire in the United States. Only three years later there were 350 local chapters. In 1989 the organization moved into Canada, and local groups emerged throughout the 1990s. Opponents of MADD have described the organization as a reincarnation of the "dry" organizations of earlier in the century, but MADD spokespersons have defended their position by insisting that they campaign not against alcohol itself but against the consequences of drunkenness. For MADD, this meant shaming and criminalizing those who drove their vehicles under the influence of alcohol. Sensing the extent of negative public reaction toward drunk drivers who killed innocent people, the liquor industry came to support MADD. After all, the industry maintained, drinking itself was not at fault; rather it was how much people drank and how they behaved once they were under the influence of alcohol that posed problems. Individuals, therefore, and not the industry were responsible for their own alcohol use and should assume the consequences of their actions.[107]

Since the 1990s, the attempt to exert state control through the criminal law has received much attention through successful lobbying by MADD. The group has advocated changes such as a mandatory prison sentences for repeat offenders, and lowering the legal blood alcohol content for drivers, first from 0.10% to 0.08%, and later to 0.05%.

Some groups, such as Quebec's Comité permanent de lutte à la toxicomanie, have pushed the idea of targeting individuals with "high-risk alcohol consumption" and "reduc[ing] the harm associated with that consumption." For these groups, state policies should focus on ways of reducing alcohol abuse and its harmful consequences.[108] This has meant setting up programs, such as Opération Nez Rouge (Operation Red Nose), to change the behaviour of people who drink. Founded in 1984 by mathematics professor and head coach of the swimming team at Laval University, Jean-Marie De Koninck, this organization offers rides home with volunteers to individuals who have been drinking. De Koninck started Operation Red Nose out of his concern that more than 50 percent of fatal car accidents were due to impaired drivers. Since individuals who drink in public places are reluctant to leave their cars behind, De Koninck came up with the idea of offering these individuals the possibility of being driven back home in their own car. The first Operation Red Nose started in December 1984, and the initiative has mushroomed elsewhere in Canada, particularly during the end-of-year holiday season. In Quebec it has been used to raise funds for the Laval swimming team. In other parts of the country the proceeds of have been given to youth and amateur sports organizations.[109]

Thus, although the Criminal Code addresses and provides sanctions against impaired driving, an educational approach has also been used effectively to change drinking behaviour. These campaigns have targeted young people, and MADD and Operation Red Nose have both attempted to change Canadians' relationship with drinking. The liquor industry itself, government

Cartoonist Aislin (Terry Mosher) alludes to a new attitude toward alcohol: If you drink, you should not drive—leave your keys with the bartender. *Drunk Drivers*, November 25, 1987, McCord Museum, M987.217.114.

liquor boards, police forces, and the media have repeatedly hammered home the message "If you drink, don't drive." The trend to appoint a "designated," sober driver to transport friends and relatives who have been drinking is a notable result of these concerted efforts.

A NEW ADDICT: GOVERNMENTS AND GAMBLING

In 1892, gambling activities had been declared illegal in Canada. Although the federal legislature had amended the Criminal Code over the years to include some exceptions—notably allowing lotteries and gambling for charitable purposes, and at agricultural fairs and exhibitions—Canadians who gambled were taking part in a criminal activity. But, depending on where they lived in the country, they did not always have to worry too much about breaking the law. The province of Quebec was notorious for not enforcing the Criminal Code provisions, which made a city like Montreal a paradise for gamblers. The reluctance of Quebec police forces to enforce the federal policy stemmed from their perception that there were more pressing forms of crime to be concerned about. The Roman Catholic Church did not favour gambling prohibition and continued to request an exemption for its gambling activities organized for fundraising purposes. Quebec municipal politicians also joined the campaign for a more liberal gambling policy. Against the backdrop of the Great Depression in 1933 and again in 1936, Montreal mayor Camillien Houde proposed a city lottery to help the unemployed and invited the Quebec government to press the federal government to amend the Criminal code. After 1945 the Montreal city council pushed without much success the idea of a lottery for charitable purposes. Quebec's provincial politicians put forward a new narrative and encouraged their federal counterparts to soften their public policy on gambling. Because of the Great Depression, the province invoked in 1934 its delicate budgetary situation and pleaded for lotteries as a new source of revenue. If they were allowed, the provincial government would be able to increase spending on welfare and education. In 1950, the Maurice Duplessis government promoted the creation of a provincial lottery. This time, the revenues would be allocated to education and hospitals. However, the federal government refused to change the Criminal Code.[110]

The province of Quebec was not the only government to argue in favour of liberalizing gambling policy. British Columbia politicians also pressed for change. Furthermore, sometimes citizens themselves took the initiative. In a referendum held in 1932, Vancouver residents voted for the legalization of lotteries. In 1934, the Victoria city council passed a resolution demanding the legalization of lotteries.

Although these initiatives were insufficient to change the federal government policy on gambling,[111] the appeals rang out as far as Parliament Hill in Ottawa, and during the Great Depression, the Senate debated various bills regarding the legalization of lotteries.[112] However, political will was insufficient to amend the Criminal Code in the face of vocal and passionate gambling opponents. Protestant churches were particularly resistant. They reminded politicians, and others who wanted to weaken the federal policy, that gambling destroyed individuals and their families, both morally and financially. Furthermore, gambling as a social fundraising activity undermined philanthropic work.

Gamblers and proponents of a more liberal gambling policy had to wait until 1967 for a major public policy shift. As a part of the omnibus bill, Minister of Justice Pierre E. Trudeau introduced amendments to the Criminal Code that authorized the provinces and the federal government to operate lotteries.

Other institutions could also operate lotteries, provided they received a provincial licence. In the latter case, the lottery had to be operated for charitable purposes.

These changes resulted from mobilization by new pressure groups. Powerful forces had developed a new narrative for gambling and gradually silenced opponents, such as Protestant religious organizations and women's groups. These forces were part of a broad coalition that included private interests eager for profit and churches and charitable organizations that relied on gambling to subsidize their philanthropic activities. Proponents argued that gambling was a respectable activity that could raise money for the public good. In addition, public opinion had shifted. When asked about gambling in national surveys, Canadians were now expressing their preference for a more liberal policy. Public support for legalized lotteries and sweepstakes was at 69 percent in 1955, 73 percent in 1967, and 79 percent when the federal government amended the Criminal Code in 1969.[113]

The loose coalition in favour of gambling counted on the support of municipal politicians who believed that it was in the state's best interest to take control away from criminal elements. Besides the Quebec and British Columbia governments, other provincial governments now reached the conclusion that the time had come to reverse course on the gambling issue. In the 1960s, the Ontario government appointed a committee—the Morton Committee on Gambling—to review lottery, gambling, and sports betting activities. The committee concluded, in unequivocal terms, that the federal policy was a complete failure: "Attempts to enforce morality in these areas were futile, encouraged underground criminality, and undermined respect for the law."[114] The committee observed that attempts at enforcement were ineffectual, and that the federal government should change its policy based on the "lottery for a legitimate purpose" argument. In justifying the creation of provincial lotteries, politicians explained that the profits generated by lottery tickets sales would be spent on welfare programs and other socially oriented initiatives that would be for the greater public good. Anticipating arguments from opponents, they emphasized that prohibition as a public policy was a failure and did not prevent individuals from gambling. Since large numbers of Canadians chose to violate the law, their behaviour, and the lack of enforcement, undermined the law as a deterrent. When politicians and gambling proponents acknowledged the persuasive force of this kind of social disobedience, they also decried the consequences of leaving the criminal underworld in charge of gambling. They believed citizens would become victims of criminal elements who would prey upon those who became financially vulnerable because of their losses. If there were a state monopoly, they argued, indebted gamblers would not have to fear for their safety, unlike what they would face if they were unable to repay debts contracted with criminal elements, biker gangs, or the Mafia. In order to put an end to a failed policy and deliver a serious blow to the criminal world, the federal government now considered the state monopoly of gambling a better public policy.[115]

The Quebec government was the first to take advantage of the changes to the Criminal Code and created a lottery. The other provinces followed suit, and even the federal government instituted Lotto-Canada, to finance the costs of the 1976 Montreal Olympics. The federal initiative became an additional source of tension in the already acrimonious field of provincial and federal relations. When the Progressive Conservative Party came to power for a brief period in 1979, Prime Minister Joe Clark announced that the federal government was no longer in the lottery business and would leave the field to

Cartoonist Serge Chapleau refers to the new narrative of using gambling revenues to finance health care and welfare programs: *Video Poker Revenues to Be Directed to Health Care/"Better luck next time ...,"* 2001. McCord Museum, M2002.131.6.

provinces. In 1985, the federal government of Progressive Conservative Brian Mulroney further amended the Criminal Code to give provincial governments exclusive jurisdiction over lotteries. At the same time, slot and video poker machines were legalized and put under provincial control. With the creation of casinos, state involvement in gambling activities continued to increase. The first provincially operated casino opened its doors in Winnipeg in 1989, and others sprang up across the country in the following years. Some Aboriginal communities, inspired by similar initiatives by American Indians, decided to invest resources in building and operating casinos.[116] More recently, governments have further expanded the range of gambling activities under state control. In 2010, the Ontario Lottery and Gaming Corporation announced that it would offer online gambling, in order to tap into the more than $400 million Ontarians spent every year on gambling websites operating outside of the country.[117]

The decision in the 1990s by provincial governments to operate casinos triggered a public debate. Provincial governments stressed the economic spinoffs and benefits, not only for communities where casinos were built, but also for society in general. They claimed that casinos would be net job creators. Also, they would be part of the redevelopment of urban areas affected by the closure of factories. They would attract tourist dollars and would constitute a "lucrative" source of revenue for the government, allowing it to keep personal income and other tax rates low. Thus, in the middle of an economic recession in the 1990s, provincial governments, such as those of Quebec and Ontario, authorized the opening of casinos. Twenty years later, the Ontario government made the construction of a casino in Toronto a key component of its deficit-fighting strategy.

Politicians and other government officials also stressed the "social" benefits of casinos. Individuals who liked to gamble and those looking for new leisure activities could now go to a well run, state-owned casino facility. At the same time, the expansion of state-controlled gambling activities posed a dilemma for politicians. While elected officials had found a surefire way to increase revenues, they had to come to terms with the fact that the state bore responsibility for individuals who developed an addiction.[118]

Consequently, while desirous to undermine opposition to state gambling activities, the government apparatus developed and advertised prevention strategies and programs for gambling addiction. During the nineteenth century, moral reformers had attributed this behaviour to a lack of self-control. Now, in 1980, the American Psychiatric Association labelled gambling addiction a mental illness. Consequently, individuals who had this mental illness would require health-oriented treatments. At the same time, gamblers themselves pushed for the medicalization of their condition. Gamblers Anonymous, which emerged in Los Angeles in the 1950s, influenced the debate on how to deal with individuals who were addicted to gambling or who demonstrated signs of compulsive gambling. They challenged those who argued that gamblers could put an end to their destructive habit if only they had the will to do so, by contending that it was not a matter of will, but rather of illness. These organizations shaped the Canadian debate on gambling, since gamblers and members of the medical community used these developments to promote a health-oriented solution for compulsive gamblers.[119]

The debate over the government's role in helping to treat problem gamblers is ongoing. Newspaper reports on studies and investigations that assess the effectiveness of government programs for problem gamblers have found they have inadequate resources or are not systematically enforced. For instance, casinos have programs built around the concept of "responsible" gambling, where individuals can register for a self-exclusion program. They may be denied access due to their recognized addiction or forced to leave the premises if their financial losses are excessive.

Investigations revealing poor enforcement have led opponents to ask if the financial benefits from gambling compromise the state's interest in helping addicted gamblers. A 2009 study published in the *Globe and Mail* revealed that one-third of government gambling revenue came from addicted gamblers. Casinos have also developed incentives—gifts, such as free tickets to cultural and sport events, and subsidies directly to bus companies that transport players—for regular players, including individuals with a gambling addiction. Loto-Québec has been by far the most generous of Canadian lottery and gaming corporations in subsidizing privately owned bus companies for bringing in customers—often senior citizens—when casinos are not crowded.[120] News reporting on gamblers is often augmented with personal stories of addiction and of the tragedies—excessive debt burden, divorce, depression, and sometimes suicide—that befall some individuals. In reaction to their financial losses, some have launched lawsuits against governments. In ruling on a claim brought forth by Paul Burrell of Nova Scotia, the province's Supreme Court found that there was no "legal basis to find the province or casino responsible for the actions of problem gamblers."[121]

According to opponents, the liberalization of gambling has led provincial governments to develop an "addiction" to gambling revenues. Ostensibly, with the rise of neoliberalism and of the notion that corporate taxes must be decreased to create a favourable environment for investors and job creators, state control of gambling activities has offered an enticing, if not irresistible way to increase revenues, while benefiting from an activity that some would

Table 2   Gambling Revenues as Share of Provincial Budget

Provinces	1999-2000	2003-2004
Alberta	4.58%	5.10%
British Columbia	2.50%	5.50%
Manitoba	4.01%	2.90%
New Brunswick	2.59%	3.50%
Newfoundland	4.41%	4.30%
Nova Scotia	5.08%	4.30%
Ontario	3.37%	3.80%
Prince Edward Island	2.19%	3.00%
Quebec	3.06%	3.30%
Saskatchewan	4.68%	4.60%

Source: Jason J. Azmier, *Gambling in Canada 2001: An Overview* (Calgary: Canadian West Foundation, 2001), 3; *Gambling in Canada 2005: Statistics and Context* (Calgary: Canadian West Foundation, 2005), 7.

still regard as sinful. Table 2 demonstrates that gambling has constituted an important source of revenues for provincial governments. Some governments have even been contemplating ways to increase the profitability of gambling. Commenting on the possibility of contracting out the lottery in Ontario, Premier Kathleen Wynne acknowledged that "what we need to do is make sure that we're maximizing that revenue stream."[122] The Ontario Lottery and Gaming Corporation "brought $3.2-billion in revenue" in 2012 and "$1-billion in profit" to the provincial government.[123]

DRUGS: LET'S HELP YOUNG WHITE KIDS

In 1923, in their ceaseless campaign against drugs, moral reformers scored another victory. That year, the federal government criminalized the possession, trafficking, importation, and exportation of marijuana. At this time, although marijuana was not an issue of public concern, it was for a few moral reformers. These individuals counted on those in positions of authority to use their power to transform their demands into law. One of these moral reformers was Alberta judge Emily Murphy, the first woman appointed, in 1916, to the judiciary. Before being appointed police magistrate for Edmonton and later for Alberta, Murphy was involved in the national campaign for women to get the right to vote. Drug use also concerned her. As a judge, she handled cases of Chinese individuals charged with illicit drug use. She also toured Vancouver drug dens and observed first-hand what drug use did to people.

These experiences prompted her to write articles for *Maclean's* magazine and to publish *The Black Candle*, a book painting an alarming picture of drug use in the country. By the end of her book, readers would likely wonder why the state was not doing something to prevent individuals from using substances that had severe health, social, and moral consequences.[124] With Murphy's book in hand, moral reformers put pressure on the federal government. Prime Minister Mackenzie King, who was known for his anti-drug views, rose to the challenge with new legislation.

But until the 1960s, drug use in general was not a significant public concern. Newspapers printed occasional stories of people arrested for possession and of others addicted to opiates. Police forces were particularly active in the enforcement of the federal drug legislation. Arrests and crackdowns on drug users, who were mostly white, urban, working-class men living in British Columbia, helped the RCMP to justify its requests for additional human and financial resources. By and large, physicians, who found that drug addicts tended to be difficult patients, left the field to law enforcement officers. Nevertheless, after 1945 the development of the disease narrative for drug addiction, like that for alcoholism, gained some supporters within the medical community. Despite that, physicians did not question the state's approach of sending drug users and addicts to jail for a short or long period of time, depending on the nature of their offence. Social workers were another group that asserted its authority when it came to controlling drug use. They claimed a right to rehabilitate drug users, but like physicians, they did not challenge the state drug policy founded on repression.[125]

In 1961, the federal government revised its drug legislation by increasing the penalties. The Narcotic Control Act included cocaine, heroin, marijuana, morphine, and opium in the definition of a narcotic. These changes reflected the new commitments that Canada had undertaken after signing an international agreement, the 1961 Single Convention on Narcotic Drugs. Among other terms, this agreement forced its signatories to repress marijuana use. The maximum penalty for anyone convicted of trafficking, importing, or exporting increased from 14 years in prison to a life sentence. In the case of possession, the maximum penalty was raised to seven years in jail. In spite of these longer potential prison terms, legislators agreed with health professionals that rehabilitation and treatment for drug addicts would require more flexible sentencing. As a result, the Narcotic Control Act gave judges the discretion to send a drug addict to a treatment centre.[126]

With the emergence of counterculture in Canada and the rest of the industrialized world during the 1960s, a wave of new drug experimentation and habits emerged: individuals took LSD and other hallucinogens, and smoked marijuana more regularly. In 1963, Harvard University dismissed Dr. Timothy Leary after he administered LSD to his students. His dismissal did not end his career. On the contrary, he toured the United States and promoted drugs as a means to unleash inner energy and creativity. American poet Allen Ginsberg pushed actively for the legalization of marijuana.

News reports fanned the flames of a moral panic, fuelled by police officers, concerned parents, and medical experts who maintained that an increasing number of young people were consuming illegal drugs. Sometimes the new drugs were blamed for deaths, as in the case of John Stern, a 20-year-old music student who committed suicide in Toronto in 1967. The *Globe and Mail* headline was unequivocal regarding the cause of the death: "Sampled LSD, Youth Plunges from Viaduc [*sic*]."[127] The father blamed drug proponents like Leary for his son's death and urged politicians to ban the deadly substance. Print and televised media emphasized the grave harm that drug users inflicted on their bodies. For example, sniffing glue could cause serious brain damage. Some expressed the fear that experimenting with an illegal drug, even only once, could be sufficient to lead to addiction or to encourage consumption of more powerful opiates.[128]

Marijuana use became a social phenomenon. Young people and many from the middle class smoked marijuana, knowingly defying the law and challenging the social order. Among young people, hippies symbolized the rebellious youth spirit, an eagerness to create a more open society that would allow creativity and free spirit to rule. By embracing marijuana, young adults, university students, and hippies gave a political focus to their action and forced a debate on the regulation of illicit drugs. They questioned the logic of criminalizing marijuana, while more powerful, legal drugs, prescribed by physicians and protected by what they referred to as the "medical establishment," remained freely available and could cause much more harm to the body than a puff of marijuana. They challenged the "habit-forming and dangerous step towards stronger drugs" narrative that was used to justify the criminalization of marijuana. They emphasized personal freedom and argued that the possession of marijuana was, after all, a harmless activity that involved only the user him or herself. The defiant gesture of smoking a joint in public proclaimed that repression as a state policy was a failure, and, since a growing number of people were picking up the marijuana habit, the defiant hippies put the power of the law as a deterrent to the test.[129]

Physicians were divided over marijuana use. This drug was central to a larger debate over how physicians should handle the new social habit of consuming drugs for non-medicinal purposes. Although some physicians doubted that drug use was inherently harmful and pointed out that Canadians lived in a society that relied on drugs for medical cures and various acceptable forms of leisure, others shared the opponents' fears of the short- and long-term consequences of illegal drugs for an individual's health. The latter were resolute in decrying the dangers of marijuana, even while they acknowledged that studies on the matter had proved inconclusive. Some physicians dismissed the inconclusive studies and argued it was better to be cautious than to let people indulge in drugs and face potentially dire outcomes.

The thalidomide crisis reinforced this cautious approach. At the beginning of the 1960s, physicians prescribed this drug to pregnant women to suppress morning sickness. Although the drug was approved by the medical community, disturbing news reports were soon appearing about "thalidomide babies" born with missing arms and legs. In 1962, the federal government banned the drug, but this episode gave a black eye to the medical community and the pharmaceutical industry.[130]

Besides adhering to the cautionary principle, which encouraged physicians and the Canadian Medical Association to oppose the legalization of marijuana, the medical establishment also wanted to protect its territory from additional state drug regulation. Physicians, but in particular the drug industry and the Council on Drug Abuse, spent time and energy to establish a clear distinction between abuse and misuse. Fearing an expansion of state control, the drug industry reminded Canadians that legal drugs did not kill people unless they were misused. In the case of illegal drugs, they were always abused and raised the likelihood of death.[131]

Drug proponents exploited the divisions within the medical community to promote their cause. Marijuana users argued that physicians simply wanted to protect their position of authority and their monopoly over health issues. The debate on the dangers of marijuana use among physicians demonstrated, according to proponents, that non-scientific concerns, such as values, beliefs, and biases, tainted their "scientific" judgment.

The ranks of marijuana opponents included several groups: concerned parents, anxious religious leaders, alarmed teachers, local and provincial police officers, politicians, and judges. In the context of the intergenerational conflicts that had arisen in the sixties, opponents of illicit drugs opted for a repressive approach. Since the medical community could not definitively state the long-term health effects of an illicit drug such as marijuana, opponents pressed government officials to keep these substances illegal and to repress those who possessed, cultivated, imported, exported, and sold them. They argued that legal control over drugs would best serve the public interest. However, these same opponents sometimes felt uncomfortable when the authoritarian approach affected white adolescents and adults who were arrested in possession of marijuana. Under these circumstances, the moral crusaders wondered if repression was actually the best approach.

The state addressed the drug issue by offering a variety of sometimes contradictory solutions. The drug debate pitted health departments against the Royal Canadian Mounted Police. In their attempts to provide some answers and offer viable public policy options, provincial health departments and the federal Department of Health and Welfare drew on the expertise of institutions such as the Addiction Research Foundation of Ontario, the Narcotic Addiction Foundation of British Columbia, and Quebec's Office de la prévention et du traitement de l'alcoolisme et des autres toxicomanies. Provincial governments had set up these organizations to assist them in designing educational and treatment programs concerning alcohol and drug use in schools and in society in general. These organizations and health departments believed that a scientific approach, in which health treatments would be paramount, was the best option in the current context of moral panic over illicit drug use. They developed a strategy to assess how many users there were and to analyze the health effects of specific illegal drugs, marijuana in particular. In their attempts to determine the number of users, the extent of usage, and the type of drugs, the vast majority of such studies were conducted among high school students in urban centres. Investigators either asked participants to self-report or to indicate how many individuals they knew who used drugs. In 1970, findings showed that a certain number of youths had tried marijuana, but their numbers were below 20 percent. This was still a significant increase from studies conducted two years earlier, when less than 10 percent of students had reported using marijuana at least once.[132] Studies of university students in 1969 and in 1970 reported that about 20 percent of them had used marijuana.

Scientists were cautious when interpreting these results. Since the public debate was about drugs as a social problem, addiction foundations insisted that it was not illicit drugs, but alcohol that was more of a problem. If society wanted a serious debate about drug use and misuse and about how to educate Canadians on these issues, it should focus its resources on alcohol. At the same time, most provincial health departments and the federal Department of Health and Welfare believed that educational programs and clinical treatments were superior to any fear-mongering campaigns aimed at discouraging individuals from experimenting with drugs.[133]

In reaction to the number of marijuana offences committed under the Narcotic Control Act, the RCMP took an alarmist stance. Their data indicated a trend toward increased drug use, which had not yet reached a plateau at the end of the 1960s. In their eyes, this was sufficient grounds on which to conclude that Canada had a serious drug problem. To eradicate the problem, the RCMP pleaded for repression. They argued that easing drug policies at this time was misguided and that doing so would exacerbate the problem. The RCMP feared that any move toward softening public policy on marijuana would encourage drug proponents to press for additional changes.[134]

The situation of members of the white middle class—some women, but mostly men—who occasionally smoked marijuana became a social concern. The Commission of Inquiry into the Non-Medical Use of Drugs, known as the Le Dain Commission, estimated that up to 1.5 million Canadians had used marijuana by 1970. Confronted with this situation, the federal government thought that legalization was not an option, but decriminalization should be considered in a bid to prevent these people from carrying criminal records. In a speech at the annual meeting of the Canadian Pharmaceutical Association on August 19, 1968, Minister of National Health and Welfare John Munro stated that he doubted "giving criminal records to several thousand curious kids each year serves any very worthwhile social purpose." Although the minister condemned marijuana use, he questioned the legal approach: "The teenager who tries pot at a Saturday night party because someone has some and passes it around and everyone else tries it may be very foolish, but he isn't a criminal, at least not in the sense that I think of criminals."[135]

RCMP and Toronto Drug Squad officers seized more than 150 pounds of marijuana on November 22, 1968. York University Libraries, Clara Thomas Archives & Special Collections, Toronto Telegram fonds, ASC00718.

The federal government amended its legislation in 1969. An individual arrested in possession of cannabis could be tried by either summary conviction—a maximum sentence of up to six months in jail and/or a $1,000 fine for a first offence and twelve months in jail and/or a $2,000 fine for subsequent offences—or indictment, which carried a sentence of up to seven years. The federal government had contemplated the possibility of decriminalizing marijuana, but abandoned the idea. In contrast to the legal regime regarding liquor and sexual deviance, international treaties and conventions constrained the federal government's ability to formulate an independent drug policy. Civil servants asserted that Canada's international obligations meant legalization was out of the question. Canada and the United States had been leaders in making the case that drug use affected every country and required a co-ordinated international response. Following the Second World War, and especially with the growth of recreational drug use in the 1960s, there were renewed efforts, initiated primarily by the United States, to reduce the worldwide supply of drugs by strengthening the international system of drug control. Canada subscribed to the overall goal of reducing illicit traffic and ensuring a stable drug supply for medical and research activities. It was among the first countries to ratify the Single Convention on Narcotic Drugs in 1961.[136]

South of the border, President Richard Nixon launched his war on drugs—something he hoped would become international in scope—and marijuana became a prime target. He did not hesitate to close the border with Mexico for a few days in 1969, due to what he considered to be the lack of commitment on the part of Mexican authorities in repressing the illegal trade. Fearing similar consequences if Canada did not take the war on drugs seriously, drug opponents continued to make their case for stricter controls to the federal government.[137]

The marijuana issue re-emerged in the 1990s. Pot advocates updated their narrative and argued that marijuana use was beneficial to individuals suffering from multiple sclerosis and AIDS.[138] In an attempt to force politicians' hands, individuals asked the courts to grant them the right to smoke. In 2000, the Alberta Court of Queen's Bench ruled that the federal drug policy was unconstitutional, since it did not allow medicinal marijuana. For its part, the Ontario Court of Appeal invalidated the legislation prohibiting possession of marijuana and gave the federal government 12 months to reconsider its options.[139] In reaction, the Department of Health issued the Marijuana Medical Access Regulations. Under these new regulations, critically ill individuals and those with chronic illnesses could legally use marijuana with the permission of a committee of two physicians.[140] Like opponents who had rejected the therapeutic abortion committees set up in 1969, those who needed marijuana for

Amid debate over the medicinal properties of marijuana, cartoonist Aislin (Terry Mosher) antici-
pated the day when Canadians would get marijuana at the drugstore: *Marijuana as Pain-Killer*, 1998.
McCord Museum, M2002.119.35.

medical reasons, and others critical of the federal drug legislation, denounced
the policy. Furthermore, the Canadian Medical Association and local chiefs
of police, such as the Toronto chief of police, Julian Fantino, asked the federal
government to decriminalize marijuana.[141]

Parliamentarians intervened in the debate. The Senate Special Committee on Illegal Drugs, formed in 2000 and chaired by Senator Pierre Claude
Nolin, and the House of Commons Special Committee on Non-Medical Use
of Drugs, appointed a year later, agreed that the war on drugs was costly and
inefficient. They also acknowledged that the time had come to embrace the
harm-reduction approach and abandon repression. Each committee, however,
made a separate recommendation. The Senate Committee recommended the
legalization of marijuana and a state monopoly of its sale. The House of Commons Committee favoured decriminalization for possession and cultivation of

Some were surprised by the broad demographic that supported the legalization of marijuana: *Legalize Marijuana!,* Aislin (Terry Mosher), 1993. McCord Museum, M997.53.92.

marijuana of less than 30 grams. But even the Commons Committee members disagreed among themselves, since the conservative Canadian Alliance MPs recommended a lesser amount: 6 grams.[142]

Ultimately, the federal government dropped the legalization of marijuana, since this option violated both the 1988 United Nations Convention Against Illicit Traffic in Narcotic Drugs and Psychotropic Substances, and the 1961 Single Convention on Narcotic Drugs. Instead, in May 2003, Jean Chrétien's Liberal government introduced a bill decriminalizing the possession of less than 15 grams of marijuana.[143] The Canadian Association of Chiefs of Police and the American government both lobbied to kill the proposal. The United States ambassador to Canada and the U.S. National Drug Control Policy director warned Canadians and the federal government that decriminalization was not an option. It did not sit well with the American war on drugs, and there was a fear that British Columbia pot growers would inundate the United States with their product.[144]

Over the last years, some U.S. states—Colorado and Washington—have legalized marijuana. In Canada, the debate resurfaced in 2013. In July, the leader of the Liberal Party, Justin Trudeau, suggested legalizing marijuana since the drug policy based on repression has been a failure, a judgment shared by some legal experts and health specialists. For its part, the NDP favours the decriminalization of marijuana for possession of small quantities. Although opposed to these public policy options, the Harper government is exploring the Canadian Chiefs of Police's proposal of imposing a fine for anyone in possession of a small amount of marijuana. This may become an issue during the next federal election, scheduled to take place in 2015.

TOBACCO: A HEALTH THREAT AND AN ANNOYING HABIT

Smoking continued to be a popular and generally accepted activity during the first half of the twentieth century. In 1971, 47 percent of the Canadian population aged 15 and over smoked. For men, smoking was a rite of passage to adulthood. For women, smoking in the privacy of their own and their friends' homes was not a concern, but it was a different story if they claimed the right to smoke in public. Only with the emergence of the "new woman" as an ideal of feminine equality in the 1920s did smoking in public places begin to become respectable for women.[145]

The number of women who smoked varied considerably, according to cultural factors. For example, "a private survey conducted by the Canadian Daily Newspaper Association in 1956 indicated that about 68 per cent of francophone women in Montreal and 28 per cent of Anglophones admitted to smoking." In 1965, official data on the number of smokers became available and Canadians learned that 39 percent of women and 62 percent of men smoked.[146] However, there was no indication of the number of cigarettes that women smoked daily.

The consumption of cigarettes increased partly because of a social environment supportive of a tobacco culture. For instance, Canadians sent cigarettes overseas to soldiers during the Second World War. But the tobacco industry was also active in supporting this culture. It developed marketing strategies, first in print media, then in movies and on the radio, and beginning in 1952 on television, which had begun to transform the communications landscape. Marketing campaigns reinforced the notion that smoking was a highly fashionable activity and a respectable pastime. Advertisements included images of women smoking cigarettes as being sexy, sophisticated, or empowered.

Woman smoking, *Toronto Telegram*, January 29, 1966. York
University Libraries, Clara Thomas Archives & Special Collections, Toronto Telegram fonds, ASC00717.

Cigarette ads told women that smoking was sexy and empowering: billboard advertising Winchester
cigarettes, 1940. Glenbow Archives, NA-4072-38.

Tobacco ads shaped culture and targeted in particular young people by populating their minds with characters such as the Marlboro man.[147]

Opponents of tobacco use failed in their fight to enforce prohibition as a public policy. Although they convinced most provinces—except Quebec and Manitoba—to prohibit the sale of tobacco products to minors, the provincial regulations were ineffective and enforcement agencies had few resources.[148] Despite their conviction and enthusiasm, anti-tobacco campaigners faced a decidedly steep uphill battle as their opponents—including a tobacco industry protecting its own interests—were well organized, resourceful, and capable of mounting a powerful lobby and sustaining it for the long haul. Furthermore, they fought against a socially acceptable habit. Nevertheless, opponents of tobacco use refused to throw in the towel.

The tide turned in their favour with the emergence of studies on the health consequences of smoking. At the end of the nineteenth century, as mentioned in the previous chapter, the narrative justifying prohibition had been based on notions of exercising self-control and declining to use a substance, even if naturally grown, to find pleasure. The health dangers of smoking now shaped a new narrative. It was in the 1950s that the first scientific reports on the health consequences of tobacco use were released. Though these studies linked tobacco use to illnesses such as lung cancer, most of them never reached the mainstream media. For its part, the Canadian Cancer Society stated that there was a possible link between cancer and smoking in 1951. A decade later, the narrative on health risks gained momentum. On June 17, 1963, in the House of Commons, Minister of National Health and Welfare Judy LaMarsh declared that there was "scientific evidence that cigarette smoking is a contributory cause of lung cancer, and that it may also be associated with chronic bronchitis and coronary hearth disease."[149] Following this statement, LaMarsh announced that the federal government would launch a campaign in 1965 to discourage Canadians from smoking. Since the minister was preoccupied with youths, she assembled some of them to meet with health experts at a conference in Ottawa and discussed strategies for discouraging youths from smoking.[150] Seven months after LaMarsh's declaration in the House of Commons, in January 1964 the U.S. Surgeon General's Advisory Committee on Smoking and Health, established by the Kennedy administration, released a report linking serious illnesses, including lung cancer, heart disease, and pulmonary emphysema, to smoking cigarettes. However, the committee did not state categorically that nicotine led to smoking addiction: "Smokers and users of tobacco in other forms usually develop some degree of dependence upon the practice, some to the point where significant emotional disturbances occur if they are deprived of its use." According to the committee, "evidence indicates this dependence to be psychogenic in origin."[151] Canadian smokers reacted to the U.S. report by reducing their cigarette consumption, but only momentarily.[152]

The tobacco industry fought back by questioning the validity of existing scientific studies on health effects and preparing to launch studies of its own. In 1954, the Big Six tobacco companies (Philip Morris, R.J. Reynolds, Lorillard, American Tobacco, Liggett and Myers, and Brown and Williamson) formed a research group called the Tobacco Industry Research Council, to study "the effects of smoking on the body." In fact, it spent its resources on a public relations campaign. The industry questioned the methodology of scientific research that had linked cancer and smoking, raised doubts about researchers' conclusions, and insisted that further studies were required, since there was "no conclusive scientific evidence."[153] They reminded governments that any public policy leaning toward prohibition would fail, as demonstrated by the failure of alcohol prohibition, both in Canada and particularly in the United States. They also insisted that smoking was a personal choice, and that consequently people could quit smoking if they wished. This last assertion denied any link between nicotine and addiction.[154] Moreover, the tobacco industry developed new types of cigarettes and marketed them as "safer" in the 1950s. New filtered cigarettes were labelled as "the greatest health protection in cigarette history."[155] But promoting a safer product was tricky. By marketing cigarettes as "safer," Pamela Pennock argues, the tobacco industry tacitly indicated "there was something dangerous" about their product.[156] In 1976, the industry introduced "light" cigarettes to the market. Light cigarettes had a lower tar level than "regular" cigarettes. These new cigarettes became extremely popular and had captured 40.1 percent of the cigarette market by 1979.[157]

In the second half of the 1960s, the anti-smoking lobby used education as a weapon in their battle. They did not ask for a ban but instead promoted educational campaigns on the ill effects of smoking and advocated for the mandatory placement of warning labels on cigarette packages. However, the anti-smoking lobby underestimated both the power of the industry to convey its views to policy-makers and the addictive power of cigarettes. Subsequently, the anti-smoking coalition has launched a series of initiatives to reduce the number of smokers and the risks associated with smoking and has pressured governments to use their regulatory powers to influence the conduct of smokers. Its ranks have included individual physicians, groups such as Physicians for a Smoke-Free Canada, which was founded in 1985; the Canadian Cancer Society; and municipal, provincial, and federal departments of health. More recently, current and former smokers, themselves ill from cigarette use, have joined this broad coalition. Before their deaths respectively in 2003 and 2006, Barb Tarbox, a former model who died of brain and lung cancer at the age

One Tobacco-related Death Every 8 Seconds, by Serge Chapleau, 1999. McCord Museum, M2001.99.59.

of 41, and Heather Crowe, a waitress who claimed to have developed lung cancer from second-hand smoke in her work environment, became powerful advocates warning about the deadly effects of second-hand smoke.

Since governments have targeted education and the dissemination of information on the dangers of smoking cigarettes, the tobacco industry has reacted by undermining the call for greater state intervention. In June 1964, the tobacco industry announced that its members would comply with a 10-rule code setting "standards of cigarettes advertising." According to this code, cigarettes would not be advertised "immediately adjacent" to schools. Advertisements would target only adults and they would not be broadcast on television before 9 p.m. Furthermore, the tobacco industry would not promote the idea that cigarettes were "essential to romance, prominence, success, or personal advancement" and would abstain from stating that "smoking a particular brand is better for health than smoking any other brand of cigarettes."[158] The industry's decision to self-regulate worked in pre-empting legislative action. The federal government was reluctant to interfere with the ability of the industry to advertise its products. But the number of studies linking smoking to lung cancer and other diseases increased tremendously in the 1970s. Furthermore, the industry's code did not work since manufacturers could refuse to comply with it, as did Rothmans of Pall Mall in 1985. These studies and the inability of the industry to self-regulate convinced the anti-smoking coalition, in particular the Canadian Cancer Society and government health officials, that the tobacco industry's ability to advertise had to be circumscribed so that the counter-narrative, linking smoking to cancer, would have its full impact on smokers. By 1988, the state offensive against tobacco marketing restricted the industry's sponsorship of cultural and sports events. Furthermore, the federal government obliged the tobacco industry to put warning labels on their products. The Tobacco Products Control Act authorized Health Canada to regulate the content of the health warning messages. During the same period and pressured by the anti-smoking lobby, leading newspapers announced that they would no longer print tobacco advertising, and CBC made a similar announcement. Starting in 1988, the public broadcaster no longer accepted ads from the tobacco industry.[159] But the industry scored a victory against the federal government in 1995. The Supreme Court of Canada ruled that a total ban "on tobacco advertising was an unjustified infringement" of the Charter of Rights and Freedoms. Although a majority of judges would allow a partial ban, they claimed that the federal government "failed to introduce evidence to demonstrate that attributed health warnings would be any less effective than unattributed warnings."[160] Following the court decision, the tobacco industry announced that it would continue to self-regulate and limit advertisements.

Despite this setback, the coalition scored a series of decisive victories as it pressured the government to require that the tobacco industry include on cigarette packages bigger labels, graphic images, and stronger warnings about the devastating long-term health effects. These new warning labels became a battleground between opponents to smoking and the industry. A further victory occurred in December 2010, when federal Minister of Health Leona Aglukkaq informed the tobacco industry they would have to incorporate even larger and more graphic warnings labels on their packages.[161]

The coalition also pressed the state to attack smokers in their wallets. Through increased taxes on cigarettes, the anti-smoking lobby hoped to achieve two goals: to reduce the number of smokers, and to hurt the tobacco industry financially. Although governments did increase taxes on tobacco products in the 1970s and the 1980s, there was a backlash, mounted partly by the tobacco industry. The high price of cigarettes at the end of the 1980s fuelled a tax revolt by smokers. Many of them began to buy contraband cigarettes on Aboriginal reserves near Cornwall and Montreal. The scale of this civil disobedience forced governments to lower taxes on tobacco products.

Although taxes on "sinful" activities are usually popular among voters, especially among those who abstain from a particular "vice" or "vices," there is a limit to a state's ability to increase taxes without triggering a taxpayers' revolt. Once the tobacco tax had reached a level that made substantial black market trading profitable, governments moved to revise their tax rates. In 1994, the federal government lowered tobacco excise taxes, and provincial governments in New Brunswick, Nova Scotia, Ontario, Quebec, and Prince Edward Island made similar cuts. At the time of this revolt, there were those who suspected the tobacco industry was involved in some way. News reports and an RCMP investigation confirmed that cigarettes destined for the American market had found their way back to Canada, and that the cigarette industry had turned a blind eye when their shipments "disappeared" and mysteriously reappeared on this side of the border. In 2003, JTI-Macdonald, Rothmans, Benson & Hedges, and Imperial Tobacco Canada Ltd. were charged with violating the federal Excise Act. Five years later, Rothmans, Benson & Hedges, and Imperial Tobacco Canada Ltd. pleaded guilty and admitted their role in smuggling, reaching an agreement with the Crown by which they would pay $1.15 billion to the federal government and ten provinces over a 15-year period.[162]

The anti-tobacco coalition also targeted the product's accessibility to consumers. In 1994, Ontario became the first province to ban the sale of cigarettes in drugstores and vending machines. This latter change made it increasingly difficult for adolescents and young adults to buy cigarettes, since it was illegal in the province to sell to anyone under the age of 19.[163]

As part of its campaign to reduce exposure to second-hand smoke, the anti-smoking coalition focused attention on spaces where smokers could light up. Opponents launched a series of campaigns to create smoke-free environments. First, the coalition targeted shared and public means of transportation such as buses, trains, and airplanes. However, the transportation industry was nervous about losing customers and passengers who smoked and were reluctant to impose a total smoking ban. For example, in 1985, the bus company Greyhound guaranteed that 50 percent of the seats on its buses would be reserved for non-smokers.[164] For its part, Voyageur Colonial opted to install plastic barriers separating smokers from non-smokers. A year later, the bus company offered entirely smoke-free buses on certain routes, before eventually banning smoking on all its buses. Via Rail started a policy of reserving two-thirds of its seats for non-smokers. In 1986, this Crown corporation restricted smoking to certain train cars, before banning it entirely. The same year, Air Canada offered domestic, smoke-free flights in the busy Montreal-Toronto-Ottawa triangle, and in 1987 the federal government announced a ban on smoking on domestic flights, which took effect in 1990. The federal

By creating smoke-free working environments, smokers have to either quit smoking or take breaks: *No Smoking Regulations*, by Aislin (Terry Mosher), 1987. McCord Museum, M987.244.29.

government targeted international flights but airlines argued that this deci-sion would be detrimental to their activities. Anti-smoking groups and flight-attendant unions pressed the federal government to go ahead anyway, which it did in 1994 despite opposition from airline companies.[165]

As well, the coalition targeted the workplace, and gradually, employers banned their employees from smoking on the job. Smokers who could not quit the habit had to smoke outside or in designated smoking areas. Going outside was a pleasant enough solution on a warm summer's day but dreadful in the depths of winter. The City of Toronto made workplaces smoke-free in 1999, and all the provinces followed suit during the next decade.[166] The enforce-ment of smoke-free workplaces also had to apply to the entertainment and restaurant industries. To compensate for the likelihood that smokers would boycott restaurants and bars where smoking was banned, these establishments were permitted to create designated smoking rooms within their premises, to be monitored by municipal and provincial health departments. Fearing colossal financial losses, many restaurant and bar owners condemned this interference with how they could conduct their business.

However, the expected consumer backlash did not materialize, partly because Canadians were awakening to the dangers of second-hand smoke. The tragic story of Heather Crowe, alluded to above, who worked for 40 years in Ottawa bars and restaurants, helped alert Canadians to these devastating effects. Although she never smoked in her life, Crowe learned in 2002 that she had lung cancer; she died four years later. After her diagnosis, she worked with Physicians for a Smoke-Free Canada. Crowe embarked on a speaking tour during which she shared her experience and encouraged Canadians to support people who worked in bars and restaurants and who put their lives on the line every day because of deadly second-hand smoke.[167] Since the beginning of the twenty-first century, all provinces have banned smoking in restaurants and bars, and Canadians are now accustomed to non-smoking environments. Governments have even targeted the notion of private space. Smoking in an automobile in the presence of a child is now an offence in all provinces and territories, except Alberta, Quebec, and the Northwest Territories. Since 2009, the government of British Columbia has forbidden individuals from smoking in an automobile if someone under the age of 16 is present. Enforcement constitutes the weakest link in this new offensive. Municipalities have also targeted outdoor areas. Recently cities like Barrie and Ottawa in Ontario, and Kelowna and Vancouver in British Columbia, have passed municipal bylaws forbidding smoking in municipal parks and on city beaches.[168] Although the anti-smoking coalition has applauded these measures, others have questioned their enforceability. Most cities posted signs and expected that individuals would comply with the ban, betting on the fact that Canadians have, for the past 40 years, internalized the assumption that they should restrict their smoking when they leave their own home.

Besides restricting access to cigarettes, educating smokers when they buy cigarettes, and reducing the ability to smoke in public, the anti-smoking coalition has developed a new weapon: lawsuits. Inspired by similar initiatives by some American states, provincial governments have been suing tobacco companies in the hope of recouping some of the health costs for the treatment of individuals with smoke-related illnesses. In 1998, the Quebec government sued JTI-Macdonald Corporation, Imperial Tobacco Canada, Rothmans, and Benson & Hedges Inc., seeking $10,000 in damages for each and every one of the estimated 1.8 million smokers in Quebec. After many delays and appeals, the case was argued before the Quebec Superior Court in 2012 (at the time of writing, the outcome was still to be decided).[169] In 2003, Kenneth Knight, a representative of a group of smokers in British Columbia, went to court against Imperial Tobacco Canada to press for financial compensation for being "tricked into thinking so-called mild or light cigarettes were less harmful than regular cigarettes."[170] Knight asked for a permanent injunction that would prevent Imperial Tobacco Canada "from marketing or selling 'light' or 'mild' cigarettes and a refund for all the cigarettes he and any other members of the class paid to purchase the allegedly misrepresented cigarettes."[171]

The tobacco industry has continued to fight back against these threats. Besides attacking the health dangers narrative, it has challenged governments that have obliged them to affix to their packages labels with graphic images of individuals dying of cancer. More recently, the industry has launched lawsuits to force the federal government to share the health costs that the industry has been asked to bear. The industry's argument—that governments permit individuals to smoke—has not been remarkably successful to date.[172] For instance, in the *Knight* case in 2004, Imperial Tobacco Canada argued that the government of Canada "should be required to pay any damages, should they be determined" since it manufactured light cigarettes "to comply with federal requirements."[173] However, the Supreme Court of Canada rejected the tobacco company's claim. In their decision in July 2011, the judges stated, "When Canada directed the tobacco industry about how it should conduct itself, it was doing so in its capacity as a government regulator that was concerned about the health of Canadians. Under such circumstances, it is unreasonable to infer that Canada was implicitly promising to indemnify the industry for acting on its request."[174]

In its attempts to influence and control the conduct of others, the anti-smoking coalition has been hugely successful. The 2011 Canadian Tobacco Use Monitoring Survey by Statistics Canada revealed only "17 percent of Canadians over the age of 15 identified themselves as smokers," the lowest level since 1999. Twenty percent of men described themselves as smokers, and 14 percent of women. The anti-smoking coalition had another reason to rejoice: only 12 percent of Canadians between the ages of 15 and 19 smoked, according to this survey. Notwithstanding these encouraging numbers, the Canadian Cancer Society interpreted these findings as a call for further action.[175]

Cartoonist Vance Rodewalt questioned the rebellious aspect associated with youths smoking cigarettes, January 17, 1995. Glenbow Archives, M-9457-48.

CONCLUSION

"Vices" have continued to generate public debate throughout the twentieth and early twenty-first centuries. Individuals, organized lobby groups, and state and non-state institutions weighed in during these years, hoping to shape public policies. More recently, courts have joined the social debate on how to regulate abortion, gambling, homosexuality, and drug use.

Some behaviours that used to be called vices acquired new names. They have become "health issues," a reflection of the growing influence of health professionals in these debates. However, some people who had been designated as suffering from an illness, such as homosexuals, successfully challenged this health-related label. Others, such as prostitutes, formerly accused of vice, raised their voices to claim that they had been doing legitimate work and did not encourage promiscuity. Churches and religious groups challenged those who claimed that birth control and, in particular, abortion were strictly medical procedures. For them, the decision did not belong exclusively to women. If the growth of the medical discourse has led to a greater influence for physicians—as the tobacco issue has illustrated—it has not meant that they have a monopoly on how gambling, homosexuality, drug and alcohol use, and abortion should be debated.

Governments have continued to regulate what used to be called vices. Since 1920, politicians and bureaucrats have developed new narratives to justify state monopolies over activities such as selling alcohol and gambling. State control, these proponents have argued, is the preferable option, since it eliminates criminal elements and guarantees new sources of revenue for the public good. At the same time, governments have revisited the boundaries between the private and public spheres. Some politicians have undertaken to redraw these boundaries, as Pierre Trudeau did with the 1967 omnibus bill. At the same time, as developments regarding abortion, gambling, and homosexuality reveal, various social and State actors have increasingly used the courts to implement their own agendas.

Conclusion

Through this exploration of the history of vice we have seen how Canadians have navigated living together in an increasingly diverse society. We have also gauged the extent of their ability to govern the conduct of others, whether through institutions of church and state, or collectively, in the context of civil society. When addressing the issues of abortion, alcohol and drug use, gambling, homosexuality, prostitution, and smoking, Canadians have responded in a variety of ways: condemnation, repression, prohibition; but also defiance, resistance, and tolerance. These responses have varied through time and from region to region, depending on the issues and the people involved.

Individuals have tried to govern not only themselves but also the conduct of others, and not always successfully. Prior to the arrival of Europeans, Aboriginal peoples had their own values, rules, and regulations. Missionaries strove to impose a different moral order, but they largely failed. Various economic, political, and social factors limited the newcomers' ability to force Aboriginals to adopt new ways, whether through internalization of values or through inculcation.

When Europeans settled permanently in the St. Lawrence Valley and the Maritimes during the seventeenth century, they brought with them a set of beliefs about acceptable behaviours. While churches enforced a moral order dictated by Roman Catholic or Protestant doctrine, and more or less effectively regulated their members, they could not manage the lives of those who did not belong to their faith. Baptist and Presbyterian religious tribunals could issue harsh punishments for vice, particularly for women; however, these tribunals largely lost their effectiveness during the Industrial Revolution. Although the Roman Catholic Church continued to rely on confession as a means of regulating the conduct of its flock, the church's ability to enforce its moral order was constrained until the mid-nineteenth century by a severe shortage of priests.

Local communities also attempted to regulate individuals' behaviour. From the seventeenth to the middle of the nineteenth century, most settlers lived in relatively small villages. They had their own codes of acceptable behaviour, especially in the realm of gender relations. A community might resort to a charivari in the case of a transgression that challenged the boundaries of appropriate relations, such as an old woman marrying a much younger man, because this type of union could stir up resentment among small-town residents. Communities organized charivaris despite the objections of church and government officials. For them, the charivari was a rebellious gesture that constituted a direct challenge either to the church's authority over moral issues or the state's power to sanction marriage.

During the colonial era, there were various ways for individuals to escape attempts by others to regulate their conduct. Those who did not want to be the victims of a charivari could move out of the village. Others, who wanted to avoid the wrath of a priest or a religious tribunal, could leave their church. However, all these options had significant economic, social, personal, and familial consequences. Individuals who resisted the external mechanisms that governed a person's conduct could lose access to familial, religious, and community resources. Some chose to break free anyway, as cases brought before Presbyterian and Baptist tribunals illustrate. Men, more often than women, would vanish rather than face their judges.

The Industrial Revolution radically transformed society in the second half of the nineteenth century. This period of economic and social turmoil led determined Christians from various denominations to launch a massive, sustained campaign targeting a series of vices that caused, according to them, social upheaval and decay. People's drinking and gambling habits, their use of drugs for recreational purposes, their attempts to control the size of their families, and their uncontrolled sexual activity—and particularly sexual activity in public spaces with the risk of disease—profoundly bothered and sometimes shocked certain Christians. In their eyes, these realities had become serious social problems. Accordingly, these Christians felt compelled to force upon others their beliefs about how individuals should govern themselves. They believed drinkers, gamblers, homosexuals, prostitutes, tobacco users, recreational drug users, and people who used contraceptives inflicted moral, health, social, and economic misery upon themselves and others. The family, as the cornerstone of society, was under siege, and so were the gender divisions that confined men primarily to the role of breadwinners and women to that of housewives and mothers. Christian faith justified the actions of opponents of vice, since they fervently believed that they were living through a period of moral decline. In response, Christian individuals, groups, and Protestant churches initiated a movement of social and political engagement. Moral reformers talked to each other; read news articles and books on how to attack the social evil at work; exchanged ideas on mobilization and arguments on how to provoke social change; and attended regional, provincial, national, and sometimes international conferences on how to transform society in order to build the kingdom of God on earth. A sense of urgency compelled them to take action. Temperance crusader Letitia Youmans justified her activism by claiming that to do nothing was a crime.

These determined individuals, animated by their Christian faith, offered solutions to the ills they apprehended, but their opponents regarded their proposals as too radical, since they threatened individuals' livelihoods and large sectors (brewing and distilling, for example) of the national economy. At first, the reformers advocated temperance, self-control of one's sexual impulses, and abstinence from gambling and drug use. These advocates initially believed that getting sufficient numbers of individuals to take the temperance pledge would suffice to quell the liquor trade and other interconnected vices such as prostitution, gambling, and drug use. They thought that if they could eliminate one, the others would follow like dominoes. Their goal was to create a Canada free of vice, by channelling individuals' wills toward this goal.

Gradually, moral reformers came to realize that individual willpower was insufficient to eradicate abortion, alcohol, drugs, gambling, homosexuality, and prostitution. The time had come to force the state to embrace and enforce their solutions. The politicization of this movement dominated the public sphere in the second half of the nineteenth century. Battles erupted all over the country, at the municipal, provincial, and federal levels. Geographically, the focus of the anti-vice campaigns varied considerably: British Columbia was at the centre of the moral panic over drug use. During the prohibition debates, the dry side was particularly strong in the Maritimes and Ontario. Quebec was less favourable than other provinces to restricting gambling and the liquor trade.

In general, the Roman Catholic Church was wary of the moral reform movement as a Protestant-led campaign with the potential to make inroads among Catholics. However, this did not prevent the Catholic church from strongly supporting state repression of abortion, birth control, and prostitution. Nevertheless it pleaded for more tolerant public policies regarding alcohol use, gambling, and tobacco, at the end of the nineteenth century in this last case.

In response to this broad social mobilization and the increasing politicization of debates over vice, the government used various means to deal with these issues. Politicians came to agree that the state could have a role in implementing a morally based order as a means to bring social peace. The state used legislation to strengthen the Christian moral order, by reinforcing criminal penalties for those seeking or performing an abortion. It criminalized homosexual acts, contraceptives, and the dissemination of information about birth control. Through these actions, the state consolidated Christian beliefs that confined sexual relations to procreation. When drug use for recreational purposes became a social concern, the federal government opted to criminalize certain substances, such as opium, cocaine, and marijuana. Canada's policy was part of an international movement toward the criminalization of drugs. Other issues, such as gambling, and the prohibition of alcohol, were destined to ignite a more protracted battle.

The success of the reform movement depended on the ability of dedicated and determined Christians to reach out to other groups and build coalitions. As demonstrated by the campaign to end illicit drug use at the end of the nineteenth century, Christians from various denominations were able to enlist nationalist and labour organizations, groups with which they otherwise had little in common. These latter groups opposed unrestricted immigration and saw state-sponsored crackdowns on immigrant drug users as a means to limit entry into Canada or to deport those already here. Otherwise disparate groups were able to collaborate in cracking down on abortionists, alcohol and drug users, gamblers, homosexuals, prostitutes, and tobacco users. Physicians and other health experts have been particularly active in working with Christian groups from various denominations to repress or control vice. In the second half of the nineteenth century, health experts structured their communities as professions, with governing bodies that strictly managed access to their professional ranks and used science to establish legitimacy and ensure social respectability. At the same time, this meant that doctors and other health experts gained greater control over individuals' bodies and claimed authority to regulate the behaviour of others. The rise of specialized medical discourse and the medicalization of issues previously regarded as moral vices explains the success physicians have had in shaping public policies. Furthermore, on abortion and birth control issues, Christians from various denominations counted on physicians asserting their control over women's bodies, and women's health in general, by denouncing abortionists. In their efforts to defend what they deemed appropriate gender roles and the sanctity of marriage, Christians found allies among members of the medical community who questioned the mental health of homosexuals.

The new moral entrepreneurs—physicians—imposed their own solution for how individuals should regulate their reproductive abilities: criminalization. Although abortion and contraception were illegal, this did not deter women and men from seeking help and sometimes putting their own health in jeopardy. Like their moral reformer predecessors, physicians came to appreciate that the implementation of a public policy required will and resources. When law enforcement forces were reluctant to crack down on abortionists and women seeking abortions, physicians concluded that abortion would not disappear.

Finding allies was not sufficient to win the war. Opponents of vice updated their arguments to take advantage of new political, social, and economic situations, as during the push to enact prohibition of alcohol during and after the First World War. By linking to the war context the severe social, economic, and familial consequences of drinking, moral reformers were able to turn a behaviour already regarded as shameful and delinquent into one that was also unpatriotic. Working under the influence of alcohol in a war factory or being drunk when facing the enemy in Europe, could cost Canada its victory.

At other moments, moral reformers counted on the active support of individuals within the state apparatus. The drug issue illustrates this well. In 1907, anti-drug opponents drew on the co-operation of an individual well positioned to influence the state: William Lyon Mackenzie King. As deputy minister of labour, he investigated drug use in British Columbia following a riot that had targeted Asians. Once appointed minister, he was able to shape the writing of the first drug law and base it on the principle of repression.

Once the state, at whatever level, has decided to regulate a particular type of behaviour, law enforcement has often been episodic. At the municipal level, this has often depended on the personality of the chief of police and other local police officers. Police have typically perceived the sex trade and gambling, for example, as minor crimes, and enforcement has generally been lacking. On the other hand, enforcement of the criminalization of same-sex sexual activity, especially after the Second World War, was based on the fear that homosexuals could recruit impressionable and insecure youths and convert them to their sexual orientation. This led police to arrest supposed predators. Similarly, the criminalization of drug use motivated police forces to crack down on specific ethnic groups—mainly the Chinese—at the beginning of the twentieth century. Although law enforcement agencies have chosen to apply the law selectively, targeting specific vices and ignoring others, they have also benefited from vice. Investigations by citizens, churches, and commissions of inquiry—set up by municipalities and provincial governments—have revealed the occasional collusion between law enforcers and criminal elements, which controlled the sex trade and gambling. Vice opponents who have pressed politicians to get serious in their fight have often found denunciations to be insufficient. However, when politicians have chosen to use campaigns against vice to win election or re-election, moral reformers' requests for crackdowns have obtained a more sympathetic hearing and have sometimes led to action.

Clearly, vice opponents have not always been successful. There have always been limits to the ability to govern the self. Although the Roman Catholic

Church pressed for a ban on alcohol in the fur trade during the colonial era, the state was unwilling to give up an essential tool and jeopardize its alliances with Aboriginals in the rivalry between the French and English empires in North America. At the beginning of the twentieth century, even though politicians enacted prohibition to regulate relations between Canadians and alcohol, they still allowed several exceptions. First, the federal government did not prohibit the possession of alcohol. Second, it permitted the manufacture of alcohol to continue in operation. Third, individuals, if they could find a physician willing to give them a prescription, could still legitimately buy alcohol.

Broadly speaking, the state has been in the business of regulating vice since the colonial era. From the seventeenth century on, it largely opted to support the Christian moral order. Since the late 1960s, however, it has decided to move out of "the bedrooms of the nation," at least with regard to some aspects of sexual relations. By legalizing homosexual acts, contraceptives, and birth control information, facilitating access to abortion, and redefining marriage as a union between two individuals, the state has redrawn the boundaries of acceptable sexual behaviour. In the case of other vices, state actions have led to a growth of the bureaucracy and its regulatory power. The liquor trade and gambling are cases in point. Since the colonial era, the sale of alcohol has been an indispensable source of revenue for the state, and during the prohibition debate in the second half of the nineteenth century, politicians expressed their reluctance to lose this source by putting an end to the liquor trade. In the 1920s, the decision by various provinces to replace prohibition with a form of liquor control conferred a monopoly over the sale of alcohol to the state. Although production remained under private ownership, state-owned or -controlled sales have become an invaluable source of public revenue. Although liberalism has characterized the implementation of public policies since the 1960s, the state remains a crucial actor in the regulation of alcohol. When gambling became legal in 1969, provinces that had already asked for lotteries as a means to support welfare programs and other state initiatives were quick to create them and, since then, have expanded their range to include casinos, video lottery machines, and, more recently, online gambling. At the same time, the continued criminalization of drugs such as opium, cocaine, and marijuana, to name a few, has led the state to allocate additional financial and human resources to police forces, courts, and prisons. Thus, the evolving regulation of certain vices has contributed to the expansion of state bureaucracies.

Since the repatriation of the constitution in 1982, there has been a judicialization of morally based issues. Individuals, organized lobby groups, manufacturers, and the state have brought the courts increasingly into the debate on abortion, marriage, medicinal marijuana, and tobacco use. Before 1982, opponents to morally based laws sometimes challenged the state's authority. For example, some asked the courts to rule on the constitutionality of the Canada Temperance Law. However, the inclusion of the Charter of Rights and Freedoms in the Canadian constitution has meant that the courts are now a powerful recourse for social actors who desire to impose or refute a particular moral agenda. Courts have not always favoured a liberal approach. If the Canadian Charter of Rights and Freedoms has played a role in liberalizing abortion and redefining marriage, it has not helped those seeking a less coercive approach on drugs.[1]

When we analyze the historical dimensions of moral regulation in Canada, it is apparent that repression has tended to characterize how collectivities, churches, and the state have dealt with deviations from established norms. Conversely, we can find numerous instances where individuals, groups, and corporations have found ways to fight back and gain access to alcohol, drugs, abortion, contraceptives, birth control information, and tobacco products. Some paid a heavy penalty when forced to confront local communities, churches, police forces, or the justice system. Class, ethnicity, gender, and age determined the sporadic and unequal enforcement of the law. In comparison to some other groups, white, upper-class men have rarely been bothered by enforcement or severe penalties. When caught—if they were even targeted to begin with—they could afford to pay leading lawyers to get them acquitted of charges or receive a reduced sentence. On the other hand, an Irish Catholic prostitute in Toronto in 1856, a labourer drinking in dry Moncton during the years of the Canada Temperance Act, a Chinese drug user in Vancouver in 1910, or a black prostitute in Halifax in 1920 were all likely to be targeted. Some of these individuals escaped law enforcement by luck or because of clumsy work by police gathering evidence. Those who were caught, particularly during moral-panic-driven crackdowns, faced the consequences of the law. In these circumstances, these individuals denounced the regulations and laws regulating their behaviour.

The regulation of vice has changed over time. This should give us pause for reflection: Why do we change our behaviour? Do we change in order to comply with what is expected of us? Do we internalize the behaviour that society expects us to adopt? Do we agree with these "acceptable" behaviours because we have been conditioned to do so? Is it a conscious and willing decision on our part? Or do we select the regulations that we deem reasonable and develop various strategies of resistance (active or passive) to others? According to Foucault, the fact that we internalize certain behaviours demonstrates not only the reach of the concept of power and the resourcefulness of those who exercise it, but also, at the same time, its diffuse and amorphous nature. Self-regulation is an illustration of how successful the concept of regulation can be as a strategy. At the same time, institutions, and in particular the state through its monopoly of legitimate violence, have the means to punish those who do not comply with behaviours defined as morally and socially acceptable. Morally based policies have often been championed by individuals and groups who concluded that their power of persuasion was limited by powerful interests opposed to regulation of alcohol, drugs, gambling, tobacco, or sexuality. Believing that these "powerful" interests interfered with their agenda, they included the state as part of their means for enforcing their views and making Canada the Good.

NOTES

NOTES TO INTRODUCTION

1 Noreen Rasback, "Vices Pay, if You Have a Stake in Them," *Globe and Mail*, August 29, 2009, B8.

2 This definition is partly inspired by Jim Leitzel, *Regulating Vice: Misguided Prohibitions and Realistic Controls* (New York: Cambridge University Press, 2008).

3 Colum Hourihane (ed.), *Virtue & Vice: The Personifications in the Index of Christian Art* (Princeton, NJ: Index of Christian Art, Department of Art and Archaeology, Princeton University in association with Princeton University Press, 2000).

4 Gabriele Taylor, *Deadly Vices* (Oxford: Clarendon, 2006), 8.

5 Leitzel, *Regulating Vice*, 4–5; Thomas Hurka, *Virtue, Vice, and Value* (New York: Oxford University Press, 2001); Craig Taylor, *Moralism: A Study of a Vice* (Montreal & Kingston: McGill-Queen's University Press, 2012); Taylor, *Deadly Vices*.

6 Alan Hunt, *Governing Morals: A Social History of Moral Regulation* (Cambridge: Cambridge University Press, 1999), 9.

7 Suzanne Morton, *At Odds: Gambling and Canadians, 1919–1969* (Toronto: University of Toronto Press, 2003), 15.

8 Matthew Hayday, *Bilingual Today, United Tomorrow: Official Languages in Education and Canadian Federalism* (Montreal & Kingston: McGill-Queen's University Press, 2005); Michael Howlett and M. Ramesh, *Studying Public Policy: Policy Cycles and Policy Subsystems* (Toronto: Oxford University Press, 1995); John W. Kingdon, *Agendas, Alternatives and Public Policies* (New York: Harper Collins, 1995); Vincent Lemieux, *Les cheminements de l'influence: Systèmes, stratégies et structures du politique* (Quebec: Les Presses de l'Université Laval, 1979); Vincent Lemieux, *L'étude des politiques publiques: Les acteurs et leur pouvoir*, 2nd ed. (Quebec: Les Presses de l'Université Laval, 2002); Jennifer A. Stephen, *Pick One Intelligent Girl: Employability, Domesticity, and the Gendering of Canada's Welfare State, 1939–1947* (Toronto: University of Toronto, 2007).

9 Kenneth J. Meier, *The Politics of Sin: Drugs, Alcohol, and Public Policy* (Armonk, NY: M. E. Sharpe, 1994), 16.

10 Meier, *The Politics of Sin*.

NOTES TO CHAPTER 1

1 Jacques Cartier, *The Voyages of Jacques Cartier*, with an introduction by Ramsay Cook (Toronto: University of Toronto Press, 1993), 21.

2 Cartier, *The Voyages of Jacques Cartier*, 68.

3 Cartier, *The Voyages of Jacques Cartier*, 68.

4 Cartier, *The Voyages of Jacques Cartier*, 68.

5 Cartier, *The Voyages of Jacques Cartier*, 68.

6 Cartier, *The Voyages of Jacques Cartier*, 68.

7 Cartier, *The Voyages of Jacques Cartier*, 69.

8 Cartier, *The Voyages of Jacques Cartier*, 69.

9 Cartier, *The Voyages of Jacques Cartier*, 22, 70.
10 Samuel de Champlain, *Voyages of Samuel de Champlain* (New York: Barnes and Noble, 1967), 131–132.
11 Léo-Paul Desrosiers, *Iroquoisie*, tome 1 (Quebec: Septentrion, 1998), 23.
12 "Distribution and Size of the Beothuk Population, Leadership and Communal Activities," http://www.heritage.nf.ca/aboriginal/beo_distribution.html.
13 Carole Blackburn, *Harvest of Souls: The Jesuit Missions and Colonialism in North America, 1632–1650* (Montreal: McGill-Queen's University Press, 2000), 134.
14 Samuel de Champlain, *Voyages and Discoveries*, in W. Vernon Kinietz, *The Indians of the Western Great Lakes, 1615–1760* (Ann Arbor: University of Michigan Press, 1965), 93.
15 Champlain, *Voyages and Discoveries*, 94.
16 Champlain, *Voyages and Discoveries*, 94; Bruce Trigger, *The Children of Aataentsic: A History of the Huron People to 1660* (Montreal: McGill-Queen's University Press, 1987), 48–50.
17 Peter Baskerville, *Sites of Power: A Concise History of Ontario* (Don Mills, ON: Oxford University Press, 2005), 7; Alan D. McMillan and Eldon Yellowhorn, *First Peoples in Canada* (Vancouver: Douglas & McIntyre, 2004), 77–86, 117.
18 Nicolas Perrot, "Memoir on the Manners, Customs, and Religion of the Savages of North America," in Kinietz, *The Indians of the Western Great Lakes, 1615–1760*, 271.
19 Blackburn, *Harvest of Souls*, 61.
20 Antoine Denis Raudot, "Memoir Concerning the Different Indian Nations of North America," in Kinietz, *The Indians of the Western Great Lakes, 1615–1760*, 367.
21 Robert-Lionel Séguin, *La vie libertine en Nouvelle-France au XVIIe siècle*, vol. 1 (Montreal: Leméac, 1972), 38.
22 Bruce G. Trigger, *The Huron: Farmers of the North* (New York: Holt, Rinehart and Winston, 1969), 64–65.
23 Trigger, *The Children of Aataentsic*, 367.
24 Séguin, *La vie libertine en Nouvelle-France au XVIIe siècle*, 40–41.
25 David Hackett Fischer, *Champlain's Dream* (New York: Simon & Schuster Paperbacks, 2008), 339, 341; Kinietz, *The Indians of the Western Great Lakes, 1615–1760*, 92.
26 Quoted in Gary Kinsman, *The Regulation of Desire: Homo and Hetero Sexualities* (Montreal: Black Rose Books, 1996), 92.
27 Kinsman, *The Regulation of Desire*, 93.
28 Séguin, *La vie libertine en Nouvelle-France au XVIIe siècle*, 102–103. Sagard mentioned another similar case in his *Histoire du Canada* published in 1636.
29 *A Short Abridgment of Christian Doctrine* (1728), 20.
30 Brenda Margaret Appleby, *Responsible Parenthood: Decriminalizing Contraception in Canada* (Toronto: University of Toronto Press, 1999), 110.
31 M. Duchesneau, "Memoir on the Western Indians, 13 September 1681," in E. B. O'Callaghan, ed., *Documents Relative to the Colonial History of the State of New York*, vol. 9 (Albany, 1855), 162.
32 Cartier, *The Voyages of Jacques Cartier*, 52.
33 Catherine Ferland, *Bacchus en Canada: Boissons, buveurs et ivresses en Nouvelle-France* (Quebec: Septentrion, 2010), 228.
34 Ferland, *Bacchus en Canada*, 229–230.
35 Trigger, *The Children of Aataentsic*, 462.
36 Raudot, "Memoir," in Kinietz, *The Indians of the Western Great Lakes, 1615–1760*, 344.
37 Ferland, *Bacchus en Canada*.
38 Paul Le Jeune, S. J., *Québec Relations: 1635, 1636, 1637*, edited by Lucien Campeau (Rome: Institutum Historicum Societatis Iesu, Quebec: Presses de l'Université Laval, 2004), 190.
39 Le Jeune, S. J., *Québec Relations: 1635, 1636, 1637*, 312.
40 Ferland, *Bacchus en Canada*, 250.
41 Abbé Raynal, *A Philosophical and Political History of the Settlements and Trade of the Europeans in the East and West Indies*, vol. 6, trans. J. O. Justamond (London: A. Strahan and T. Cadell, 1788), 514.

42   Jim R. Miller, *Skyscrapers Hide the Heavens: A History of Indian–White Relations in Canada*, 3rd ed. (Toronto: University of Toronto Press, 2000), 59.

43   Paul Le Jeune, S. J., *Québec Relations: 1635, 1636, 1637*, 189.

44   M. Duchesneau, "Memoir on the Western Indians, 13 September 1681," in E. B. O'Callaghan, ed., *Documents Relative to the Colonial History of the State of New York*, vol. 9 (Albany, 1855), 162.

45   Fischer, *Champlain's Dream*, 378; Ferland, *Bacchus en Canada*, 257–58; Claiborne A. Skinner, *The Upper Country: French Enterprise in the Colonial Great Lakes* (Baltimore: Johns Hopkins University Press, 2008), 20.

46   Ferland, *Bacchus en Canada*, 256–260.

47   McMillan and Yellowhorn, *First Peoples in Canada*, 83.

48   Elisabeth Tooker, *An Ethnography of the Huron Indians, 1615–1649* (Syracuse, NY: Syracuse University Press, 1991), 116.

49   Trigger, *The Children of Aataentsic*, 84.

50   Cartier, *The Voyages of Jacques Cartier*, 69–70.

51   Paul Le Jeune, S. J., *Québec Relations: 1635, 1636, 1637*, 223.

52   Trigger, *The Children of Aataentsic*, 280.

53   Trigger, *The Children of Aataentsic*, 62–63.

54   Trigger, *The Children of Aataentsic*, 41, 62–63.

55   Kinietz, *The Indians of the Western Great Lakes, 1615–1760*, 69.

56   Miller, *Skyscrapers Hide the Heavens*, 54.

57   Miller, *Skyscrapers Hide the Heavens*, 42.

NOTES TO CHAPTER 2

1   Adolph B. Benson, *Peter Kalm's Travel in North America*. The English Version of 1770, vol. 2 (New York: Dover Publications, 1964), 422.

2   Susanna Moodie, *Roughing It in the Bush*, 2nd ed. (London: Richard Bentley, 1852), http://digital.library.upenn.edu/women/moodie/roughing/roughing.html#I-11.

3   Lucien Lemieux, *Une histoire religieuse du Québec* (Montreal: Les Éditions Novalis, 2010).

4   Serge Gagnon, *Plaisir d'amour et crainte de Dieu: Sexualité et confession au Bas-Canada* (Sainte-Foy, QC: Les Presses de l'Université Laval, 1990), 99.

5   Terence J. Ray, *A History of Canadian Catholics: Gallicanism, Romanism, and Canadianism* (Montreal & Kingston: McGill-Queen's University Press, 2002), 24.

6   N. E. S. Griffiths, *From Migrant to Acadian: A North American Border People 1604–1755* (Montreal & Kingston: McGill-Queen's University Press, 2005), 311.

7   Gagnon, *Plaisir d'amour et crainte de Dieu*, 99–100.

8   Terry Crowley, "The French Regime to 1760," in Terrence Murphy and Roberto Perin, eds., *A Concise History of Christianity in Canada* (Toronto: Oxford University Press, 1996), 41.

9   Gagnon, *Plaisir d'amour et crainte de Dieu*, 44.

10   Terrence Murphy, "The English-Speaking Colonies to 1854," in Murphy and Perin, *A Concise History of Christianity in Canada*, 121.

11   John D'Emilio and Estelle B. Freedman, *Intimate Matters: A History of Sexuality in America* (New York: Harper & Row Publishers, 1988), 18.

12   Patrice Corriveau, *Judging Homosexuals: A History of Gay Persecution in Quebec and France*, trans. Käthe Roth (Vancouver: UBC Press, 2011), 22–39; D'Emilio and Freedman, *Intimate Matters*.

13   Elizabeth Abbott, *A History of Marriage* (Toronto: Penguin Canada, 2010), 15.

14   D'Emilio and Freedman, *Intimate Matters*, 4.

15   D'Emilio and Freedman, *Intimate Matters*, 79.

16   Peter Ward, *Courtship, Love, and Marriage in Nineteenth-Century English Canada* (Montreal & Kingston: McGill-Queen's University Press, 1990), 39–40.

17   Robert-Lionel Séguin, *La vie libertine en Nouvelle-France au XVIIᵉ siècle*, vol. 1 (Montreal: Leméac, 1972), 74–75.

18 Séguin, *La vie libertine en Nouvelle-France au XVIIe siècle*, 75–76.
19 Séguin, *La vie libertine en Nouvelle-France au XVIIe siècle*, 84–88.
20 André Lachance, *Crimes et criminels en Nouvelle-France* (Montreal: Boréal, 1984); Collectif Clio, *L'histoire des femmes au Québec depuis quatre siècles*, 2nd ed. (Montreal: Le Jour, 1992), 137–138.
21 Collectif Clio, *L'histoire des femmes au Québec depuis quatre siècles*, 137–138.
22 Mary Anne Poutanen, "'The Homeless, the Whore, the Drunkard, and the Disorderly: Contours of Female Vagrancy in the Montreal Courts, 1810–1842," in Kathryn McPherson, Cecilia Morgan, and Nancy M. Forestell, eds., *Gendered Pasts: Historical Essays in Femininity and Masculinity in Canada* (Don Mills, ON: Oxford University Press, 1999), 32.
23 Poutanen, "The Homeless, the Whore, the Drunkard, and the Disorderly," 41.
24 Corriveau, *Judging Homosexuals*, 41.
25 Lachance, *Crimes et criminels en Nouvelle-France*, 130.
26 Corriveau, *Judging Homosexuals*, 36.
27 Edith G. Firth, "Alexander Wood," *Dictionary of Canadian Biography*, http://www.biographi .ca/009004-119.01-e.php?BioId=37856.
28 Gary Kinsman, *The Regulation of Desire: Homo and Hetero Sexualities* (Montreal: Black Rose Books, 1996), 100.
29 Lynne Marks, "No Double Standard?: Leisure, Sex, and Sin in Upper Canadian Church Discipline Records, 1800–1860," in McPherson, Morgan, and Forestell, *Gendered Pasts: Historical Essays in Femininity and Masculinity in Canada*, 48–52.
30 Marks, "No Double Standard?," 59.
31 Gagnon, *Plaisir d'amour et crainte de Dieu*, 99–101; Ward, *Courtship, Love, and Marriage in Nineteenth-Century English Canada*, 21.
32 Mandements des Évêques de Québec, "Circulaire avant départ pour la France," 1690, quoted in Corriveau, *Judging Homosexuals*,177, note 28.
33 Gagnon, *Plaisir d'amour et crainte de Dieu*, 100–113.
34 "Pope Gregory XIV," *The Embryo Project Encyclopedia*, http://embryo.asu.edu/view/ embryo:127770.
35 Wendy Mitchinson, *The Nature of Their Bodies: Women and Their Doctors in Victorian Canada* (Toronto: University of Toronto Press, 1991), 134–35; Constance Backhouse, *Petticoats and Prejudice: Women and Law in Nineteenth-Century Canada* (Toronto: Osgoode Society, 1991), 147.
36 Lachance, *Crimes et criminels en Nouvelle-France*, 36; Backhouse, *Petticoats and Prejudice*, 113–14, 123.
37 Lachance, *Crimes et criminels en Nouvelle-France*, 36.
38 Collectif Clio, *L'histoire des femmes au Québec depuis quatre siècles*, 85; Gagnon, *Plaisir d'amour et crainte de Dieu*, 125–126.
39 Brenda Margaret Appleby, *Responsible Parenthood: Decriminalizing Contraception in Canada* (Toronto: University of Toronto Press, 1999), 100.
40 André Lachance and Sylvie Savoie, "Violence, Marriage, and Family Honour: Aspects of the Legal Regulation of Marriage in New France," in Jim Phillips, Tina Loo, and Susan Lewthwaite, eds., *Essays in the History of Canadian Law*, vol. 5, *Crime and Criminal Justice* (Toronto: Osgoode Society for Canadian Legal History, 1994), 169, note 16.
41 Lachance and Savoie, "Violence, Marriage, and Family Honour," 152.
42 Lachance and Savoie, "Violence, Marriage, and Family Honour," 149, 152, 161.
43 Backhouse, *Petticoats and Prejudice*, 167–70.
44 Andrée Lévesque, *Making and Breaking the Rules: Women in Quebec, 1919–1939* (Toronto: McClelland & Stewart, 1994), 76.
45 Edward Shorter, *Written in the Flesh: A History of Desire* (Toronto: University of Toronto Press, 2005), 90–93; Lachance and Savoie, "Violence, Marriage, and Family Honour," 157.
46 Natalie Zemon Davis, "Charivari, Honor and Community in Seventeenth-Century Lyon and Geneva," in John J. MacAloon, ed., *Rite, Drama, Festival, Spectacle: Rehearsals Toward*

a Theory of Cultural Performance (Philadelphia: Institute for the Study of Human Issues, 1984), 42–57.

47 Loretta T. Johnson, "Charivari/Shivaree: A European Folk Ritual on the American Plains," *Journal of Interdisciplinary History* 20, no. 3 (Winter 1990): 374–376.

48 Brian D. Palmer, "Discordant Music: Charivaris and Whitecapping in Nineteenth-Century North America," *Labour/Le Travail* 3 (1978): 17.

49 Johnson, "Charivari/Shivaree: A European Folk Ritual on the American Plains," 376; Alan Greer, *The Patriots and the People: The Rebellions of 1837 in Rural Lower Canada* (Toronto: University of Toronto Press, 1993), 69–86.

50 Tina Loo and Carolyn Strange, *Making Good: Law and Moral Regulation in Canada, 1867–1939* (Toronto: University of Toronto Press, 1997), 35; Johnson, "Charivari/Shivaree: A European Folk Ritual on the American Plains," 376.

51 René Hardy, "Le charivari: divulguer et sanctionner la vie privée," in Manon Brunet and Serge Gagnon, eds., *Discours et pratiques de l'intime* (Quebec: Institut québécois de recherche sur la culture, 1993), 47–69.

52 Pauline Greenhill, *Make the Night Hideous: Four English-Canadian Charivaris, 1881–1940* (Toronto: University of Toronto Press, 2010).

53 Collectif Clio, *L'histoire des femmes au Québec depuis quatre siècles*, 100.

54 Catherine Ferland, *Bacchus en Canada: Boissons, buveurs et ivresses en Nouvelle-France* (Quebec: Septentrion, 2010), 27–66.

55 Benson, *Peter Kalm's Travel in North America*, 535.

56 Ferland, *Bacchus en Canada*, 129–131.

57 Ferland, *Bacchus en Canada*, 126.

58 Julia Roberts, *In Mixed Company: Taverns and Public Life in Upper Canada* (Vancouver: UBC Press, 2009), 59.

59 Craig Heron, *Booze: A Distilled History* (Toronto: Between the Lines, 2003), 30–31.

60 Heron, *Booze*, 35.

61 Ferland, *Bacchus en Canada*, 65–166; Griffiths, *From Migrant to Acadian*, 311.

62 Ferland, *Bacchus en Canada*, 128, 160–164.

63 Ferland, *Bacchus en Canada*, 240–246; John A. Dickinson, "Native Sovereignty and French Justice in Early Canada," in *Crime and Criminal Justice*, 29–30.

64 Ferland, *Bacchus en Canada*, 263–65.

65 In her study of alcohol use in Upper Canada, Roberts mentions "ninety-six percent of the tavern licences issued in the colony belonged to men." *In Mixed Company*, 153.

66 Roberts, *In Mixed Company*, 103.

67 Heron, *Booze*, 40.

68 Roberts, *In Mixed Company*, 90.

69 Roberts, *In Mixed Company*, 92.

70 Carl L. Hart and Charles Ksir, *Drugs, Society & Human Behaviour*, 14th ed. (New York: McGraw-Hill, 2011), 199; Sharon Anne Cook, "*Through Sunshine and Shadow*": The Woman's Christian Temperance Union, Evangelicalism, and Reform in Ontario, 1874–1930* (Montreal & Kingston: McGill-Queen's University Press, 1995), 20.

71 Quoted in Roberts, *In Mixed Company*, 78.

72 Michel Labrosse, *The Lottery from Jacques Cartier's Day to Modern Times: Sidelights on the History of Lotteries in Québec*, trans. Alan Brown (Montreal: Stanké, 1985), 75–78.

73 John C. Burnham, *Bad Habits: Drinking, Smoking, Taking Drugs, Gambling, Sexual Misbehaviour, and Swearing in American History* (New York: New York University Press, 1993), 147–50.

74 Suzanne Morton, *At Odds: Gambling and Canadians, 1919–1969* (Toronto: University of Toronto Press, 2003), 7; Burham, *Bad Habits*, 147–150.

75 Magaly Brodeur, *Vice et corruption à Montréal, 1892–1970* (Quebec: Les Presses de l'Université du Québec, 2011), 20.

76 Ferland, *Bacchus en Canada*, 128.

77　Labrosse, *The Lottery from Jacques Cartier's Day to Modern Times*, 64.
78　Roberts, *In Mixed Company*, 82; Labrosse, *The Lottery from Jacques Cartier's Day to Modern Times*, 79.
79　Benson, *Peter Kalm's Travel in North America*, 510.
80　Quoted in Griffiths, *From Migrant to Acadian*, 312.

NOTES TO CHAPTER 3

1　Letitia Youmans, *Campaign Echoes* (Toronto: William Briggs, 1893), 90.
2　Ruth Elizabeth Spence, *Prohibition in Canada* (Toronto: Ontario Branch of the Dominion Alliance, 1919), xiii.
3　Alan Hunt, *Governing Morals: A Social History of Moral Regulation* (Cambridge: Cambridge University Press, 1999), 9.
4　Hunt, *Governing Morals*, 4.
5　Hunt, *Governing Morals*, 2.
6　Hunt, *Governing Morals*, 7.
7　Quoted in Paul T. Phillips, *A Kingdom on Earth: Anglo-American Social Christianity, 1880–1940* (University Park: Pennsylvania State University Press, 1996), 21–22.
8　Sharon Anne Cook, *"Through Sunshine and Shadow": The Woman's Christian Temperance Union, Evangelicalism, and Reform in Ontario, 1874–1930* (Montreal & Kingston: McGill-Queen's University Press, 1995), 11.
9　Phillips, *A Kingdom on Earth*, 21–22.
10　Neil Semple, *The Lord's Dominion: The History of Canadian Methodism* (Montreal & Kingston: McGill-Queen's University Press, 1996).
11　Phyllis Airhart, *Serving the Present Age: Revivalism, Progressivism, and the Methodist Tradition in Canada* (Montreal & Kingston: McGill-Queen's University Press, 1992); Ramsay Cook, *The Regenerators: Social Criticism in Late-Victorian English Canada* (Toronto: University of Toronto Press, 1985).
12　Peter Ward, *Courtship, Love, and Marriage in Nineteenth-Century English Canada* (Montreal & Kingston: McGill-Queen's University Press, 1990), 37; James G. Snell, "'The White Live for Two': The Defence of Marriage and Sexual Morality in Canada, 1890–1914," *Histoire sociale/Social History* 16, no. 31 (May 1983): 111–128.
13　Elizabeth Abbott, *A History of Marriage* (Toronto: Penguin Canada, 2010), 22.
14　O. Kendall White Jr., "Mormonism in America and Canada: Accommodation to the Nation-State," *Canadian Journal of Sociology/Cahiers canadiens de sociologie* 3, no. 2 (Spring 1978): 161–181; Charles A. Cannon, "The Awesome Power of Sex: The Polemical Campaign Against Mormon Polygamy," *Pacific Historical Review* 43, no. 1 (February 1974): 61–82.
15　Sarah Carter, *The Importance of Being Monogamous: Marriage and Nation Building in Western Canada to 1915* (Edmonton: University of Alberta Press and Athabasca University Press, 2008).
16　Lynne Marks, "No Double Standard?: Leisure, Sex, and Sin in Upper Canadian Church Discipline Records, 1800–1860," in Kathryn McPherson, Cecilia Morgan, and Nancy M. Forestell, eds., *Gendered Pasts: Historical Essays in Femininity and Masculinity in Canada*, 63.
17　Collectif Clio, *L'histoire des femmes au Québec depuis quatre siècles*, 2nd ed. (Montreal: Le Jour, 1992), 229.
18　Judith Fingard, *The Dark Side of Life in Victorian Halifax* (Porters Lake, NS: Pottersfield Press, 1989), 99.
19　Christopher St. George Clark, *Of Toronto the Good. A Social Study: The Queen City of Canada as It Is* (Montreal: Toronto Publishing Company, 1898), 90.
20　John D'Emilio and Estelle B. Freedman, *Intimate Matters: A History of Sexuality in America* (New York: Harper & Row Publishers, 1988), 153; Hunt, *Governing Morals*; Carolyn Strange, *Toronto's Girl Problem: The Perils and Pleasures of the City, 1880–1930* (Toronto: University of Toronto Press, 1995); Mariana Valverde, *The Age of Light, Soap, and Water: Moral Reform in English Canada, 1885–1925* (Toronto: McClelland and Stewart, 1991), 77–78.

21 John R. Graham, "William Lyon Mackenzie King, Elizabeth Harvie, and Edna: A Prostitute Rescuing Initiative in Late Victorian Toronto," *Canadian Journal of Human Sexuality* 8, no. 1 (Spring 1999): 47–60; "A Real Companion and Friend: The Diary of William Lyon Mackenzie King," October 19, 1894, http://www.collectionscanada.gc.ca/king/index-e.html.

22 Constance Backhouse, *Petticoats and Prejudice: Women and Law in Nineteenth-Century Canada* (Toronto: Osgoode Society, 1991), 234.

23 Tamara Myers, *Caught: Montreal's Modern Girls and the Law, 1869–1945* (Toronto: University of Toronto Press, 2006).

24 Carolyn Strange, "From Modern Babylon to a City upon a Hill: The Toronto Social Survey Commission of 1915 and the Search for Sexual Order in the City," in Roger Hall, William Westfall, and Laurel Sefton MacDowell, eds., *Patterns of the Past: Interpreting Ontario's History* (Toronto: Dundurn Press, 1988), 255–277; Alan Hunt, "Measuring Morals: The Beginning of the Social Survey Movement in Canada, 1913–1917," *Histoire sociale/Social History* 35, no. 69 (2002): 88–105; Phillips, *A Kingdom on Earth*.

25 Fingard, *The Dark Side of Life in Victorian Halifax*, 100.

26 Patrick A. Dunae, "Sex, Charades, and Census Records: Locating Female Sex Trade Workers in a Victorian City," *Histoire sociale/Social History* 42, no. 84 (November 2009): 267–297.

27 Backhouse, *Petticoats and Prejudice*; Fingard, *The Dark Side of Life in Victorian Halifax*.

28 Backhouse, *Petticoats and Prejudice*, 233.

29 Fingard, *The Dark Side of Life in Victorian Halifax*, 105.

30 Clark, *Of Toronto the Good*, 86.

31 Alan F. J. Artibise, *Winnipeg: A Social History of Urban Growth, 1874–1914* (Montreal & Kingston: McGill-Queen's University Press, 1975); James H. Gray, *Red Lights on the Prairies* (Toronto: Macmillan of Canada, 1971); Andrée Lévesque, "Éteindre le 'Red Light': Les réformateurs et la prostitution à Montréal, 1865–1925," *Urban History Review/Revue d'histoire urbaine* 17, no. 3 (February 1989): 191–201.

32 Backhouse, *Petticoats and Prejudice*, 236.

33 Backhouse, *Petticoats and Prejudice*; Gray, *Red Lights on the Prairies*.

34 Backhouse, *Petticoats and Prejudice*, 237.

35 Backhouse, *Petticoats and Prejudice*, 241; Fingard, *The Dark Side of Life in Victorian Halifax*; Gray, *Red Lights on the Prairies*.

36 Serge Gagnon, *Religion, Moralité, Modernité* (Quebec: Presses de l'Université Laval, 1999), 91; Wendy Mitchinson, *The Nature of Their Bodies: Women and Their Doctors in Victorian Canada* (Toronto: University of Toronto Press, 1991); Angus McLaren, *The Trials of Masculinity: Policing Sexual Boundaries, 1870–1930* (Chicago: University of Chicago Press, 1997); Angus McLaren, *Our Own Master Race: Eugenics in Canada, 1885–1945* (Toronto: McClelland & Stewart, 1990).

37 Andrée Lévesque, *Making and Breaking the Rules: Women in Quebec, 1919–1939* (Toronto: McClelland & Stewart, 1994), 93; Angus McLaren, "Illegal Operations: Women, Doctors, and Abortion, 1886–1939," *Journal of Social History* 26, no. 4 (Summer 1993): 797–816.

38 *Canada Lancet* 7 (1875), 289 quoted in Backhouse, *Petticoats and Prejudice*, 149.

39 Mitchinson, *The Nature of Their Bodies*, 128; Angus McLaren and Arlene Tigar McLaren, *The Bedroom and the State: The Changing Practices and Politics of Contraception and Abortion in Canada, 1880–1997*, 2nd ed.(Don Mills, ON: Oxford University Press, 1997), 11.

40 McLaren, *Our Own Master Race*, 104.

41 Mitchinson, *The Nature of Their Bodies*, 126, 133–134, 146.

42 Backhouse, *Petticoats and Prejudice*, 166.

43 Strange, *Toronto's Girl Problem*, 71; Lévesque, *Making and Breaking the Rules*, 93; McLaren, "Illegal Operations: Women, Doctors, and Abortion, 1886–1939"; Backhouse, *Petticoats and Prejudice*, 162.

44 Mitchinson, *The Nature of Their Bodies*, 148; Collectif Clio, *L'histoire des femmes au Québec depuis quatre siècles*, 187, 189.

45 McLaren, *The Trials of Masculinity*, 30–31, 158–159; D'Emilio and Freedman, *Intimate Matters*, 126.

46   Patrice Corriveau, *Judging Homosexuals: A History of Gay Persecution in Quebec and France* (Vancouver: UBC Press, 2011, translated by Käthe Roth), 85.

47   Cook, "*Through Sunshine and Shadow*," 20–21; Darren Ferry, "'To the Interests and Conscience of the Great Mass of the Community:' The Evolution of Temperance Societies in Nineteenth-Century Central Canada," *Journal of the Canadian Historical Association*, New Series 14 (2003): 137–163.

48   Jan Noel, *Canada Dry: Temperance Crusades before Confederation* (Toronto: University of Toronto Press, 1995), 172–174.

49   Fingard, *The Dark Side of Life in Victorian Halifax*; Youmans, *Campaign Echoes*, 91.

50   Ferry, "'To the Interests and Conscience of the Great Mass of the Community'": 142–143, 148–149; Noel, *Canada Dry*, 37–38.

51   Cook, "*Through Sunshine and Shadow*"; Craig Heron, *Booze: A Distilled History* (Toronto: Between the Lines, 2003); Valverde, *Age of Light, Soap, and Water*; Youmans, *Campaign Echoes*.

52   Roderick Stewart and Sharon Stewart, *Phoenix: The Life of Norman Bethune* (Montreal & Kingston: McGill-Queen's University Press, 2011), 5–8.

53   Ferry, "'To the Interests and Conscience of the Great Mass of the Community'": 142–143.

54   Ferry, "'To the Interests and Conscience of the Great Mass of the Community'": 155.

55   Heron, *Booze*, 11.

56   John C. Burnham, *Bad Habits: Drinking, Smoking, Taking Drugs, Gambling, Sexual Misbehaviour, and Swearing in American History* (New York: New York University Press, 1993), 59; Heron, *Booze*, 67.

57   Cheryl Krasnick Warsh, "'Oh, Lord, Pour a Cordial in her Wounded Heart'. The Drinking Woman in Victorian and Edwardian Canada," in Cheryl K. Warsh, ed., *Drink in Canada: Historical Essays* (Montreal & Kingston: McGill-Queen's University Press, 1993): 76–80.

58   Quoted in Warsh, "'Oh, Lord…'": 83.

59   Warsh, "'Oh, Lord…'"

60   Warsh, "'Oh, Lord, Pour a Cordial in her Wounded Heart'"; Gagnon, *Religion, Moralité, Modernité*, 94–95.

61   Mimi Ajzenstadt, "Racializing Prohibitions: Alcohol Laws and Racial/Ethnic Minorities in British Columbia, 1871–1927," in John McLaren, Robert Menzies, and Dorothy E. Chunn, eds., *Regulating Lives: Historical Essays on the State, Society, the Individuals, and the Law* (Vancouver: UBC Press, 2002), 97–119.

62   Heron, *Booze*, 102.

63   Ajzenstadt, "Racializing Prohibitions," 97–119.

64   Greg Marquis, "Alcohol and the Family in Canada," *Journal of Family History* 29, no. 3 (July 2004): 313.

65   Jacques-Paul Couturier, "Prohibition or Regulation? The Enforcement of the Canada Temperance Act in Moncton, 1881–1896," in Warsh, ed., *Drink in Canada*, 144–165.

66   Couturier, "Prohibition or Regulation," 151–152.

67   Couturier, "Prohibition or Regulation."

68   Couturier, "Prohibition or Regulation."

69   Couturier, "Prohibition or Regulation," 162–164.

70   Jean Hamelin and Nicole Gagnon, *Histoire du catholicisme québécois: Le XXe siècle. Tome 1 1898–1940* (Montreal: Boréal Express, 1984).

71   Benoit Dostie and Ruth Dupré, "'The People's Will': Canadians and the 1898 Referendum on Alcohol Prohibition," *Explorations in Economic History* 49, no. 4 (2012): 503–504.

72   Hamelin and Gagnon, *Histoire du catholicisme québécois: Le XXe siècle*.

73   John Herd Thompson, *The Harvests of War: The Prairies West, 1914–1918* (Toronto: McClelland and Stewart, 1978), 97.

74   Thompson, *The Harvests of War*, 99.

75   Hamelin and Gagnon, *Histoire du catholicisme québécois: Le XXe siècle*, 216.

76   Hamelin and Gagnon, *Histoire du catholicisme québécois: Le XXe siècle*.

77   Heron, *Booze*, 183.

78   The three small towns are Dresden, Elora, and Tillsonburg. Rebecca Beausaert, "Benevolence, Bicycles, and Quilting Bees: Leisure, Gender, and Class in Small-Town Ontario, 1870–1914," PhD dissertation, York University, 2013, 338.

79   Kevin B. Wamsley, "State Formation and Institutionalized Racism: Gambling Laws in Nineteenth and Early Twentieth Century Canada," *Sport History Review* 29 (1998): 77–85.

80   Burnham, *Bad Habits*; Suzanne Morton, *At Odds: Gambling and Canadians, 1919–1969* (Toronto: University of Toronto Press, 2003).

81   Burnham, *Bad Habits*; Morton, *At Odds*.

82   Magaly Brodeur, *Vice et corruption à Montréal, 1892–1970* (Quebec: Les Presses de l'Université du Québec, 2011).

83   Brodeur, *Vice et corruption à Montréal, 1892–1970*; Michel Labrosse, *The Lottery from Jacques Cartier's Day to Modern Times: Sidelights on the History of Lotteries in Québec*, trans. Alan Brown (Montreal: Stanké, 1985), 82.

84   Labrosse, *The Lottery from Jacques Cartier's Day to Modern Times*, 83–84.

85   Brodeur, *Vice et corruption à Montréal, 1892–1970*, 23.

86   Douglas A. Brown, "Thoroughbred Horse-Racing Receives an Imperialist Nod: The Parliamentary Debate on Legalizing Gambling in Canada, 1910," *International Journal of the History of Sport* 11, no. 2 (August 1994): 252–269; Greg Marquis, "Vancouver Vice: The Police and the Negotiation of Morality, 1904–1935," in Hamar Foster and John McLaren, eds., *Essays in the History of Canadian Law*, vol. 6, *British Columbia and the Yukon* (Toronto: Osgoode Society for Canadian Legal History, 1995): 242–273.

87   Colin S. Campbell, ed. *Gambling in Canada: The Bottom Line* (Vancouver: Criminology Research Centre, School of Criminology at Simon Fraser University, 1994), viii; Morton, *At Odds*, 10–12; Labrosse, *The Lottery from Jacques Cartier's Day to Modern Times*, 102.

88   Brodeur, *Vice et corruption à Montréal, 1892–1970*.

89   Julia Buxton, *The Political Economy of Narcotics: Production, Consumption, & Global Markets* (Black Point, Canada; London; New York: Fernwood Publishing, 2006), 15; Burnham, *Bad Habits*, 112–113; Holly Marie Karibo, "Ambassadors of Pleasure: Illicit Economies in the Detroit–Windsor Borderland, 1945–1960," PhD dissertation, University of Toronto, 2012; Clayton Mosher, "The Legal Response to Narcotic Drugs in Five Ontario Cities, 1908–1961," PhD dissertation, University of Toronto, 1992, 35, quoted in Karibo's dissertation.

90   Catherine Carstairs, "Deporting 'Ah Sin' to Save the White Race: Moral Panic, Racialization, and the Extension of Canadian Drug Laws in the 1920s," *Canadian Bulletin of Medical History/Bulletin canadien d'histoire de la médecine* 16, no. 1 (1999): 65–88; Daniel J. Malleck, "'Its Baneful Influences Are Too Well Known': Debates over Drug Use in Canada, 1867–1908," *Canadian Bulletin of Medical History/Bulletin canadien d'histoire de la médecine* 4 (1997): 263–288.

91   R. MacGregor Dawson, *William Lyon Mackenzie King: A Political Biography, 1874–1923* (Toronto: University of Toronto Press, 1958), 146–147; W. L. Mackenzie King, *Report into the Losses Sustained by the Chinese Population of Vancouver, B.C. on the Occasion of the Riots in that City in September, 1907* (Ottawa: S. E. Dawson, 1908).

92   Glenn F. Murray, "Cocaine Use in the Era of Social Reform: The Natural History of a Social Problem in Canada, 1880–1911," *Canadian Journal of Law and Society/Revue canadienne de droit et société* 2 (1987): 29–43.

93   Kenneth J. Meier, *The Politics of Sin: Drugs, Alcohol, and Public Policy* (Armonk, NY: M. E. Sharpe, 1994).

94   Jarrett Rudy, *The Freedom to Smoke: Tobacco Consumption and Identity* (Montreal & Kingston: McGill-Queen's University Press, 2005).

95   Cheryl Krasnick Warsh, "Smoke and Mirrors: Gender Representation in North American Tobacco and Alcohol Advertisements before 1950," *Histoire sociale/Social History* 31 (1999): 183–221; Rudy, *The Freedom to Smoke*.

96   Sharon Anne Cook, *Sex, Lies and Cigarettes: Canadian Women, Smoking, and Visual Culture, 1880–2000* (Montreal & Kingston: McGill-Queen's University Press, 2012), 26.

97   Cook, "Through Sunshine and Shadow," 54.

98   Valverde, *Age of Light, Soap, and Water*, 71; Rob Cunningham, *Smoke & Mirrors: The Canadian Tobacco War* (Ottawa: International Development Research Centre, 1996), 32; Pamela E. Pennock, *Advertising Sin and Sickness: The Politics of Alcohol and Tobacco Marketing, 1950–1990* (DeKalb, IL: Northern Illinois University Press, 2007).

99   Youmans, *Campaign Echoes*, 92.

100 Rudy, *The Freedom to Smoke*, 22–23.

101 Rudy, *The Freedom to Smoke*, 22, 25.

102 Rudy, *The Freedom to Smoke*, 22, 93.

103 "His Tongue Cut Out," *Globe*, March 30, 1904, 9; "Result of Smoking, *Globe*, January 21, 1905, 5; "Smoking and the 'Flu,'" *Toronto Star*, October 21, 1918, 7.

104 *Daily Mail and Empire*, November 19, 1898, 20; March 11, 1899, 7; "Tobacco Heart Cured by Millburn's Heart and Nerve Pills," *Toronto Star*, December 9, 1915, 11.

105 Rudy, *The Freedom to Smoke*, 96–100.

106 Rudy, *The Freedom to Smoke*, 99, 103.

107 "To Prohibit Cigarettes," *Globe*, March 24, 1904, 8.

108 "House Discusses Cigarette Evil," *Globe*, March 5, 1907, 10; "War on the Cigarette. W.C.T.U. Deputation See Sir Wilfrid Laurier," *Globe*, December 3, 1907, 4; Rudy, *The Freedom to Smoke*, 102–105.

109 Cook, *Sex, Lies and Cigarettes*, 46.

110 Cook, *Sex, Lies and Cigarettes*, 46; Rudy, *The Freedom to Smoke*, 102–105.

111 Spence, *Prohibition in Canada*, xiii.

NOTES TO CHAPTER 4

1   Quoted in Leslie Ann Jeffrey and Gayle MacDonald, *Sex Workers in the Maritimes: Talk Back* (Vancouver: UBC Press, 2006), 227.

2   Andrée Lévesque, *Making and Breaking the Rules: Women in Quebec, 1919–1939* (Toronto: McClelland & Stewart, 1994), 88.

3   Lévesque, *Making and Breaking the Rules*, 89–90.

4   Angus McLaren, *The Trials of Masculinity: Policing Sexual Boundaries, 1870–1930* (Chicago: University of Chicago Press, 1997), 71.

5   McLaren, *The Trials of Masculinity*, 86.

6   *Report of the Committee on the Operation of the Abortion Law* (Ottawa: Minister of Supply and Services Canada, 1977), 66.

7   Brenda Margaret Appleby, *Responsible Parenthood: Decriminalizing Contraception in Canada* (Toronto: University of Toronto Press, 1999), 3.

8   Angus McLaren, *Our Own Master Race: Eugenics in Canada, 1885–1945* (Toronto: McClelland & Stewart, 1990), 77, 84; Angus McLaren and Arlene Tigar McLaren, *The Bedroom and the State: The Changing Practices and Politics of Contraception and Abortion in Canada, 1880–1997*, 2nd ed. (Don Mills, ON: Oxford University Press, 1997).

9   McLaren, *Twentieth-Century Sexuality: A History* (Oxford, UK; Malden, MA: Blackwell, 1999), 82.

10   *Casti Connubii Encyclical of Pope Pius XI on Christian Marriage to the Venerable Brethren, Patriarchs, Primates, Archbishops, Bishops, and Other Local Ordinaries Enjoying Peace and Communion with the Apostolic See*, http://www.vatican.va/holy_father/pius_xi/encyclicals/documents/hf_p-xi_enc_31121930_casti-connubii_en.html.

11   Appleby, *Responsible Parenthood*, 64; McLaren and McLaren, *The Bedroom and the State*, 96.

12   Andrea Tone, *Devices and Desires: A History of Contraceptives in America* (New York: Hill and Wang, 2001), 237; McLaren, *Twentieth-Century Sexuality: A History*, 82.

13   Appleby, *Responsible Parenthood*, 29.

14   Jennifer Wells, "Everything You Know about the Sexual Revolution Is Wrong," *Toronto Star*, May 8, 2010, IN1, IN4.

15 Christabelle Sethna, "The Evolution of the Birth Control Handbook: From Student Peer-Education Manual to Feminist Self-empowerment Text, 1968–1975," *Canadian Bulletin of Medical History/Bulletin canadien d'histoire de la médecine* 23, no. 1 (2006): 89–118.

16 Appleby, *Responsible Parenthood*, 3; "Fine Man $100 for Advertising Contraceptives," *Globe and Mail*, April 26, 1964, 4.

17 Appleby, *Responsible Parenthood*, 71.

18 "Catholics May Use Contraceptives Now," *Globe and Mail*, April 9, 1966, 6; *Globe and Mail*, April 12, 1967.

19 Bernard Asbell, *The Pill: A Biography of the Drug That Changed the World* (New York: Random House, 1995).

20 United Church of Canada, Abortion: A Study, 39–40, quoted in Bruce Douville, "The Uncomfortable Pew: Christianity, The New Left, and the Hip Counterculture in Toronto, 1965–1975," PhD dissertation, York University, 2011, 411.

21 United Church of Canada, Twenty-Fifth General Council, 169, quoted in Douville, "The Uncomfortable Pew," 412.

22 Douville, "The Uncomfortable Pew," 408.

23 The Canadian Catholic Conference, "Pastoral Statement on Proposed Change of Canadian Law on Abortion," in E. F. Sheridan, ed., *Love Kindness! The Social Teaching of the Canadian Catholic Bishops (1958–1989): A Second Collection* (Toronto: Editions Paulines and Jesuit Centre for Social Faith and Justice, 1991), 136.

24 *Encyclical Letter Humanae Vitae of the Supreme Pontiff Paul VI to his venerable brothers the Patriarchs, Archbishops, Bishops, and other local Ordinaries in Peace and Communion with the Apostolic See, to the Clergy and Faithful of the Whole Catholic World, and to all Men of Good Will, on the Regulation of Birth*, http://www.vatican.va/holy_father/paul_vi/encyclicals/documents/hf_p-vi_enc_25071968_humanae-vitae_en.html.

25 Paul Litt, *Elusive Destiny: The Political Vocation of John Napier Turner* (Vancouver: UBC Press, 2011), 101.

26 Appleby, *Responsible Parenthood*, 31, 35–36.

27 Appleby, *Responsible Parenthood*, 43.

28 Appleby, *Responsible Parenthood*, 44.

29 The Gallup Poll of Canada (Toronto: Canadian Institute of Public Opinion, 1952, 1961, 1965, 1967, and 1968).

30 The Gallup Poll of Canada (Toronto: Canadian Institute of Public Opinion, 1965).

31 John English, *Just Watch Me: The Life of Pierre Elliott Trudeau, 1968–2000* (Toronto: Knopf Canada, 2009).

32 Litt, *Elusive Destiny*, 98–99.

33 *Encyclical Letter Humanae Vitae*, http://www.vatican.va/holy_father/paul_vi/encyclicals/documents/hf_p-vi_enc_25071968_humanae-vitae_en.html113.

34 English, *Just Watch Me*, 112.

35 Quoted in Litt, *Elusive Destiny*, 101. Litt does not know the name of the Dominican theologian.

36 Quoted in Litt, *Elusive Destiny*, 102.

37 English, *Just Watch Me*, 249.

38 *Report of the Committee on the Operation of the Abortion Law*, 110.

39 Beth Palmer, "'Lonely, tragic, but legally necessary pilgrimages': Transnational Abortion Travel in the 1970s," *Canadian Historical Review* 92, no. 4 (December 2011): 637–664; Christabelle Sethna and Steve Hewitt, "Clandestine Operations: The Vancouver Women's Caucus, the Abortion Caravan, and the RCMP," *Canadian Historical Review* 90, no. 3 (September 2009): 463–495.

40 Diane Lamoureux, "La lutte pour le droit à l'avortement (1969–1981)," *Revue d'histoire de l'Amérique française* 37, no. 1 (1983): 84–85.

41 *R. v. Morgentaler* 1 S.C.R. 30, Supreme Court of Canada, January 28, 1988, http://scc.lexum.org/en/1988.html.

42 *R. v. Morgentaler* 3 S.C.R. 463, Supreme Court of Canada, September 30, 1993, http://scc
    .lexum.org/en/1993.html.

43 Ingrid Peritz, "G20 Maternal Health," *Globe and Mail*, June 19, 2010, A1, A15; Oliver Moore, "No
    Takers for Abortion Debate in New Brunswick," *Globe and Mail*, September 30, 2010, A11.

44 Michaela Freund, "The Politics of Naming: Constructing Prostitutes and Regulating Women
    in Vancouver, 1939–45," in John McLaren, Robert Menzies, and Dorothy E. Chunn, eds.,
    Regulating Lives: Historical Essay on the State, Society, the Individual, and the Law (Vancou-
    ver: UBC Press, 2002), 231–258.

45 Danielle Lacasse, *La prostitution feminine à Montréal, 1945–1970* (Montreal: Boréal, 1994),
    38–47.

46 Lacasse, *La prostitution feminine à Montréal*, 38–47.

47 Lacasse, *La prostitution feminine à Montréal*, 38–47.

48 Holly Marie Karibo, "Ambassadors of Pleasure: Illicit Economies in the Detroit–Windsor
    Borderland, 1945–1960," PhD dissertation, University of Toronto, 2012.

49 Jeffrey and MacDonald, *Sex Workers in the Maritimes*.

50 Lacasse, *La prostitution feminine à Montréal*.

51 Jeffrey and MacDonald, *Sex Workers in the Maritimes*.

52 "Red Light District Pitched for Toronto Island. But Residents Aren't Keen about Coun.
    Mammoliti's 'Brothel Island' Idea," CBC News, March 23, 2011, http://www.cbc.ca/news/
    canada/toronto/story/2011/03/23/mammoliti-sextrade-toronto-island.html; Jeffrey and
    MacDonald, *Sex Workers in the Maritimes*.

53 Jeffrey and MacDonald, *Sex Workers in the Maritimes*, 124–125.

54 Lacasse, *La prostitution feminine à Montréal*.

55 Lacasse, *La prostitution feminine à Montréal*.

56 Karlene Faith, *Unruly Women: The Politics of Confinement and Resistance* (Vancouver: Press
    Gang Publishers, 1993), 80–81; Jeffrey and MacDonald, *Sex Workers in the Maritimes*.

57 Jeffrey and MacDonald, *Sex Workers in the Maritimes*, 224.

58 *Hutt v. The Queen* 2 S.C.R. 476, Supreme Court of Canada, February 7, 1978, http://scc
    .lexum.org/en/1978.html.

59 Kirk Makin, "Court Strikes Down Federal Prostitution Law," *Globe and Mail*, September 29,
    2010, A13.

60 Patrice Corriveau, *Judging Homosexuals: A History of Gay Persecution in Quebec and France*,
    trans. Käthe Roth (Vancouver: UBC Press, 2011), 82.

61 Reg Whitaker, Gregory S. Kealey, and Andrew Parnaby, *Secret Service: Political Policing in
    Canada from the Fenians to Fortress America* (Toronto: University of Toronto Press, 2012),
    191.

62 Daniel J. Robinson and David Kimmel, "The Queer Career of Homosexual Security Vetting
    in Cold War Canada," *Canadian Historical Review* 75, no. 3 (1994): 340.

63 Whitaker, Kealey, and Parnaby, *Secret Service*, 191.

64 Quoted in Corriveau, *Judging Homosexuals*, 83; Gary Kinsman and Patrizia Gentile, *The
    Canadian War on Queers: National Security as Sexual Regulation* (Vancouver: UBC Press,
    2010).

65 Corriveau, *Judging Homosexuals*, 93–94.

66 Stuart Chambers, "Pierre Elliott Trudeau and Bill C-150: A Rational Approach to Homo-
    sexual Acts, 1968–69," *Journal of Homosexuality* 57, no. 2 (2010): 249–266.

67 Laurier L. LaPierre, "Trudeau's 'Indelible Imprint," *XTra!*, May 21, 2009, 16.

68 *Klippert v. the Queen*, S.C.R. 822, Supreme Court of Canada, November 7, 1967, http://scc
    .lexum.org/en/1967.html.

69 "Timeline, Same-Sex Rights in Canada," CBC News, http://www.cbc.ca/news/canada/
    story/2012/01/12/f-same-sex-rights.html.

70 LaPierre, "Trudeau's 'Indelible Imprint," 15.

71 Ian McKay, "Sarnia in the Sixties (or The Peculiarities of the Canadians)," in Karen Dubinsky
    et al., eds., *New World Coming: The Sixties and the Shaping of Global Consciousness* (Toronto:
    Between the Lines, 2009), 33.

72   English, *Just Watch Me*, 115.

73   English, *Just Watch Me*, 118.

74   We Demand, The August 28th Gay Day Committee, *The Body Politic*, Issue 1 (Nov.–Dec. 1971) Reprinted in *Flaunting It!*, 1982, http://www.clga.ca/Material/Records/docs/wedemand.html.

75   Sylvain Larocque, *Gay Marriage: The Story of a Canadian Social Revolution* (Toronto: James Lorimer, 2006), 15–21.

76   "Ontario Unable to Register Same-Sex Marriages," January 15, 2001, http://www.samesexmarriage.ca/press/pressrelease_refused.html; Elaine and Anne's Affidavit, Court File No. 39/2001, Ontario Superior Court of Justice (Divisional Court), Metropolitan Community Church of Toronto (applicant) and the Attorney General of Canada and the Attorney General of Ontario (Respondents), http://www.samesexmarriage.ca/legal/elaine_and_anne_affidavit.html.

77   Larocque, *Gay Marriage*, 71–73, 87–88.

78   Reference re Same-Sex Marriage, 2004 SCC 79, 3 S.C.R. 698, Supreme Court of Canada, December 9, 2004, http://scc.lexum.org/en/2004/2004scc79/2004scc79.html.

79   "Timeline, Same-Sex Rights in Canada," CBC News.

80   Gloria Galloway, "Ottawa Rejects Call to Halt Gay Marriage," *Globe and Mail*, January 20, 2005, A1.

81   "Same-sex Marriage: Canadian Public Opinion Polls 1996 to 2002," http://www.religioustolerance.org/hom_marz.htm.

82   Tonda MacCharles, "Canadians Split over Same-Sex Marriage," *Toronto Star*, February 12, 2005, A1.

83   Aloysius Ambrozic, "An Open Letter: Why the Rush on Same-Sex Marriage?" *Globe and Mail*, January 19, 2005, A19; Gloria Galloway, "Ottawa Rejects Call to Halt Gay Marriage," *Globe and Mail*, January 20, 2005, A1.

84   "The Vatican's Reach, the Politician's Duty," *Globe and Mail*, August 1, 2003, A16.

85   Michael Valpy, "An Archbishop's Ire: In Newfoundland a Priest Is Scolded for His Comments on Gay Marriage," *Globe and Mail*, August 19, 2003, A2; "Time Line, Same-sex Rights in Canada," CBC News.

86   Michael Riordan, *The First Stone: Homosexuality and the United Church* (Toronto: McClelland and Stewart, 1990); Douville, "The Uncomfortable Pew," 522.

87   "Time Line, Same-sex Rights in Canada," CBC News.

88   "Statement from the House of Bishops to the Members of General Synod," May 1, 2007, in *History of Statements and Resolutions about Homosexuality. Anglican Church of Canada General Synod and House of Bishops*, 14, http://www.anglican.ca/faith/files/2010/10/hsrh.pdf.

89   Wendy Stueck, "Canada Would Become Magnet for Polygamy if Law Struck Down, Court Told," *Globe and Mail*, November 23, 2010, A6; "B.C. Civil Rights Group Backs Polygamists," *Toronto Star*, March 18, 2011, A12; Wendy Stueck and Justine Hunter, "Anti-Polygamy Law Constitutional: B.C. Attorney General Shirley Bond Says Province Won't Take Immediate Legal Action Against Polygamists in Bountiful," *Globe and Mail*, November 24, 2011, A8.

90   "Foreign Couple's Divorce a First for Same-Sex Unions Solemnized in Canada," *Globe and Mail*, September 10, 2013 (online edition).

91   Craig Heron, *Booze: A Distilled History* (Toronto: Between the Lines, 2003).

92   Jim Leitzel, *Regulating Vice: Misguided Prohibitions and Realistic Controls* (Cambridge and New York: Cambridge University Press, 2008).

93   Italics are author's. Line Beauchesne, "Setting Public Policy on Drugs: A Choice of Social Values," in Edgar-André Montigny, ed., *The Real Dope: Social, Legal, and Historical Perspectives on the Regulation of Drugs in Canada* (Toronto: University of Toronto Press, 2011), 26.

94   Heron, *Booze*; Dan Malleck, *Try to Control Yourself: The Regulation of Public Drinking in Post-Prohibition Ontario, 1927–44* (Vancouver: UBC Press, 2012).

95   Mariana Valverde, *Diseases of the Will: Alcohol and the Dilemmas of Freedom* (Cambridge and New York: Cambridge University Press, 1998), 9.

96   Valverde, *Diseases of the Will*; Dale Barbour, "Drinking Together: The Role of Gender in Changing Manitoba's Liquor Laws in the 1950s," in Esyllt W. Jones and Gerald Friesen, eds., *Prairie Metropolis: New Essays on Winnipeg Social History* (Winnipeg: University of Manitoba Press, 2009); Robert A. Campbell, *Sit Down and Drink Your Beer: Regulating Vancouver's Beer Parlours, 1925–1954* (Toronto: University of Toronto Press, 2001); Malleck, *Try to Control Yourself.*

97   Beauchesne, "Setting Public Policy on Drugs," 32–33; Heron, *Booze*; Alberta Gaming and Liquor Commission, "Liquor History & Facts," http://aglc.ca/liquor/liquorhistoryandfacts.asp.

98   Jane Taber, "Merchants Push for Liquor Sales," *Globe and Mail*, August 5, 2013, A4.

99   Keith Leslie, "Corner Stores Want Right to Sell Alcohol," *Globe and Mail*, July 26, 2012, A10.

100 Richard Mackie, "Unloading Key Assets Not Harris Priority LCBO Has Done Well and Won't Be Sold; Future of TV Network Remains in Doubt," *Globe and Mail*, May 27, 1998, A5.

101 Keith Leslie, "Wynne Rejects Call to Sell Alcohol in Convenience Stores," *Globe and Mail*, October 30, 2013, A8.

102 "Vices Top Oil and Gas Revenues in Alberta," Jason Fekete and Renata D'Aliesio, *National Post*, August 27, 2010, A6; Keith Leslie, "Corner Stores Want Right to Sell Alcohol," *Globe and Mail*, July 26, 2012, A10.

103 Pamela E. Pennock, *Advertising Sin and Sickness: The Politics of Alcohol and Tobacco Marketing, 1950–1990* (DeKalb: Northern Illinois University Press, 2007), 26; Valverde, *Diseases of the Will.*

104 Erika Dyck, *Psychedelic Psychiatry: LSD from Clinic to Campus* (Baltimore: Johns Hopkins University Press, 2008), 54.

105 Pennock, *Advertising Sin and Sickness*, 26; Valverde, *Diseases of the Will*, 19.

106 Pennock, *Advertising Sin and Sickness*, 27.

107 John C. Burnham, *Bad Habits: Drinking, Smoking, Taking Drugs, Gambling, Sexual Misbehaviour, and Swearing in American History* (New York: New York University Press, 1993), 80–81.

108 Beauchesne, "Setting Public Policy on Drugs," 43.

109 "History," Opération Nez Rouge/Operation Red Nose, http://operationnezrouge.com/en/home.html.

110 Michel Labrosse, *The Lottery from Jacques Cartier's Day to Modern Times: Sidelights on the History of Lotteries in Québec*, trans. Alan Brown (Montreal: Stanké, 1985), 110–129; Suzanne Morton, *At Odds: Gambling and Canadians, 1919–1969* (Toronto: University of Toronto Press, 2003), 186–190; Brodeur, *Vice et corruption*, 94–104.

111 Labrosse, *The Lottery from Jacques Cartier's Day to Modern Times*, 110.

112 "Sweepstakes Bill Again Is Presented," *The Globe*, February 12, 1932, 3.

113 Morton, *At Odds*, 181.

114 Litt, *Elusive Destiny*, 97.

115 Burnham, *Bad Habits*, 167; Campbell, *Gambling in Canada.*

116 Colin S. Campbell, ed., *Gambling in Canada: The Bottom Line* (Vancouver: Criminology Research Centre, School of Criminology at Simon Fraser University, 1994), vii–ix.

117 Adam Radwanski, "Ontario's Premier Dad Rolls Dice on Online Gambling," *Globe and Mail*, August 11, 2010, A6; Tanya Talaga, "Toronto Could Get Temporary Casino until Site Built," *Toronto Star*, March 14, 2012, A6.

118 Campbell, *Gambling in Canada.*

119 Campbell, *Gambling in Canada*; Morton, *At Odds*, 177.

120 Lisa Priest, "A Family Man's Tragic Transformation," *Globe and Mail*, October 3, 2009, A10; "Casinos Spend Millions to Make Losers Feel Like Winners; Addicts Get Gifts to Come Back, but No Help to Stay Away," *Globe and Mail*, October 3, 2009, A1, A11; "The Million-Dollar Club: Losing Big, Losing Often," *Globe and Mail*, October 5, 2009, A4; "Wheels of Fate Aren't Always Kind to Seniors," *Globe and Mail*, October 6, 2009, A15.

121 "Gambling Addict Loses Lawsuit Against Casino," *Toronto Star*, October 9, 2012, A16.

122 Adrian Morrow, Elizabeth Church, and Marina Strauss, "Wynne Urges Expanded Lottery System to Maximize Revenue for Province," *Globe and Mail*, February 26, 2013, A6.

123 Elizabeth Church and Tara Perkins, "Ontario's Privatization Gamble; Bidding Has Begun for Province's Lottery Business as Gaming Commission Presses for a High-Tech Makeover," *Globe and Mail*, February 25, 2013, A1.

124 Catherine Carstairs, *Jailed for Possession: Illegal Drug Use, Regulation, and Power in Canada, 1920–1961* (Toronto: University of Toronto Press, 2006).

125 Carstairs, *Jailed for Possession*.

126 Reginald Whitaker, *Drugs and the Law: The Canadian Scene* (Toronto: Methuen, 1969), 42–43.

127 "Sampled LSD, Youth Plunges from Viaduct," *Globe and Mail*, March 20, 1967, 1.

128 Marcel Martel, *Not This Time: Canadians, Public Policy and the Marijuana Question, 1961–1975* (Toronto: University of Toronto Press, 2006); Marcel Martel, "Setting Boundaries: LSD Use and Glue Sniffing in Ontario in the 1960s," *The Real Dope*.

129 Martel, *Not This Time*.

130 The German manufacturer of thalidomide issued an apology and asked for forgiveness, in September 2012. Stephanie Findlay, "Thalidomide Maker Finally Issues Apology," *Toronto Star*, September 1, 2012, A2.

131 Martel, *Not This Time*.

132 Reginald G. Smart and Dianne Fejer, "The Extent of Illicit Drug Use in Canada: A Review of Current Epidemiology," in Paul C. Whitehead, Carl F. Grindstaff, and Craig L. Boydell, eds., *Alcohol and Other Drugs: Perspectives on Use, Abuse, Treatment and Prevention* (Toronto: Holt, Rinehart and Winston of Canada, 1971), 144, 146.

133 Martel, *Not This Time*.

134 Martel, *Not This Time*.

135 "Munro Hints at Eased Marijuana Sentences," *Globe and Mail*, August 20, 1968, 1.

136 Martel, *Not This Time*.

137 Martel, *Not This Time*.

138 Krista Foss, "The Transformation of Mary Jane," *Globe and Mail*, November 24, 1998, C10; Krista Foss, "Chronically Ill Cheer Marijuana Trials," *Globe and Mail*, March 5, 1999, A12.

139 "Ottawa doit changer sa loi sur la marijuana," *Le Soleil*, August 1, 2000, A7. "Ailing Alberta Man Wins Right to Grow Pot," *Globe and Mail*, December 12, 2000, A6.

140 Colin Freeze and Carolyn Abraham, "Marijuana Regulation Draws Fire," *Globe and Mail*, July 31, 2001, A1, A8.

141 "Fantino Urges Decriminalizing of Marijuana," *Globe and Mail*, June 3, 2000, A25.

142 Senate Special Committee on Illegal Drugs, *Cannabis: Our Position for a Canadian Public Policy* (Ottawa: 2002), 42, 46; Brian Laghi and Kim Lunman, "Parliamentary Committee to Recommend New Pot Law," *Globe and Mail*, December 11, 2002, A10; House of Commons Special Committee on Non-Medical Use of Drugs, *Policy for the New Millennium: Working Together to Redefine Canada's Drug Strategy* (Ottawa: 2002).

143 "Ottawa's Marijuana Plans Get Pat from UN Agency," *Globe and Mail*, June 5, 2003, A11; Janice Tibbetts, "Liberals' Pot Bill Denounced; Even Caucus Opposes Plan," *National Post*, May 28, 2003, A4.

144 Kim Lunman, "U.S. Fears Change in Marijuana Laws," *Globe and Mail*, December 13, 2002, A9; "Cellucci Repeats Warning over Decriminalizing Pot," *Globe and Mail*, May 3, 2003, A4.

145 Rob Cunningham, *Smoke & Mirrors: The Canadian Tobacco War* (Ottawa: International Development Research Centre, 1996), 14–15; Burnham, *Bad Habits*, 97–98.

146 Sharon Anne Cook, *Sex, Lies and Cigarettes: Canadian Women, Smoking, and Visual Culture, 1880–2000* (Montreal & Kingston: McGill-Queen's University Press, 2012), 42.

147 Cunningham, *Smoke & Mirrors*, 40–41; Cook, *Sex, Lies and Cigarettes*; Burnham, *Bad Habits*, 103–106.

148 Jarrett Rudy, *The Freedom to Smoke: Tobacco Consumption and Identity* (Montreal & Kingston: McGill-Queen's University Press, 2005), 102–103.

149 *House of Commons Debates*, June 17, 1963, pp. 1213–1214.
150 "LaMarsh Cigarets Hit the Deck," *Toronto Star*, June 17, 1963, 1; "Judy May Filter 'Romantic' Cigaret Ads," *Toronto Star*, June 18, 1963, 4; Peter Trueman, "Ottawa Seeks Teen Ideas for Anti-Smoking Campaign," *Toronto Star*, May 13, 1965, 25; Cook, *Sex, Lies and Cigarettes*, 47–48; Cunningham, *Smoke & Mirrors*, 45–51.
151 U.S. Public Health Service, *Smoking and Health: Report of the Advisory Committee to the Surgeon General of the Public Health Service* (Washington, DC: GPO, 1964), 350.
152 Cook, *Sex, Lies and Cigarettes*, 42.
153 Pennock, *Advertising Sin and Sickness*, 99.
154 Burnham, *Bad Habits*, 283–88.
155 Pennock, *Advertising Sin and Sickness*, 100; Cunningham, *Smoke & Mirrors*, 45–46.
156 Pennock, *Advertising Sin and Sickness*, 101.
157 Cook, *Sex, Lies and Cigarettes*, 50–51.
158 Cigarette Advertising Code of Canadian Tobacco Manufactures, June 19, 1964, http://legacy.library.ucsf.edu/tid/zrc54e00/pdf;jsessionid=ED4ACFD820CC1DE64DBBF084DB51C81D.tobacco03.
159 Cook, *Sex, Lies and Cigarettes*, 322.
160 Cunningham, *Smoke & Mirrors*, 65–77, 82.
161 *Proposed New Labelling Requirements for Tobacco Products. Consultation Paper* (Health Canada, 1999), 3, http://www.tobaccolabels.ca/health/canada19; Cook, *Sex, Lies and Cigarettes*, 47–52; Paul Taylor, "Tough on Bisphenol A, Dithering on Cigarette Packages," *Globe and Mail*, December 31, 2010, L6.
162 Trevor Haché, "Imperial and Rothmans Admit Guilt in 1990s Cigarette Smuggling Crimes," August 19, 2008, Non-Smokers' Rights Association, http://www.nsra-adnf.ca/cms/index.cfm?group_id=1522.
163 "Ontario Passes Tough New Anti-Smoking Legislation," http://www.cbc.ca/archives/categories/health/public-health/butting-out-the-slow-death-of-smoking-in-canada/ontario-passes-tough-new-anti-smoking-legislation.html.
164 Cecil Foster, "Greyhound Butts Out Smoke," *Globe and Mail*, June 21, 1985, B11.
165 Doug Yonson, "Voyageur Bans Smoking on Some Ottawa–Montreal Runs," *Ottawa Citizen*, June 21, 1986, A12; David Gersovitz, "Scoring Points on Planes, Trains, Buses: Non-Smokers Clear the Air," *Globe and Mail*, February 23, 1985, T4; Cunningham, *Smoke & Mirrors*, 113–114.
166 André Picard, "Smoking Ban Linked to Drop in Hospitalizations," *Globe and Mail*, April 13, 2010, A7.
167 "The Heather Crowe Campaign," http://www.smoke-free.ca/heathercrowe/.
168 Ian Bailey, "Vancouver Extends Smoking Crackdown; City Widens War on Tobacco with Ban at Parks and Beaches, with Almost All Public Spaces off Limits," *Globe and Mail*, April 21, 2010, A11; Adrian Nieoczym, "You Can't Smoke in Kelowna—but Don't Expect to See the Signs. B.C. City Passed a Ban on Public Smoking, but Was Unable to Afford the Signage Alerting the Public to the New Law," *Globe and Mail*, March 8, 2011, A3; "Anti-Smoking Efforts in Canada and Abroad," http://www.cbc.ca/news/health/story/2009/09/29/f-smoking-bans-tobacco.html.
169 "Tobacco Lawyers Attack Expert Witness Before Testimony in Quebec," Canadian Press, November 26, 2012, http://www.cbc.ca/news/canada/montreal/story/2012/11/26/mtl-tobacco-lawsuit-to-hear-from-robert-proctor.html.
170 Steve Rennie, "Does Ottawa Share Responsibility for the Costs of Smoking?" *Globe and Mail*, July 29, 2011, A4; "Federal Government Not Liable in Smoking Lawsuits, Court Rules," *Toronto Star*, July 30, 2011, A10; Les Perreaux, "Tobacco Firms Face All-out Assault in Courts," *Globe and Mail*, March 10, 2012, A6.
171 "Tobacco Litigation: Canadian Efforts to Hold Tobacco Companies Accountable," http://www.smoke-free.ca/litigation/webpages/Knight.htm.
172 Rennie, "Does Ottawa Share Responsibility for the Costs of Smoking?"; "Federal Government Not Liable in Smoking Lawsuits, Court Rules," *Toronto Star*, July 30, 2011, A10.

173   "Tobacco Litigation: Canadian Efforts to Hold Tobacco Companies Accountable."

174   *R. v. Imperial Tobacco Canada Ltd.*, 2011. SCC 42, 29 July 2011, http://scc.lexum.org/decisia
-scc-csc/scc-csc/scc-csc/en/item/7957/index.do.

175   Michelle McQuigge, "Smoking Rates Hit an All-Time Low," *Globe and Mail*, September 8,
2011, L6.

NOTE TO CONCLUSION

1   This activism is not unique to morally based issues. There is a similar trend in the language
issue. See Marcel Martel and Martin Pâquet, *Speaking Up: A History of Language and Politics
in Canada and Quebec,* trans. Patricia Dumas (Toronto: Between the Lines, 2012).

BIBLIOGRAPHY

BOOKS AND ARTICLES

Abbott, Elizabeth. *A History of Marriage*. Toronto: Penguin Canada, 2010.

Airhart, Phyllis. *Serving the Present Age: Revivalism, Progressivism, and the Methodist Tradition in Canada*. Montreal: McGill-Queen's University Press, 1992.

Appleby, Brenda Margaret. *Responsible Parenthood: Decriminalizing Contraception in Canada*. Toronto: University of Toronto Press, 1999.

Artibise, Alan F. J. *Winnipeg: A Social History of Urban Growth, 1874–1914*. Montreal & Kingston: McGill-Queen's University Press, 1975.

Asbell, Bernard. *The Pill: A Biography of the Drug That Changed the World*. New York: Random House, 1995.

Azmier, Jason J. *Gambling in Canada 2001: An Overview*. Canada West Foundation, www.cwf.ca, 2001.

Azmier, Jason J. *Gambling in Canada 2005: Statistics and Context*. Canada West Foundation, www.cwf.ca, 2005.

Backhouse, Constance. *Petticoats and Prejudice: Women and Law in Nineteenth-Century Canada*. Toronto: Osgoode Society, 1991.

Baskerville, Peter. *Sites of Power: A Concise History of Ontario*. Toronto: Oxford University Press, 2005.

Benson, Adolph B. *Peter Kalm's Travel in North America: The English Version of 1770*. New York: Dover Publications, 1964.

Blackburn, Carole. *Harvest of Souls: The Jesuit Missions and Colonialism in North America, 1632–1650*. Montreal & Kingston: McGill-Queen's University Press, 2000.

Bradbury, Bettina. *Wife to Widow: Lives, Laws, and Politics in Nineteenth-Century Montreal*. Vancouver: UBC Press, 2011.

Brodeur, Magaly. *Vice et corruption à Montréal, 1892–1970*. Quebec: Les Presses de l'Université du Québec, 2011.

Brown, Douglas A. "Thoroughbred Horse-Racing Receives an Imperialist Nod: The Parliamentary Debate on Legalizing Gambling in Canada, 1910." *International Journal of the History of Sport* 11, no. 2 (August 1994): 252–269.

Brunet, Manon, and Serge Gagnon. *Discours et pratiques de l'intime*. Quebec: Institut québécois de recherche sur la culture, 1993.

Burnham, John C. *Bad Habits: Drinking, Smoking, Taking Drugs, Gambling, Sexual Misbehaviour, and Swearing in American History*. New York: New York University Press, 1993.

Buxton, Julia. *The Political Economy of Narcotics: Production, Consumption, and Global Markets*. Black Point, Canada; London; New York: Fernwood Publishing, 2006.

Campbell, Colin S., ed. *Gambling in Canada: The Bottom Line*. Vancouver: Criminology Research Centre, School of Criminology at Simon Fraser University, 1994.

Campbell, Robert. *Demon Rum or Easy Money? Government Control of Liquor in British Columbia from Prohibition to Privatization*. Ottawa: Carleton University Press, 1991.

Campbell Robert A. *Sit Down and Drink Your Beer: Regulating Vancouver's Beer Parlours, 1925–1954*. Toronto: University of Toronto Press, 2001.

Cannon, Charles A. "The Awesome Power of Sex: The Polemical Campaign Against Mormon Polygamy." *Pacific Historical Review* 43, no. 1 (February 1974): 61–82.

Carstairs, Catherine. "Deporting 'Ah Sin' to Save the White Race: Moral Panic, Racialization, and the Extension of Canadian Drug Laws in the 1920s." *Canadian Bulletin of Medical History/Bulletin canadien d'histoire de la médecine* 16, no. 1 (1999): 65–88.

Carstairs, Catherine. *Jailed for Possession: Illegal Drug Use, Regulation, and Power in Canada, 1920–1961*. Toronto: University of Toronto Press, 2006.

Carter, Sarah. *The Importance of Being Monogamous: Marriage and Nation Building in Western Canada to 1915*. Edmonton: University of Alberta Press, 2008.

Cartier, Jacques. *The Voyages of Jacques Cartier*, with an introduction by Ramsay Cook. Toronto: University of Toronto Press, 1993.

Cassel, Jay. *The Secret Plague: Venereal Disease in Canada, 1838–1939*. Toronto: University of Toronto Press, 1987.

Casti Connubii Encyclical of Pope Pius XI on Christian Marriage to the Venerable Brethren, Patriarchs, Primates, Archbishops, Bishops, and Other Local Ordinaries Enjoying Peace and Communion with the Apostolic See. http://www.vatican.va.

Chambers, Stuart. "Pierre Elliott Trudeau and Bill C-150. A Rational Approach to Homosexual Acts, 1968–69." *Journal of Homosexuality* 57, no. 2 (2010): 249–266.

Champlain, Samuel de. *Voyages of Samuel de Champlain*. New York: Barnes and Noble, 1967.

Chenier, Elise. *Strangers in Our Midst: Sexual Deviancy in Postwar Ontario*. Toronto: University of Toronto Press, 2008.

Clark, Christopher St. George. *Of Toronto the Good: A Social Study. The Queen City of Canada as It Is*. Montreal: Toronto Publishing Company, 1898.

Cliche, Marie-Aimée. "L'infanticide dans la région de Québec (1660–1969)." *Revue d'histoire de l'Amérique française* 44, no. 1 (été 1990): 31–59.

Cohen, Stanley. *Folk Devils and Moral Panics: The Creation of the Mods and Rockers*. London: MacGibbon & Kee, 1972.

Collectif Clio. *L'histoire des femmes au Québec depuis quatre siècles*, 2nd ed. Montréal: Le Jour, 1992.

Comacchio, Cynthia. *The Dominion of Youth: Adolescence and the Making of Modern Canada, 1920–1950*. Waterloo: Wilfrid Laurier University Press, 2006.

Cook, Ramsay. *The Regenerators: Social Criticism in Late Victorian English Canada*. Toronto: University of Toronto Press, 1985.

Cook, Sharon Anne. *Sex, Lies and Cigarettes: Canadian Women, Smoking, and Visual Culture, 1880–2000*. Montreal & Kingston: McGill-Queen's University Press, 2012.

Cook, Sharon Anne. *"Through Sunshine and Shadow": The Woman's Christian Temperance Union, Evangelicalism, and Reform in Ontario, 1874–1930*. Montreal & Kingston: McGill-Queen's University Press, 1995.

Corriveau, Patrice. *Judging Homosexuals: A History of Gay Persecution in Quebec and France*. Translated by Käthe Roth. Vancouver: UBC Press, 2011.

Cunningham, Rob. *Smoke & Mirrors: The Canadian Tobacco War*. Ottawa: International Development Research Centre, 1996.

D'Emilio, John, and Estelle B. Freedman. *Intimate Matters: A History of Sexuality in America*. New York: Harper & Row Publishers, 1988.

Dawson, R. MacGregor. *William Lyon Mackenzie King: A Political Biography, 1874–1923*. Toronto: University of Toronto Press, 1958.

Desrosiers, Léo-Paul. *Iroquoisie*, vol. 1. Quebec: Septentrion, 1998.

Dostie, Benoit, and Ruth Dupré. "'The people's will': Canadians and the 1898 Referendum on Alcohol Prohibition." *Explorations in Economic History* 49, no. 4 (2012): 498–515.

Dubinsky, Karen, et al., eds. *New World Coming: The Sixties and the Shaping of Global Consciousness*. Toronto: Between the Lines, 2009.

Dunae, Patrick A. "Sex, Charades, and Census Records: Locating Female Sex Trade Workers in a Victorian City." *Histoire sociale/Social History* 42, no. 84 (November 2009): 267–297.

Encyclical Letter Humanae Vitae of the Supreme Pontiff Paul VI to his venerable brothers the Patriarchs, Archbishops, Bishops, and other local Ordinaries in Peace and Communion with the Apostolic See, to the Clergy and Faithful of the Whole Catholic World, and to all Men of Good Will, on the Regulation of Birth. http://www.vatican.va.

English, John. *Just Watch Me: The Life of Pierre Elliott Trudeau, 1968–2000*. Toronto: Knopf Canada, 2009.

Faith, Karlene. *Unruly Women: The Politics of Confinement and Resistance*. Vancouver: Press Gang Publishers, 1993.

Ferland, Catherine. *Bacchus en Canada. Boissons, buveurs et ivresses en Nouvelle-France*. Quebec: Septentrion, 2010.

Ferry, Darren. "'To the Interests and Conscience of the Great Mass of the Community:' The Evolution of Temperance Societies in Nineteenth-Century Central Canada." *Journal of the Canadian Historical Association*, New Series 14 (2003): 137–163.

Fingard, Judith. *The Dark Side of Life in Victorian Halifax*. Porters Lake, NS: Pottersfield Press, 1989.

Fischer, David Hackett. *Champlain's Dream*. New York: Simon & Schuster Paperbacks, 2008.

Foucault, Michel. *Discipline and Punish : The Birth of the Prison*. New York: Vintage, 1979.

Foucault, Michel. *The History of Sexuality*. London: Allen Lane, 1978.

Gagnon, Serge. *Plaisir d'amour et crainte de Dieu. Sexualité et confession au Bas-Canada*. Sainte-Foy, QC: Les Presses de l'Université Laval, 1990.

Gagnon, Serge. *Religion, Moralité, Modernité*. Quebec: Presses de l'Université Laval, 1999.

Graham, John R. "William Lyon Mackenzie King, Elizabeth Harvie, and Edna: A Prostitute Rescuing Initiative in Late Victorian Toronto." *Canadian Journal of Human Sexuality* 8, no. 1 (Spring 1999): 47–60.

Gray, James H. *Red Lights on the Prairies*. Toronto: Macmillan of Canada, 1971.

Greenhill, Pauline. *Make the Night Hideous: Four English-Canadian Charivaris, 1881–1940*. Toronto: University of Toronto Press, 2010.

Greer, Alan. *The Patriots and the People: The Rebellions of 1837 in Rural Lower Canada*. Toronto: University of Toronto Press, 1993.

Griffiths, Naomi E. S. *From Migrant to Acadian: A North American Border People 1604–1755*. Montreal & Kingston: McGill-Queen's University Press, 2005.

Haché, Trevor. "Imperial and Rothmans Admit Guilt in 1990s Cigarette Smuggling Crimes," August 19, 2008. Non-Smokers' Rights Association. http://www.nsra-adnf.ca/cms/index.cfm?group_id=1522.

Hall, Roger, William Westfall, and Laurel Sefton MacDowell, eds. *Patterns of the Past: Interpreting Ontario's History*. Toronto: Dundurn Press, 1988.

Hamelin, Jean, and Nicole Gagnon. *Histoire du catholicisme québécois. Le XXe siècle. Tome 1 1898-1940*. Montreal: Boréal Express, 1984.

Hart, Carl L., and Charles Ksir. *Drugs, Society and Human Behaviour*, 14th ed. New York: McGraw-Hill, 2011.

Hayday, Matthew. *Bilingual Today, United Tomorrow: Official Languages in Education and Canadian Federalism*. Montreal & Kingston: McGill-Queen's University Press, 2005.

Heron, Craig. *Booze: A Distilled History*. Toronto: Between the Lines, 2003.

Hourihane, Colum, ed. *Virtue & Vice: The Personifications in the Index of Christian Art*. Princeton, NJ: Index of Christian Art, Department of Art and Archeology, Princeton University in association with Princeton University Press, 2000.

Howlett, Michael, and M. Ramesh. *Studying Public Policy: Policy Cycles and Policy Subsystems*. Toronto: Oxford University Press, 1995.

Hunt, Alan. *Governing Morals: A Social History of Moral Regulation*. Cambridge: Cambridge University Press, 1999.

Hunt, Alan. "Measuring Morals. The Beginning of the Social Survey Movement in Canada, 1913-1917." *Histoire sociale/Social History* 35, no. 69 (2002): 88-105.

Hurka, Thomas. *Virtue, Vice, and Value*. New York: Oxford University Press, 2001.

Jeffrey, Leslie Ann, and Gayle MacDonald. *Sex Workers in the Maritimes: Talk Back*. Vancouver: UBC Press, 2006.

Johnson, Loretta T. "Charivari/Shivaree: A European Folk Ritual on the American Plains." *Journal of Interdisciplinary History* 20, no. 3 (Winter 1990): 371-387.

Jones, Esyllt W., and Gerald Friesen, eds. *Prairie Metropolis: New Essays on Winnipeg Social History*. Winnipeg: University of Manitoba Press, 2009.

King, William Lyon Mackenzie. *Diaries*. http://www.collectionscanada.gc.ca/king/index-e.html.

King, William Lyon Mackenzie. *Report into the Losses Sustained by the Chinese Population of Vancouver, B.C. on the Occasion of the Riots in that City in September, 1907*. Ottawa: S. E. Dawson, 1908.

Kingdon, John W. *Agendas, Alternatives and Public Policies*. New York: HarperCollins, 1995.

Kinietz, W. Vernon. *The Indians of the Western Great Lakes, 1615-1760*. Ann Arbor: University of Michigan Press, 1965.

Kinsman, Gary. *The Regulation of Desire: Homo and Hetero Sexualities*, 2nd ed. Montreal: Black Rose Books, 1996.

Kinsman, Gary, and Patrizia Gentile. *The Canadian War on Queers: National Security as Sexual Regulation*. Vancouver: UBC Press, 2010.

Labrosse, Michel. *The Lottery from Jacques Cartier's Day to Modern Times: Sidelights on the History of Lotteries in Québec*. Translated by Alan Brown. Montreal: Stanké, 1985.

Lacasse, Danielle. *La prostitution féminine à Montréal, 1945-1970*. Montreal: Boréal, 1994.

Lachance, André. *Crimes et criminels en Nouvelle-France*. Montreal: Boréal, 1984.

Lamoureux, Diane. "La lutte pour le droit à l'avortement (1969-1981)," *Revue d'histoire de l'Amérique française* 37, no. 1 (1983): 81-90.

Larocque, Sylvain. *Gay Marriage: The Story of a Canadian Social Revolution*. Toronto: James Lorimer & Company, 2006.

Le Jeune, Paul, S. J. *Québec Relations: 1635, 1636, 1637*, edited by Lucien Campeau. Rome: Institutum Historicum Societatis Iesu; Quebec: Presses de l'Université Laval, 2004.

Leitzel, Jim. *Regulating Vice: Misguided Prohibitions and Realistic Controls*. New York: Cambridge University Press, 2008.

Lemieux, Lucien. *Une histoire religieuse du Québec*. Montreal: Les Éditions Novalis, 2010.

Lemieux, Vincent. *Les cheminements de l'influence : Systèmes, stratégies et structures du politique*. Quebec: Les Presses de l'Université Laval, 1979.

Lemieux, Vincent. *L'étude des politiques publiques. Les acteurs et leur pouvoir*, 2nd ed. Quebec: Les Presses de l'Université Laval, 2002.

Lévesque, Andrée. "Éteindre le 'Red Light': Les réformateurs et la prostitution à Montréal, 1865–1925." *Urban History Review/Revue d'histoire urbaine* 17, no. 3 (February 1989): 191–201.

Lévesque, Andrée. *Making and Breaking the Rules: Women in Québec, 1919–1939*. Toronto: University of Toronto Press, 1994.

Litt, Paul. *Elusive Destiny: The Political Vocation of John Napier Turner*. Vancouver: UBC Press, 2011.

Little, Margaret. *"No Car, No Radio, No Liquor Permit": The Moral Regulation of Single Mothers in Ontario, 1920–97*. Toronto: Oxford University Press, 1998.

Loo, Tina, and Carolyn Strange. *Making Good: Law and Moral Regulation in Canada, 1867–1939*. Toronto: University of Toronto Press, 1997.

Lutz, John Sutton. *Makuk: A New History of Aboriginal–White Relations*. Vancouver: UBC Press, 2008.

Malleck, Daniel J. "'Its Baneful Influences Are Too Well Known': Debates over Drug Use in Canada, 1867–1908." *Canadian Bulletin of Medical History/Bulletin canadien d'histoire de la médecine* 4 (1997): 263–288.

Malleck, Dan. *Try to Control Yourself: The Regulation of Public Drinking in Post-Prohibition Ontario, 1927–44*. Vancouver: UBC Press, 2012.

Marquis, Greg. "Alcohol and the Family in Canada." *Journal of Family History* 29, no. 3 (July 2004): 308–327.

Marquis, Greg. "Vancouver Vice: The Police and the Negotiation of Morality, 1904–1935." In Hamar Foster and John McLaren, eds., *Essays in the History of Canadian Law*, vol. VI, *British Columbia and the Yukon*. Toronto: Osgoode Society for Canadian Legal History, 1995: 242–273.

Martel, Marcel. *Not This Time: Canadians, Public Policy and the Marijuana Question, 1961–1975*. Toronto: University of Toronto Press, 2006.

Martel, Marcel, and Martin Pâquet. *Speaking Up: A History of Language and Politics in Canada and Quebec*. Trans. Patricia Dumas. Toronto: Between the Lines, 2012.

Maynard, Steven. "'Horrible Temptations': Sex, Men, and Working-Class Male Youth in Urban Ontario, 1890–1935." *Canadian Historical Review* 78, no. 2 (June 1997): 191–236.

Maynard, Steven. "Through a Hole in the Lavatory Wall: Homosexual Subcultures, Police Surveillance, and the Dialectics of Discovery, Toronto, 1890–1930." *Journal of the History of Sexuality* 5, no. 2 (1994): 207–242.

McLaren, Angus. *The Bedroom and the State: The Changing Practices and Politics of Contraception and Abortion in Canada, 1880–1986*. Toronto: McClelland & Stewart, 1986.

McLaren, Angus. "Illegal Operations: Women, Doctors, and Abortion, 1886–1939." *Journal of Social History* 26, no. 4 (Summer 1993): 797–816.

McLaren, Angus. *The Trials of Masculinity: Policing Sexual Boundaries, 1870–1930*. Chicago: University of Chicago Press, 1997.

McLaren, Angus. *Twentieth-Century Sexuality: A History*. Oxford, UK; Malden, MA: Blackwell, 1999.

McLaren, Angus, and Arlene Tigar McLaren. *Our Own Master Race: Eugenics in Canada, 1885–1945*. Toronto: McClelland & Stewart, 1990.

McLaren, John P. S., Robert Menzies, and Dorothy E. Chunn, eds. *Regulating Lives: Historical Essays on the State, Society, the Individual, and the Law*. Vancouver: University of British Columbia Press, 2002.

McMillan, Alan D., and Eldon Yellowhorn. *First Peoples in Canada*. Vancouver: Douglas & McIntyre, 2004.

McPherson, Kate, Cecilia Morgan, and Nancy M. Forestell, eds. *Gendered Pasts: Historical Essays in Femininity and Masculinity in Canada*. Toronto: University of Toronto Press, 1999.

Meier, Kenneth J. *The Politics of Sin: Drugs, Alcohol, and Public Policy*. Armonk, NY: M. E. Sharpe, 1994.

Miller, Jim R. *Skyscrapers Hide the Heavens: A History of Indian–White Relations in Canada*, 3rd ed. Toronto: University of Toronto Press, 2000.

Mitchinson, Wendy. *The Nature of Their Bodies: Women and Their Doctors in Victorian Canada*. Toronto: University of Toronto Press, 1991.

Montigny, Edgar-André, ed. *The Real Dope: Social, Legal, and Historical Perspectives on the Regulation of Drugs in Canada*. Toronto: University of Toronto Press, 2011.

Moodie, Susanna. *Roughing It in the Bush*, 2nd ed. London: Richard Bentley, 1852.

Morton, Suzanne *At Odds: Gambling and Canadians, 1919–1969*. Toronto: University of Toronto Press, 2003.

Murphy, Terrence, and Roberto Perin, eds. *A Concise History of Christianity in Canada*. Toronto: Oxford University Press, 1996.

Murray, Glenn F. "Cocaine Use in the Era of Social Reform: The Natural History of a Social Problem in Canada, 1880–1911." *Canadian Journal of Law and Society/Revue canadienne de droit et société* 2 (1987): 29–43.

Myers, Tamara. *Caught: Montreal's Modern Girls and the Law, 1869–1945*. Toronto: University of Toronto Press, 2006.

Noel, Jan. *Canada Dry: Temperance Crusades before Confederation*. Toronto: University of Toronto Press, 1995.

O'Callaghan, E. B., ed. *Documents Relative to the Colonial History of the State of New York*. Albany, NY: 1855.

Palmer, Beth. "'Lonely, tragic, but legally necessary pilgrimages': Transnational Abortion Travel in the 1970s." *Canadian Historical Review* 92, no. 4 (December 2011): 637–664.

Palmer, Brian D. "Discordant Music: Charivaris and Whitecapping in Nineteenth-Century North America." *Labour/Le Travail* 3 (1978): 5–62.

Pennock, Pamela E. *Advertising Sin and Sickness: The Politics of Alcohol and Tobacco Marketing, 1950–1990*. DeKalb, IL: Northern Illinois University Press, 2007.

Phillips, Jim, Tina Loo, and Susan Lewthwaite, eds. *Essays in the History of Canadian Law*, vol. V, *Crime and Criminal Justice*. Toronto: Osgoode Society for Canadian Legal History, 1994.

Phillips, Paul T. *A Kingdom on Earth. Anglo-American Social Christianity, 1880–1940*. University Park, PA: Pennsylvania State University Press, 1996.

Ray, Terence J. *A History of Canadian Catholics: Gallicanism, Romanism, and Canadianism*. Montreal & Kingston: McGill-Queen's University Press, 2002.

Raynal, Abbé. *A Philosophical and Political History of the Settlements and Trade of the Europeans in the East and West Indies*. Translated by J. O. Justamond. 8 vols. London: A. Strahan and T. Cadell, 1788.

Riordan, Michael. *The First Stone: Homosexuality and the United Church*. Toronto: McClelland and Stewart, 1990.

Roberts, Julia. *In Mixed Company: Taverns and Public Life in Upper Canada*. Vancouver: UBC Press, 2009.

Ross, Becki. *Burlesque West: Showgirls, Sex, and Sin in Postwar Vancouver*. Toronto: University of Toronto Press, 2009.

Ross, D. Fair. "A Most Favourable Soil and Climate: Hemp Cultivation in Upper Canada, 1800–1813." *Ontario History* 96, no. 1 (spring 2004): 41–61.

Rudy, Jarrett. *The Freedom to Smoke: Tobacco Consumption and Identity*. Montreal & Kingston: McGill-Queen's University Press, 2005.

Sangster, Joan. *Regulating Girls and Women: Sexuality, Family, and the Law in Ontario*. Toronto: Oxford University Press, 2001.

Séguin, Robert-Lionel. *La vie libertine en Nouvelle-France au XVIIᵉ siècle*, vol. 1. Montreal: Leméac, 1972.

Semple, Neil. *The Lord's Dominion: The History of Canadian Methodism*. Montreal & Kingston: McGill-Queen's University Press, 1996.

Sethna, Christabelle. "The Evolution of the Birth Control Handbook: From Student Peer-Education Manual to Feminist Self-empowerment Text, 1968–1975." *Canadian Bulletin of Medical History/Bulletin canadien d'histoire de la médecine* 23, no. 1 (2006): 89–118.

Sethna, Christabelle, and Steve Hewitt. "Clandestine Operations: The Vancouver Women's Caucus, the Abortion Caravan, and the RCMP." *Canadian Historical Review* 90, no. 3 (September 2009): 463–495.

A Short Abridgment of Christian Doctrine. 1728.

Shorter, Edward. *Written in the Flesh: A History of Desire*. Toronto: University of Toronto Press, 2005.

Sioui, Georges E. *Les Wendats: Une civilisation méconnue*. Sainte-Foy, QC: Les Presses de l'Université Laval, 1994.

Skinner, Claiborne A. *The Upper Country: French Enterprise in the Colonial Great Lakes*. Baltimore, MD: Johns Hopkins University Press, 2008.

Snell, James G. "'The White Live for Two': The Defence of Marriage and Sexual Morality in Canada, 1890–1914." *Histoire sociale/Social History* 16, no. 31 (May 1983): 111–128.

Spence, Ruth Elizabeth. *Prohibition in Canada*. Toronto: Ontario Branch of The Dominion Alliance, 1919.

Stephen, Jennifer A. *Pick One Intelligent Girl: Employability, Domesticity, and the Gendering of Canada's Welfare State, 1939–1947*. Toronto: University of Toronto, 2007.

Stewart, Roderick, and Sharon Stewart. *Phoenix: The Life of Norman Bethune*. Montreal & Kingston: McGill-Queen's University Press, 2011.

Strange, Carolyn. *Toronto's Girl Problem: The Perils and Pleasures of the City, 1880–1930*. Toronto: University of Toronto Press, 1995.

Taylor, Craig. *Moralism: A Study of a Vice*. Montreal & Kingston: McGill-Queen's University Press, 2012.

Taylor, Gabriele. *Deadly Vices*. Oxford: Clarendon, 2006.

Thompson, John Herd. *The Harvests of War: The Prairies West, 1914–1918*. Toronto: McClelland and Stewart, 1978.

Tone, Andrea. *Devices and Desires: A History of Contraceptives in America*. New York: Hill and Wang, 2001.

Tooker, Elisabeth. *An Ethnography of the Huron Indians, 1615–1649*. Syracuse, NY: Syracuse University Press, 1991.

Trigger, Bruce G. *The Children of Aataentsic: A History of the Huron People to 1660*. Montreal: McGill-Queen's University Press, 1987.

Trigger, Bruce G. *The Huron: Farmers of the North*. New York: Holt, Rinehart and Winston, 1969.

Valverde, Mariana. *The Age of Light, Soap, and Water: Moral Reform in English Canada, 1885–1925*. Toronto: McClelland & Stewart, 1991.

Valverde, Mariana. *Diseases of the Will: Alcohol and the Dilemmas of Freedom*. Cambridge and New York: Cambridge University Press, 1998.

Wamsley, Kevin B. "State Formation and Institutionalized Racism: Gambling Laws in Nineteenth and Early Twentieth Century Canada." *Sport History Review* 29 (1998): 77–85.

Ward, Peter. *Courtship, Love, and Marriage in Nineteenth-Century English Canada*. Montreal & Kingston: McGill-Queen's University Press, 1990.

Warsh, Cheryl Krasnick. "Smoke and Mirrors: Gender Representation in North American Tobacco and Alcohol Advertisements before 1950." *Histoire sociale/Social History* 31 (1999): 183–221.

Warsh, Cheryl Krasnick, ed. *Drink in Canada: Historical Essays*. Montreal & Kingston: McGill-Queen's University Press, 1993.

We Demand, The August 28th Gay Day Committee, *The Body Politic*, Issue 1 (Nov.– Dec. 1971). Reprinted in *Flaunting It!*, 1982; http://www.clga.ca/Material/Records/docs/wedemand.htm.

Whitaker, Reginald. *Drugs and the Law: The Canadian Scene*. Toronto: Methuen, 1969.

White Jr., O. Kendall. "Mormonism in America and Canada: Accommodation to the Nation-State." *Canadian Journal of Sociology/Cahiers canadiens de sociologie* 3, no. 2 (Spring 1978): 161–181.

Whitehead, Paul C., Carl F. Grindstaff, and Craig L. Boydell, eds. *Alcohol and Other Drugs: Perspectives on Use, Abuse, Treatment and Prevention*. Toronto: Holt, Rinehart and Winston of Canada, 1971.

Youmans, Letitia. *Campaign Echoes*. Toronto: William Briggs, 1893.

DISSERTATIONS

Beausaert, Rebecca. "Benevolence, Bicycles, and Quilting Bees: Leisure, Gender, and Class in Small-Town Ontario, 1870–1914." PhD diss., York University, 2013.

Douville, Bruce. "The Uncomfortable Pew: Christianity, The New Left, and the Hip Counterculture in Toronto, 1965–1975." PhD diss., York University, 2011.

Karibo, Holly Marie. "Ambassadors of Pleasure: Illicit Economies in the Detroit–Windsor Borderland, 1945–1960." PhD diss., University of Toronto, 2012.

Lapointe, Mathieu. "Le Comité de moralité publique, l'enquête Caron et les campagnes de moralité publique à Montréal. 1940–1954." PhD diss., York University, 2010.

GOVERNMENT PUBLICATIONS

Canada. House of Commons Debates.

Canada. House of Commons Special Committee on Non-Medical Use of Drugs. *Policy for the New Millennium: Working Together to Redefine Canada's Drug Strategy.* Ottawa: Queen's Printer, 2002.

Canada. Health Canada. *Proposed New Labelling Requirements for Tobacco Products. Consultation Paper.* Ottawa: Queen's Printer, 1999.

Canada. *Report of the Committee on the Operation of the Abortion Law.* Ottawa: Minister of Supply and Services Canada, 1977.

Canada. Senate Special Committee on Illegal Drugs. *Cannabis: Our Position for a Canadian Public Policy.* Ottawa: Queen's Printer, 2002.

U.S. Public Health Service. *Smoking and Health: Report of the Advisory Committee to the Surgeon General of the Public Health Service.* Washington, DC: U.S. Dept. of Health, Education, and Welfare, Public Health Service, 1964.

NEWSPAPERS

Daily Mail and Empire
Globe
Globe and Mail
Le Soleil
National Post
Ottawa Citizen
Toronto Star
XTra!

WEBSITES

Air Canada
Alberta Gaming and Liquor Commission
The Canadian Broadcasting Corporation
The Embryo Project Encyclopedia
National Union of Public and General Employees
Opération Nez Rouge/Operation Red Nose
Same Sex Marriage
Smoke-Free Canada
The Supreme Court of Canada

INDEX